Hounds of the Road

Hounds of the Road

A History of the Greyhound Bus Company

Carlton Jackson

Bowling Green State University Popular Press
Bowling Green, OH 43403

Other books by Carlton Jackson
Presidential Vetoes, 1792-1945
Zane Grey
J. I. Rodale: Apostle of Nonconformity
The Great Lili
The Dreadful Month
Picking Up the Tab: The Life and Movies of Martin Ritt
Hattie: The Life of Hattie McDaniel
Forgotten Tragedy: The Sinking of HMT Rohna
Joseph Gavi: Young Hero of the Minsk Ghetto
A Social History of the Scotch-Irish
Who Will Take Our Children: The Story of the British Evacua-
    tion, 1939-1945

Fiction
Kentucky Outlaw Man
Freedom's Way

As Co-author
Foundations of Freedom
Challenge and Change
Two Centuries of Progress

As Editor
Befriending: The American Samaritans
George Washington: Frontiersman

2nd edition copyright 2001

Copyright © 1984 by Bowling Green State University Popular Press

Library of Congress Catalogue Card No.: 83-72887

ISBN: 0-87972-270-3

Contents

General Acknowledgements

I received help from so many people on this project that space and memory probably dictate against listing all of them. I will, however, give it a try.

Mr. John Hoschek of the Motor Bus Society at Trenton, New Jersey, at my request, read the entire manuscript and saved me from numerous technical errors. I thank him, and his colleague, Don Coffin, most sincerely. Emmet D. Chisum of the fantastic American Heritage Center at the University of Wyoming, went out of his way to be helpful, friendly and courteous, and I am appreciative. Mrs. Angelo Grosvenor of Walnut Creek, California, helped with certain aspects of the study. Others who come to mind include Verne Kelley, Sid Cato, Charles Kirkpatrick and James Kerrigan.

Besides Lee Whitehead, there were numerous other Greyhounders who were valuable to me, either in a material way or in helping to form certain ideas and approaches. They include Dorothy Lorant, and Messrs. E.W. Simmons, John Adkins, Frederick Dunikoski, Joe Black, Kenneth White and D.H. Behnke. I thank them all for their contributions. The Greyhound employees I thank the most, however, are the drivers, past and present. They are a fabulous group of people—a veritable national resource in terms of social and transportation history.

Here at home I was aided at length by the librarians at Western Kentucky University, by student assistants Walter Hixson and Bruce Trammell; and by grants from the University's Research Committee. To each librarian, student and member of the research committee: thank you.

And, of course, my gratitude goes to my rapidly increasing family: Bev, Steve, Colleen; Hilary; Dan, Grace, Travis, Megan; Matthew. And—as always—Pat.

Specific Acknowledgements

Russell Byrd, for quotes from *Russ's Bus.*
Broad, Khourie & Schultz, for excerpts from "The Saga of Mt. Hood Stages."
Kelly Crocker, for quotes from "Flecha Amarilla."
Greyhound Corporation, for photographs and quotes from *Go With Greyhound*
Marjorie Huffine, for use of David Huffine's cartoon,

Introduction to the Revised Edition

It has been 17 years since *Hounds of the Road* was first published. For much of this time, Greyhound fortunes have see-sawed between valleys and peaks. It has come close on occasions to dissolution, suffering two crippling strikes, and one Chapter 11 bankruptcy. Yet, since 1994, its fortunes seem to have reversed under the leadership of a bright young CEO, Craig Lentzsch. As chapter ten explains, his leadership has meant a world of difference in Greyhound, all the way from the executive suite to drivers on the road. I wish to thank all the Greyhound personnel, including Mr. Lentzsch, Kristin Parsley, Lyn Brown, and Ralph Borland, who helped me with this final chapter of *Hounds of the Road*.

Back in the early '80s when I was researching this book, there came a time that Greyhound in Phoenix would barely speak to me. The drivers' union, the Amalgamated Transit Union (ATU), however, helped immensely. Interestingly, the roles seem to be reversed today. The ATU did send me some material for which I thank them, and I did speak with their general counsel, but ATU president, James La Sala, for reasons known only to himself, did not respond to my requests for help.

I have enjoyed being the author of *Hounds of the Road* over the past several years. I still rode the buses after *Hounds of the Road* publication, and it was nice to be recognized by drivers and terminal managers as the person "who wrote that book" about them. One lady, or so I have heard, was a frequent bus rider. She bought several copies of *Hounds of the Road* and gave them to the drivers as souvenirs. All I can say to that, is Thank you, kind lady.

Not the least of the good things that have come my way because of *Hounds of the Road* is that it figured in getting me a senior Fulbright scholarship to Finland for a full year. One of the members of the selection committee used to come to the States every three or four years. He would buy an "Ameripass" in New York and use it to travel all over the country.

When he saw *Hounds of the Road* on my resume, he said he had to support someone who was "crazy enough to write a book about Greyhound buses." His influence and vote swayed the committee in my favor, and I became the 1989-1990 Fulbright Bicentennial Professor of American Studies at the University of Helsinki. I am proud to be one of the "Bicens" from that venerable institution.

Many individuals at Western Kentucky University helped me with this final chapter. My graduate assistant, Evan Lamberth carried out many tasks that facilitated the job. As every author knows, he would not get very far without good libraries and good librarians. I was fortunate to have the help of WKU librarian, Nancy Marshall, in finding and collecting material. I am deeply indebted to her for her superb assistance.

History Department Chair, Richard Weigel, helped in the development of this chapter. He read it, and gave useful comments. I appreciate his support.

And, finally, once again, I have the pleasure of thanking my family for their love and help. My daughters, Beverly and Hilary; my sons, Daniel and Matthew; my granddaughters, Colleen, Megan, and Katharine; and my grandsons, Travis, Patrick, and Austin. And my daughter-in-law, Grace; and my son-in-law Steve. And, as always, Pat.

Western Kentucky University   Carlton Jackson

Introduction

Why would anybody write a history of the Greyhound Bus Company? The idea first occurred to me when I rode an "Americruiser" from Bowling Green, Kentucky, to Dayton, Ohio. On the trip, a man's money was "stolen" and "they" were "after him." On that Greyhound were several "professional bus riders," some of whom had been aboard for four or five days. Those people told me about previous trips they had taken, of the persons they had met, and of the situations they had encountered. The drivers on my Dayton trip were talkative in varying degrees, and soon I realized that they, too, had many stories to tell.

The more I thought about a history of the Greyhound buses, the more attractive the idea became. I did not wish to write a "dissertation-type" treatise, based primarily on minutes of board meetings and such dusty material. If the story was worth telling, I believed, it must not be an "official history," and it must be told from the human angle.

My first job, of course, was to see if any histories were already out. There were none—at least beyond a few M.A. theses and Ph.D. dissertations. So far, so good.

The next step was to contact Public Relations at Greyhound, and see if they would put me onto some right tracks; I had the good fortune to come into contact with Mr. Lee Whitehead. Yes, he said, he would help me. And he sent printed materials from the Greyhound Tower, told me where historical material might possibly be located, and promised to line up some interviews if I could ever get out to Phoenix. I wish to thank Mr. Whitehead for his courtesies, and for his help in getting me started on my project.

Then there came the time that the top brass at Greyhound cut me off completely. I wrote to ask for interviews of additional officers, and I also inquired about their opinions of the Mt. Hood Case. (Admittedly, my timing was wrong on that one: Greyhound was just on the verge of losing an expensive lawsuit to Mt. Hood Stages in Oregon, and here was a "troublesome" historian trying to quiz them about it.)

1

For a long time I believed that it was just my inquisitiveness that caused the Greyhounders to cold-shoulder me. But then I talked with numerous knowledgeable people about the problem, and we concluded that the present Greyhound management is simply not historical-minded.

For example, there is a surfeit of material on the train industry, and even on airplanes, but very little, indeed, on inter-city buses. It may be that, as a long-time bus buff told me, "the goddamn bus industry is too stupid to blow its own horn." Or perhaps it is, as a former Greyhound executive (a friendly one, by the way, to the Corporation—not one of those dozens of ex-Greyhound officials scattered around the country rueing the day they ever saw a Scenicruiser) said, the Corporation today is ashamed of its bus operations. It had rather push the fortunes of Armour & Company, and its other subsidiaries, than to publicize its carriers. I believe neither statement, though there are some elements of truth in them.

I believe that the Greyhound management has always been made up of strong-willed people who wanted to be well thought of in the public image, even to the point, if necessary, of manipulation. Any writing done about them, therefore, would have to be "PR'd," or as the English say, "vetted." If an author chose to retain his independence (as I did) over who will read his developing manuscript and who will not, his chances of convincing Greyhound people that their buses deserve a legitimate historical treatment are slim indeed. This tendency toward the "public relations blurb," as opposed to attempts at legitimacy, is not a new thing in Greyhound history; its founder, Eric Wickman, possessed almost exactly the same traits.

As it turned out, however, very little of the material I needed came from Phoenix. It came from Laramie, Wyoming, (where there is a great Greyhound collection); from New York, Chicago, Washington, Trenton, San Francisco, and a whole bunch of other places. Beyond the source material, there were plenty of present and former Greyhound employees who shared their experiences with me. The "Greyhound Stories" were collected from many sources, primarily drivers, both active and retired. They are true, false, sad, funny, sexy, dirty and just plain silly. They are intended, loosely so, as introductions to each chapter. The appendices contain material about the bus industry in general, and not just about Greyhound specifically.

The greatest compliment I received during the research was

unintended. I contacted a former President of the Greyhound Corporation, and he was willing to help me. We arranged for me to send him a list of questions. Included among the "more acceptable" questions were one or two about Mt. Hood, and some personnel problems at Greyhound Tower. The former President's answer came back that I was "trying to stir up things," and therefore he could be of no assistance.

He was incorrect; in this study, I am not necessarily "trying to stir up things," but I must say that during my allotted time here on this earth, I'd rather do just that than to live the life of a lackey or sycophant. What I *am* trying to do is present a balanced, informative and as-accurate-as-possible *social* history of the Greyhound buses.

As a final point, I must emphasize that my study is confined *to the Greyhound buses*. I have no research interest in any other part of the Greyhound Corporation, except as those parts occasionally inter-act with bus operations.

Western Kentucky University   Carlton Jackson

"Greyhound Stories"—The Early Years

"First there was tree; the tree became a log; then man invented the wheel. Soon wheels were everywhere; on Roman war chariots, wheels on medieval sedan chairs, and wheels on oriental sail barrels.

"A French wind wagon blew in and the first bicycle rolled around to the delight of the youngsters everywhere.

"Then the carriage was built. Shortly carriage wheels were spinning all over the world.

"The discovery of steam propulsion and the internal combustion engine let inventors run wild. The English made a combustible tri-car and the Germans dreamed up a stream-lined catapult car. Shades of Jules Verne.

"Gasoline buggies were just a 'rich man's toy' until Henry Ford invented the tin lizzie. Soon the motor bus appeared on the nation's roads as a new form of transportation. That's how the largest inter-city passenger carrier in the world began. They called it Greyhound"—A Greyhound Journal.

"I see you stand like greyhounds in the slips, straining upon the start. The games of foot follow your spirit, and upon this charge cry, 'God for Harry, England, and St. George' "— Shakespeare, Henry IV, Act III.

"There be three things which go well; yea are comely and going: a greyhound and a goat also; and a king against whom there is no rising up"—King Solomon in Proverbs 30: 29, 31.

"The roads you travel so briskly
lead out of dim antiquity,
and you study the past chiefly because
of its bearing on the living present
and its promise for the future"—Lt. General James G. Harbord (U.S. Army)

An early Greyhound bus driver, Cliff Graves, recounted this story:

Graves was preparing for his trip from Hibbing to Grand Rapids. A foreigner who could not speak much English, timidly came up to Graves, holding his suitcase. Graves told him to put the suitcase in the luggage box over the rear bumper. When his trip was ready, Graves missed the foreign passenger. After looking for him for several minutes, Graves found him sitting in the luggage box, still firmly gripping his suitcase.—Scott Holtzlander, AHC.

Once, Andrew Anderson was loading his bus for a run to Grand Rapids, when a passenger showed up with a friendly bear. "Bus Andy" told him that his service was for people, not bears. The man promised to sit by the bear, saying that it would take up no more room than he did. Finally, for five dollars, Anderson took the bear on board. A few miles down the road, the bear broke out a window, and Anderson charged his owner for it. "He was really angry. The man, not the bear. The bear didn't care"—Hal Boyle, Duluth Herald, *August 11, 1951.*

Chapter One
The "Snoose Line"

Greyhound, the most enduring bus system in the United States, had its origins in the frigid climes of northern Minnesota. The place was Hibbing, seventy-five miles northwest of Duluth, incorporated as a village in 1893. It was first a lumber center, but then iron ore was discovered under its streets, and the entire village was moved two miles to the south to make way for the mine.

The discovery of ore turned Hibbing into a boom town. It attracted people from all over the United States and from several foreign countries as well. In 1901, Hibbing had a population of 3,000 with seventy saloons, and wooden sidewalks that rested on stilts. There was also the open pit iron ore mine, known as the Mahoning. In some places the ore was only four feet below the surface, which made it easy to strip. This assured Hibbing's financial future, and also its character of "rough and tumble," with miners and lumberjacks freely mingling on the village streets.

The Mahoning Iron Ore Company furnished some houses to certain classes of workers (mostly supervisory), but the majority of laborers had to acquire their own accommodations. Thus, a little settlement two miles south of Hibbing, named Alice, became the chief residential area for the Mahoning miners. (Today, Alice is known as South Hibbing.) The standard transportation for getting to work and back was footpower, augmented occasionally by a horse and buggy. There were a few cars around, of course, but they were too expensive for most of the miners to hire, let alone own.

It was into this milieu that a number of enterprising Swedes came. One was Carl Eric Wickman, and he is usually credited with being the major founder of the system that was later known as Greyhound. He was born August 7, 1887, in Mora, Sweden. He came to the United States in 1903 when he was sixteen, and went first to Arizona territory to work at a sawmill. He never did like the heat and dryness of the Southwest; when he heard from fellow immigrants that the Minnesota climate was similar to Sweden's, he traveled to Hibbing. He went to work for the mining company, operating a diamond drill. As fortune dictated, however, he was not long to remain a miner.

7

Another Swedish immigrant was Andrew Anderson (later known as "Bus Andy"). He borrowed money from his mother to come across on a cattle boat in 1900. He was a farm boy, and could not speak English. He had with him on the boat a well-made hand-carved wooden suitcase. On the way over, he found a large supply of herring in the ship's food-locker and filled his suitcase with them. Since it was spring, the herring soon spoiled, and began smelling up the vessel. Anderson did not really strike the pose of a future Greyhound executive as the ship's crew and passengers angrily made him throw his suitcase overboard with its smelly contents.[1] He came to Hibbing and worked alternately as a blacksmith's helper and a driller for the mine. Like his buddy, Eric Wickman, he yearned for something better.

Wickman was the first of the two to break away from the mines. With $3,000 in savings in 1913, he bought a franchise in Hibbing to sell Goodyear tires and Hupmobile cars.[2] Wickman, however, was not a good salesman; nobody would buy the single Hupmobile he had in stock. Finally he sold it to apparently the only person in Hibbing who wanted it—himself. The Hup was a seven-passenger touring car, so he hit upon the idea of transporting miners across the Mesaba Iron Range to and from their work. He intended for this to be only a part-time occupation, as his major interest remained in selling Goodyear tires and Hupmobiles. On his first jaunt he collected $2.25. This sum encouraged him to make other trips.

Soon Wickman's venture caught Anderson's attention. He and a friend, Oscar Wenberg, bought Eric's Hupmobile for $1,200, with the intention of starting a full-time livery service for the Hibbing-Alice miners. Before long, however, Anderson and Wenberg quarreled. It turned out that Wenberg did not know how to drive; and he also refused to learn English, which put him in bad stead with several of his clientele. Finally Wenberg sold his interest back to Wickman for $600. Nothing more, then, was heard of Wenberg in terms of Greyhound history.[3]

The Wickman-Anderson combine now began operating in earnest the route from Hibbing to Alice. They alternated on hourly runs from a saloon in Hibbing to the fire-hall in Alice. At the beginning they charged $1.50 for the round trip; when their business really began to bloom, though, they dropped the price to fifteen cents one way, and twenty-five cents round trip, keeping their earnings in a trunk at Hibbing's Palace Hotel.[4] Sometimes they could squeeze eighteen passengers into the seven capacity Hup. They put them inside, on the running boards, and some clung to the back bumpers.

Only men rode this first "air-conditioned bus" in America, "with the exhilirating air of northern Minnesota coming in freely around the windows."[5] It was rare indeed for a woman to come aboard. Most of the Hup's patrons were heavy users of snuff, so each trip was rife with puffed out lips, spitting into the wind, and a lot of dodging. Soon the Wickman-Anderson operation became known as the "Snoose Line." ("Snoose" is the Swedish word for snuff.) It was widely reported that the only way you could get a "Snoose Line" bus to stop for you was to stand on a curb and display a large, colorful snuff box to the driver, and rap loudly on it with your fingers. Though the operation was now officially known as the Hibbing Transportation Company, its reputation of being the "Snoose Line" remained with it for a long time.[6]

Wickman and Anderson faced a problem when their one Hupmobile—now stretched out by blacksmith Anderson to seat twelve people—became insufficient for the volume of trade. Therefore they began seriously to think about broadening the scope of their business.

They brought in another immigrant, Arvid Heed, who drove a Buick (or a Packard, depending on who is telling the story). Now with two cars and three drivers, the "Snoose Line" operated literally around the clock. In 1915 this new business, the Hibbing Transportation Company, bought two buses mounted on truck chassis from the White Company in Cleveland. This purchase, of course, made it necessary to hire additional drivers. They were Cliff Graves and Swan Sundstrom, both later to become prominent Greyhound officials.[7] With the new buses, the Wickman-Anderson combine became inter-city for the first time. A route was established between Hibbing and the little settlement of Nashwauk, fifteen miles to the north.

Before being in operation long, the "Snoose Line" very definitely faced some competition. Ralph Bogan, born in 1896 in Ludington, Michigan, had come to Hibbing to capitalize on the iron ore business. Instead of becoming a miner, however, he allowed his love of mechanics to guide his life. He was a widely known motorcycle racer in areas of northern Minnesota, and also one of the first individuals in Hibbing to have a care for hire.[8] When Wickman and Anderson began their bus service, Bogan—unlike some other Hibbing taxi drivers—decided to fight back.

By 1915 the round trip from Hibbing to Alice had risen to seventy-five cents. Bogan, with his Studebaker, cut the price to fifty cents. The "Snoose Line" then dropped to forty.[9] This was the first known price war between competing means of transportations in the United States. It quickly became obvious to both parties that they were killing off each other. Wickman and Anderson then did what Greyhound later became so adept at doing: they offered Bogan a partnership in their company. Thus, Bogan became the fourth member of the rapidly expanding Wickman-Anderson bus operation.[10]

In 1916 the four partners—Wickman, Anderson, Heed and Bogan—incorporated themselves as the Mesaba Transportation Company, and immediately began a dramatic expansion of services. For example, the new company had in hand a contract from the Hibbing School Board to transport pupils, particularly in the winter months. Also, the route from Hibbing to Nashwauk was extended twenty miles westward to Grand Rapids, Minnesota.

The company's first "official" bus station was at the fire house in Alice.[11] Its "Board of Directors," composed of the four partners, met regularly at the Silliman House in Hibbing, and gained a reputation in the neighborhood for shouting at one another.[12] Increasingly, their deliberations centered around extending operations to Duluth, some seventy-five miles away.

By 1918 the "Snoose Line" had taken on some more stockholders. The first one was Dominic Bretto, a fireman from Alice. He had been so fascinated watching the passengers load and unload at the station that he asked for and got an interest in the company. He died soon thereafter, and his shares were taken by E.C. Eckstrom. Still another new stockholder was Andrew Anderson, this one nicknamed "Tireshop Andy," to distinguish him from the earlier Anderson, "Bus Andy."

In 1919 the long-awaited Duluth run became a reality. The company owned a garage on Garfield Avenue in Duluth, and began to hold its stockholders' meetings at Malek's Half Way House between Duluth and Hibbing. The Mesaba Transportation Company took pride in telling the traveling public that its buses "got through," no matter what the road condition or weather.

This claim was, of course, something of an exaggeration, but not much. For heat in winter, passengers huddled around that part of the exhaust pipe that was on top of the bus's floor. They were also supplied with heated bricks for their feet, and heavy lap robes. Being part-time heated by the engine's exhaust system, there was always a pervasive smell of burning rubber on those early buses.

Graves was the first driver on the Hibbing-Duluth run. The road was of clay, covered with a thin layer of gravel. Even though the

"Snoose Line" buses were equipped with plows on their front bumpers, there was a constant danger in winter-time of becoming snow-bound. There were no towns on the route, and precious few farms, so travelers in January and February always had a good reason to be out on the road, or they stayed indoors.

In the winter of 1920 Graves set out from Hibbing to Duluth. He had only three passengers: a Hibbing policeman on his way to Rochester for rheumatism treatments at Mayo Clinic; a professional football player; and a piston ring salesman going to a convention in Duluth. About half-way on the journey, Graves took in three Finn lumberjacks.

It had been snowing all along, but about twenty miles short of Duluth, it became a blizzard. Finally the bus ran into a drift that even the plow could not penetrate. Trying to force the bus through it, Graves snapped the universal joint. He and his six passengers were thus stranded. It was ten degrees below zero. He left the motor running to get heat from the exhaust, and then set out to find help. Three miles down the road he found a cabin whose lone inhabitant was a grouchy old man who would not allow his horses to be used to pull the bus out of the snowdrift. By the time Graves got back to his bus, the temperature had dropped another ten degrees. He decided, then, to take all of his passengers to the old man's cabin. The selfish old curmudgeon, though, refused them entrance! It was only after the bus driver and some of his passengers threatened physical force that the old man relented. The room was large enough for two people, but now eleven (they had found a stranded car with a man and wife and daughter in it) were packed into it, luggage and all. It was too much for the three Finns. They left the cabin and began walking the twenty miles on into Duluth. They got there well before the bus did.[13]

In the early twenties, bus operation and bus manufacturing became two distinct divisions. The "Snoose Line," like other operatives, found that business was so good that it had to contract for its vehicles.

A pioneer in the auto-body business was C.J. Eckland who, with his brother Peter, worked in Minneapolis as early as 1905. They produced their first "bus" in 1912. They would cut a large automobile, such as a Packard or Pierce-Arrow, in half. Then they would cut channels into each end of the frame and insert a new body section. The result would be a twelve passenger touring car. Since a ventilation system was obviously necessary to rescue passengers from cigars, pipes, snuff, cigarettes and mining aromas, they built a small opening above the windshield. Air would thus circulate in the bus and exit through specially built louvres.[14]

In 1921 another set of brothers, Frank and W.B. Fageol of Oakland, California, introduced the first vehicle built specifically as a motor bus.[15] With sedan doors all along its side, it resembled a "hefty version" of some early touring cars. The new Fageol "Safety-Coach," designed with operating needs in mind, set a "new standard" in bus operations.[16]

This "new standard" encouraged Eric Wickman in 1922 to sell his interest in the Mesaba Transportation Company for $60,000, and go on to new ventures.[17] He had been with buses now for eight years, and had seen their operations grow from a jitney operation to a multi-million dollar business. Every route in Minnesota, he believed—and the entire country for that matter—was his for the taking. He bought into a small outfit called the White Bus Lines and, operating out of Duluth and Minneapolis, his business soon covered the whole of northern Minnesota. Then in 1925 Wickman's White Bus Lines merged with a Wisconsin enterprise, Superior White, to form the Northland Transportation Company.[18] This gave Wickman's activities an interstate character, and turned him into one of the "transportation giants" in the United States.

In 1925 Ralph Budd, President of the Great Northern Railroad, parted company with some of his more conservative railroading colleagues, and decided to buy into the bus industry. Instead of blaming buses for lost profits that the trains had suffered since the end of World War I, he reasoned that railroad branch lines feeding into main lines could profitably be taken over by buses. This was especially true since the trains operated on these branch lines at ninety cents a mile; and buses could run for twenty cents a mile. (See Appendix A.)

Budd, therefore, decided to buy into the largest and most efficient bus operation in Minnesota. That was Northland, headed by Eric Wickman. Budd paid $240,000 for an eighty percent interest in Northland. Wickman, with his remaining twenty percent, agreed to continue operating the system.[19]

With the help of his new-found railroad money and with the expertise of some business friends, especially Glenn Traer of Minneapolis, Wickman now organized a holding company known as the Motor Transit Corporation. This was in September, 1926, and it was the immediate predecessor to Greyhound. It was capitalized at $10 millions, and was headquartered in Delaware, the friendliest

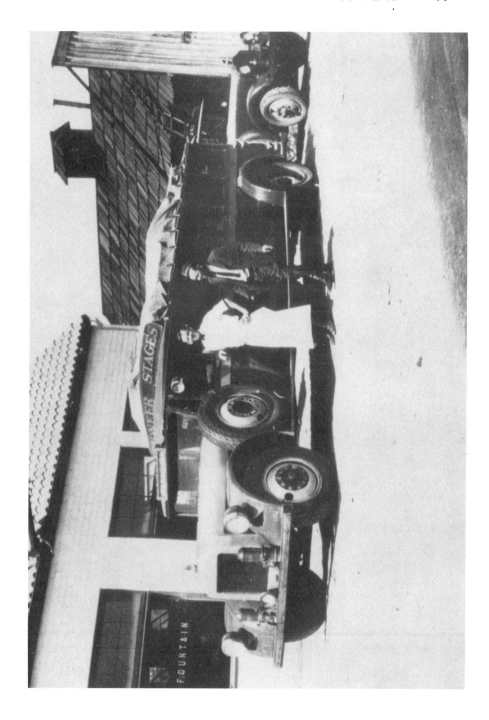

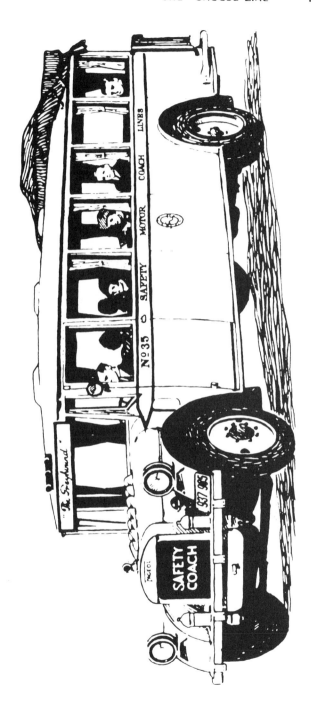

state in the Union to industrial and business amalgamation. E. C. Eckstrom was its first president, and he called his buses, "the greyhounds."

The name "greyhound" itself, and the emblem of the running dog, evolved from practices that were quite common in the early days of the industry. In olden times great pains were taken to show patrons of stagecoaches the advantages of "fast runs," "comfortable rides," and the like. Sometimes, elaborate emblems and paintings adorned these coaches: one Italian, Giovanni Cipriani, become notable in the late 18th century for his decorations of coaches. Also, the coaches were sometimes given fancy names to catch the public's eye. There were, for example, the "flying coach," and "whirlicote," in England that attracted much attention. Even after the coaches had fallen to the railroads in popularity, decorations and naming continued. The Pullman sleeper cars, for example, were often lavishly appointed and titled—all in an advertising effort to the traveling public.

It was natural, therefore, for bus lines to come up with fancy names and emblems for their own operations. Some used animal and bird names: "Jackrabbit," "Whippet," "Wolverine," "Tiger," Wolf," "Eagle," "Oriole," "White Swan," "Purple Swan," "White Bird," and "Blue Goose," while others were astronomical with "Red Star," and "Green Rocket." Sometimes they derived their name from the places they served: "Great Lakes," "Teche," (from Bayou Teche in Louisiana), "Okonogan," "Geneva Railway," "Camel City" (Winston-Salem, North Carolina), "Outer Belt," "Old South," "Wyandotte," "Old Colony," and "Tri-State." And, of course, sometimes the owners used their own names: "Bill's Stage Lines," "Ola Alden," "Benson and Ault," "Aldrich," "Dillard," and "Evans."

The practice of "stretching out" seven-passenger touring cars to accommodate twelve people caused many drivers for Wickman to call the new, low-slung product, "The Dachshund." (One can only guess at how the image of mass transportation in this country would have developed if this name had stuck). According to one story, a driver in California disliked the titles "hound" and "dachshund," that had been given to his bus, and began calling it the "greyhound." After stretching out their cars, Fageol Brothers products were usually painted gray. This helped considerably for the greyhound image to grow.

Another explanation has it that "because of dusty road conditions... the buses were painted battleship gray.... One day an inn-keeper whose hotel was located along the route remarked to...Wickman that the buses looked 'just like Greyhound dogs streaking by.' The name caught on, and Wickman adapted the slogan, 'Ride the Greyhounds.' "[20]

Probably the most accurate claim is that a Wisconsin man, Edward Stone, should be credited with "greyhound." One version is that Stone and John Wickman (Eric's brother) were in Fond du Lac, Wisconsin, trying to start a bus run to Milwaukee. One day in 1922 Stone called Wickman and said, "Let's go over to Cap Wellings for a glass of beer [despite prohibition] and talk over Milwaukee." They drove over to Cap Wellings in a bus, since neither of them had a car. On the way, Stone happened to see the bus's reflection in a store window. Its "jumping up and down" in the reflection gave its low-slung appearance the image of a dog, Stone thought—a greyhound.

Some sources say that Stone's bus that bright sun-shiny day was an old hearse. More probably, however, it was a sixteen valve, four cyclinder lengthened out White touring a car. It was painted light gray on the sides, with black trimmings for its California top. A week or so after starting the Milwaukee run, Stone took his vehicle to the sign shop of A. Jaeger in Fond du Lac, and had "THE GREYHOUND" put on just above the windows on each side. This was mid-June, 1922.[21] The earliest advertising that can be found was in the Fond du Lac *Commonwealth Reporter,* October 20, 1923. There was a picture of a Fageol bus in that day's edition, and the caption, "Take the Greyhound for business or pleasure to various places in Wisconsin." The name of the advertiser was the Eastern Wisconsin Transportation Company.

An associate of Stone's in Wisconsin was E. C. Eckstrom, from the Wickman group in Minnesota. He went to Michigan in the spring of 1924, and started a new bus company, operating between Muskegon and Grand Rapids, Michigan. He incorporated under Michigan laws in August, 1925, and named it the Safety Motor Coach Lines. He painted his buses blue and white, and put the emblem of the running dog on them. They soon became known far and wide as "the greyhounds."[22]

Then, in 1926, as we have noted, the Motor Transit Corporation was formed with Eckstrom as its President. He said that the greyhound emblem which had been standard equipment on his Michigan buses was now adapted by all MTC operations. He also reported that not only did Eric Wickman (soon to be the head) like the running dog insignia, but that he also decided that all MTC and subsequently, Greyhound, vehicles would be painted blue and white.[23]

It was somewhat ironic that with all of Wickman's activities that it was not he who sponsored the first transcontinental run. That honor fell to William E. ("Buck") Travis, who headed the giant Yelloway fleet, operating out of Denver.

At 8 o'clock, Wednesday night, September 5, 1928, the bus (built by the California Transit Company), pulled out of Los Angeles. It went to Denver on the old Santa Fe Trail; to St. Louis, it covered the United States Highway; to Pittsburgh on the old National Trail; and then to New York City on the Lincoln Highway. The distance traveled was 3,433 miles. It took five days and fourteen hours (exactly one day longer than the average train run). The transcontinental bus run came almost to the date ten years after the last of the long distance stagecoaches had been discontinued.

The Yelloway (so-named because they were painted yellow; although one wit said it was because when they broke down, the passengers could "yell away" and no-one would help them) picked up one important passenger in Pittsburgh: Buck Travis himself. He was on the bus just when the noon whistles were blowing, as it rolled down the Great White Way in Manhattan. The importance of that day to the transportation and social history of the United States was overlooked by the politicians. Travis was not greeted by any ceremonies, nor was he feted by government officials. In fact, he was totally ignored—in New York, at least. Back in Chicago, to which all MTC operations had been moved, Eric Wickman and his worried partners paid attention to this first transcontinental run—a great deal of attention—and decided to do something about it.

The Greyhound people, on Traer's advice, bought Yelloway in March, 1929, for $6,400,000, both companies' largest deals in their history. (In fact, this was the biggest transaction to date involving U.S. bus lines). The announcement of the Greyhound-Yelloway merger was made jointly by Orville Caesar of Greyhound and Travis of Yelloway:

> "The consolidation is a logical one, which will advance the standards of service rendered to the public and will afford substantial economics to the companies through the use of the same depots and facilities where the lines lie along the same route. It will enable a passenger to ride from coast to coast over the lines of a single system."[24]

A trade journal for Greyhound printed a cartoon about the merger. A Greyhound was on one side of the page, and a Yelloway on the other. Two bus drivers reached out of their windows, and shook hands. The

Greyhound driver said, "Howdy traveler—nice looking road ahead."

The Greyhound-Yelloway merger left just one major system now as real competition. That was Charles Wren's Pickwick network in California, and Greyhound saw it more as an opportunity than a threat. Shortly after the merger with Yelloway, Greyhound "persuaded Pickwick that [its] further eastward expansion was uneconomic and wasteful. Greyhound connections...could do the same job. Impressed with Greyhound's operating ability and financial resources, "Wren agreed to sell Pickwick Stages...."[25] The overall Pickwick Empire, which included some other bus lines, a hotel chain, and incipient airlines, did not totally break up until 1932.

The Yelloway merger and Pickwick acquisition were actually a combination of events that had taken place since 1925. Financial journals frequently asserted that Wickman was slow-footed at money matters—that he was a "field man" and not a "desk-jockey"—and that it was Traer who put Greyhound on a firm economic footing. The claim is not exactly accurate, for throughout the Twenties, well before the merger with Yelloway, Wickman and Caesar traveled throughout Dixie and the Midwest starting, buying, merging, and consolidating bus lines. It was vigorous, exciting work for the two young bus entrepreneurs.

Orville Swan Caesar came from Rye's Lake, Wisconsin, where, at the turn of the century, he was a mechanic in an auto repair shop. Then he became a field representative for Studebaker, based at Minneapolis. Tiring of this job, he moved on to Superior, where he proposed to sell Studebakers, Dodges, and Chandlers; and in time, the Caesar Motor Company became the largest automotive concern in northern Minnesota. Orville discovered, however, that he had a surplus of White trucks, and he was no more successful at selling them than Wickman had been with that long ago Hupmobile. Caesar and his partner, Ford Campbell, began stretching out the Whites, and putting bus bodies on them. To accommodate these new vehicles, Caesar started an inter-city bus line—from Superior to Duluth—charging a quarter for a one way journey. Then he extended his operation, by now called the Superior White Line, to Hurley, to which a trip from Superior cost $4.25. In 1925, Caesar sold out to Wickman of Northland in Minnesota, and became his partner.

The usual operating methods for these two—Wickman and Caesar—was to pour large amounts of money into an area to buy buses and to engage appropriate personnel. Then they filed "certificates of necessity" with the various state governments, showing that a dependable bus line was required. In cases where bus lines already operated, the Greyhound team offered favorable exchanges of stock, and always in no time, it seemed, the majority of stockholders in the old companies approved the transaction. In numerous instances, too, the Greyhound people were interested primarily—at first—in gaining a minority holding in an already established bus company. It was a practice also for Greyhound to team up with a railroad to buy bus lines. By the end of the decade, therefore, Greyhound either owned outright, was a co-owner, or had a minority interest in most of the bus operations east of the Mississippi. (See Appendix B).

Greyhound most assuredly did not operate in isolation. Toward the end of the Twenties, the number of bus lines in the United States ranged between three and four thousand. As one might imagine, the competition was fierce. Some "operators" accepted telephone orders, "leading to the obvious trick of sending the competition out to the end of town for a non-existent customer just to get clear use of the parking space."[26] All of this confusion and skullduggery highly motivated the industry leaders to consolidate and merge—to create uniform route and fare schedules, and in the process to kill off the "fly-by-nighters." It was this thought as much as anything else that caused the Motor Transit Corporation—on February 5, 1930—to restructure itself as the Greyhound Corporation, again under the laws of Delaware. Its headquarters, by 1930, was in the "transportation capital" of America, Chicago. The little jitney "snoose line" of 1914 had indeed covered many miles by the time it turned, in 1930, into the giant Greyhound conglomerate. It was in for a rude shock, however, as the depression-infested Thirties made their debut.

"Greyhound Stories"
Some True; Some Otherwise

Fat Lady: Driver is the bus through?
Driver: Through to where?
Fat Lady: Through shaking my body bountiful.
Driver: Falker Packing Company; next stop!—Greyhound Traveler, *March, 1929.*

Russell Byrd became known as the "singing bus driver." One woman passenger, however, did not care much for Russ's musical aptitudes:

"It was 2 A.M. The moon was full and clear. I was just going by Starvation Peak, and the inspiration that has come from those hills for generations to inspire poets of no litle stature, was working on me. I felt like singing.

"The lady in a very rude, irritable manner, raised up from her seat beside me and said 'driver, stop that infernal noise. Your fool whistling is keeping me awake.'

"Having red blood in my veins, my first impulse was to tell her to go jump in the lake. I had already seen for myself, however, that there are far better ways for putting a person in his place.

"After being quiet for a few minutes __ I __ smiled and remarked: 'You know, lady, you are right. I've been noticing the same thing. It keeps me awake, too. Now, I'll be quiet, and we can both go to sleep.'

"There was no immediate response. The lady leaned back and went to sleep for a few minutes. About ten or fifteen minutes later, she raised up with a start, and __ said, 'Oh, I'm sorry, driver; I see what you mean'."—Russell Byrd, Russ's Bus.

Russell Byrd's "happiest moments" on a bus were when he "over-ruled" one of "God's pranks" at Caliente race-track in Tia Juana, Mexico. He was taking a charter group there one day in a rain-storm that extended from Los Angeles to the Mexican border. A few passengers jokingly asked him if he could do something about the rain. He replied that it would take some doing, but he would think about it; he believed he could arrange for them to have sunshine all day at the race-track. Five miles from Caliente, however, there was still a downpour, and the bus travelers now looked forward to a wet day at the races, only to be chided by Russ for having too little faith.

Three miles from Caliente, the sun suddenly broke through. It remained sun-shiny all day. When they began their return trip late that afternoon, it started raining again exactly three miles from Caliente. Some of the passengers really did believe that Russ had a direct line to God. It was geographical rather than theological knowledge, however, that gave Russ his "insights."

"The Coast Range Mountains extend down the California coast and skip Caliente race track at Tia Juana ___ I knew that storms often paralleled the mountains on the U.S. side and abruptly quit three miles out of Tia Juana. It worked fine that day."—Russell Byrd, to the author, August 5, 1980.

*"Greyhound has a million less bumps for the travelers' rumps."—*Greyhound Traveler, *March, 1929.*

"Old buses back in the late '30s ___ never knew what air-conditioning was. All the air you got came through an open window. Once ___ [in the summertime] ___ a driver had all his windows open. A bee flew into the bus and of all places settled between the breasts of a woman passenger.

"She screamed. The driver stopped and rushed back to see what was wrong. The lady was fumbling at the front of her dress.

"The flustered driver asked, 'Lady, you want me to get the bee out of there?'

"She said, 'Hell no! I'd rather have the bee in there than you!' "—George Walker, Louisville, Kentucky.

Lady: "What seat do you want me to take?
Driver: "Any of 'em. I'm gonna take 'em all with me."—Greyhound story.

A mother took her son to the zoo. They came to the baboon cage.
"What's that? Mommy?" the boy asked.
"That's a baboon, son," she replied.
The boy looked puzzled. He said, "With that funny look on its face and all the corns on its butt, I thought it was a Greyhound bus driver.'—Another Greyhound story.

Two women on a bus had a dispute concerning a window, and they at last called the driver as a referee. "If this window is open," one declared, "I shall catch cold and probably die."
"If this window is shut," the other announced, "I shall certainly suffocate."

The two glared at each other. The driver was at a loss, but he welcomed the remarks of a man with a red nose who sat nearby. He said, "first, open the window. That will kill one. Next, shut it, and that will kill the other. Then we can have a little peace around here."—Bill Crook and Bill Morgan, Exhaust, June, 1945.

A cartoon showed a Greyhound bus hopelessly stuck in the mud. The driver addresses his passengers: "And now, ladies and gentlemen, we come to the audience participation part of our program. Everyone out and push!"—Cartoon by Wally Falk in Rearview Mirror, May, 1955.

Lady: "Driver, how long is your route?"
Driver: "Well, Ma'am, I'd say about average."—Greyhound story.

There was this bus sliding down a steep hill in slippery snow. A man said, "Driver, let me off this bus!" The driver responded: "Sir, if I could stop this damn thing, I'd get off myself."—Another Greyhound story.

"Nothing opens the door of a bus quicker at a rest stop than a bawling baby."—Old Greyhound saying.

A passenger jumped out of a moving bus one time, and headed into the desert. The driver stopped the vehicle, and caught the man. "What's the matter with you?" the driver demanded. "It's not me," said the man, "it's you. You're taking me in the other direction!"— Russell Byrd, Russ's Bus.

This driver stopped for a lady each morning who lived on the left side of a road going into Madisonville, Kentucky. He always made a left turn into her yard, without ever checking to see if anyone was passing. One morning, he maneuvered his bus as usual, only to cause a man behind him to careen off the road and turn over.
"Don't you ever give any signals?" the man asked.
"I stop here every morning," the bus driver, who was getting on in years, said, somewhat indignantly.
"Oh, excuse me," said the saintly man. "I live in Illinois, and didn't know that!"— Raymond Ogilby, Louisville, Kentucky.

"I always tried to avoid the experience of 'ships that pass in the

night,' and usually learned about my passengers. I was talking about my book, Russ's Bus, *going into Fresno, CA, and the passenger behind me asked to see one. He bought it, and then said, 'We have something in common.' I asked what and he said, 'authorship.' I asked him to tell me of one of his works, and he recited, 'The Face on the Barroom Floor.' I immediately said to him 'Robert Service?' 'The same,' he replied."—Russell A. Byrd, letter to the author, August 5, 1980.*

"Many girls walk back from rides in cars with bus drivers on account of the driver being accustomed to a larger bus."—Another old Greyhound saying.

Once Arvid Heed had a full bus coming into Hibbing, when a blizzard struck. He came to a man and a woman, waiting for the bus, and he stopped for them. The man, seeing that there was no room inside, jumped on a ladder at the bus' rear end. Heed assumed that the woman did likewise. He drove on, and nine miles later when he stopped, the man explained that Heed had left his wife behind, and angrily demanded that Heed go back for her. If Heed refused, said the man, he would see to it that Heed was fired. Heed replied, "Fire me? Hah! I'm the Vice-President of this Company!"—Attributed to Heed, or to any of the other early officers for Greyhound who started out behind the wheel.

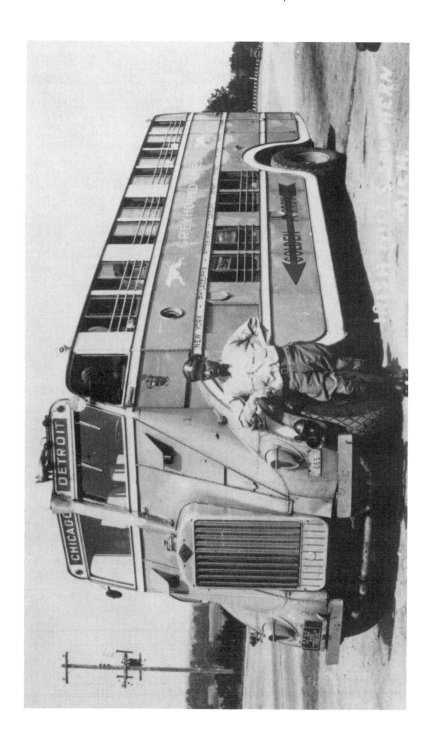

Chapter Two
Trials of the Thirties

The Greyhounds loped into 1930 as though there were no economic clouds anywhere. By now, bus travelers reflected a cross section of American society. They included salesmen (but *not* the expense account executive), workmen, housewives, tourists, sportsmen, school teachers, old people and youngsters. It was frequently asserted, with some truth, that passengers getting on and off a bus during the time it traveled a hundred miles represented the people of all America. Bus travelers tended to be persons who paid their own way for their trips. Perhaps this was why they were much more informal than those going by train, or by recently started air services. Bus people generally wore sports clothes, were very friendly, and were easy to get acquainted with.

Much of this informality had to do with the driver (whose role in latter day times is vastly different from that of his early brethren). He made numerous stops along the route, and frequently got to know his passengers by name. He collected fares in cash, and sometimes adopted the laissez-faire principle of charging "whatever the market will bear." This practice, among others, finally caused the company to hire "spotters" to ride incognito, and report erring drivers.[1] In time, the word "spotter" equated to bus drivers everywhere as "rat," "fink," "no-good busybody"—and worse.

On the longer runs, the buses did use a ticketing system. Greyhound continued a practice begun by Yelloway of issuing tickets for long-distance travel in much the way of trains. A traveler was given a ticket for each division of about three hundred miles, meaning that at least ten coupons would be necessary for coast to coast travel. Forgetful passengers, or those prone to lose things, frequently had a rough time holding on to their coupons.

Already by the Thirties, complaints poured in from disgruntled passengers about the services that were auxiliary to their travel. Greasy, stomach-turning lunch counters and cafes topped the list, followed closely by filthy toilets at rest stops and terminals. A part of the problem in these respects was that Greyhound and the other bus companies frequently leased facilities from private business concerns, and did not keep a very close watch on them. In later years, when Greyhound diversified, some of these difficulties were ameliorated (in part, by setting up a network of "Post-House Restaurants").

Another problem the travelers faced was breakdowns, often caused by dusty roads clogging up vital machinery. Though Greyhound stocked parts in all major cities so that buses could be repaired in good order, many an uncomfortable hour was spent on the road waiting for help. Drivers were instructed, during breakdowns to placate passengers by not complaining about the company's failure at good maintenance. Such complaints would only make the passenger nervous and cause him to believe that "the company is badly managed and is not safe to ride with. Always try to give an excuse that will satisfy the passengers."

Whenever a bus completed a long run and stopped at a station in a major city, it was immediately put onto a wash rack, where its exterior was scrubbed with soap and high pressure water sprays. Inside, it was cleaned by vacuum. On a regular schedule, the coach was thoroughly inspected for mechanical or safety faults. It could not leave the terminal until the resident superintendent put his stamp of satisfaction on it. (One major, even deadly, problem faced by early bus drivers and passengers was vacuum brakes, whose performances were tied directly to the operation of the engine. Frequently, if the engine died while the coach was moving, the brakes would go out, and not be strong enough to stop the bus. Some dreadful accidents happened in just this way. Air brakes were a definite improvement over the old vacuum system.)

The buses cast an imaginative image as they roared over the roads for far-away, mysterious destinations. Already they were being romanticized by the American people much in the same way the trains of an earlier era had been. In 1934, a journalist for *The New Republic*, Nathan Asch, penned a fascinating description of cross-country travel: a "snapshot of America," as it were.

Flagstaff, Arizona, said Asch, was filled with drunken cowpunchers without jobs. Meat prices had dropped so low that the area's ranchers could no longer hire any help. The unemployed cowboys then came to Flagstaff and drank away their problems.

In Gallup, New Mexico, martial law had just been called off after a coal miners' strike. Several workers in a saloon told Asch that the management had sprayed them with acid during the labor troubles. There was much talk in Gallup, and indeed throughout the Southwest, about an expected Communist-inspired general strike. The miners, noted Asch, had no forebodings about such an event.

A baby rode alone from Denver to Kansas City. It slept soundly throughout the bumps, shakes and rattles that kept all the other passengers awake. Periodically, the driver stopped and gave the baby one of six bottles that had been packed for it in a shoe box.

Out of Kansas City, Asch talked with a soldier about war. Soon everyone on the bus, except the women, was in a general discussion about warfare. Their failure to join in was caused, said Asch, not by any anti-bellicose attitudes but because of their overwhelming interests in permanent waves and clothes.

In Wheeling, West Virginia, Asch "heard class hatred" as never before. The passengers saw miners, many of whom were foreigners, going to work. A mining equipment salesman sitting near Asch said loudly about the miners, "do you know those bastards are so mean they send their own children into the state highway so they can get hit by coal trucks and then they sue the company for damages?" Asch and his fellow travelers passed on through Pittsburgh where, in 1933, over 65,000 families had to get state and federal relief. On eastward from Pittsburgh, passengers seemed to be embarrassed and apologetic for riding a bus, and Asch attributed these conditions to the supposed sophistication of eastern minds and manners—particularly as those qualities were compared with the citizenry west of the Alleghenies.

At 5 o'clock of a morning, the bus made a breakfast stop. Then it rolled on through New Jersey, and came at last to the Holland Tunnel. Emerging from it, they saw the gleaming skyscrapers of Manhattan. After a few more minutes, the driver stopped and yelled, "Everybody out! This is the end!" They were in New York City.[2]

"Bus watching" had become something of a national past-time by the Thirties. It was not unusual for people to picnic along roads in places where they knew several buses would pass. They wanted a good look at those behemoths—many with Dr. Pepper advertisements on their sides—that were rapidly changing the transportation patterns of America.

If the "bus watchers" were unusually lucky, they might get a glimpse of "Number One." This was the official bus for Greyhound executives, christened in 1928 by singer and actor Eddie Cantor. Orville Caesar used it the most, since as vice-president now of the overall Greyhound Corporation, he was generally out in the field.

Number One, a Will 1000, usually piloted by Martin Suthack, was a "hotel on wheels," with sleeping berths to accommodate nine people. Frequently it was called a "land yacht," because of its luxurious appointments and its amenities to encourage "easy living." Despite its glamorous image, it was from Greyhound One that many momentous decisions affecting American transportation were made.

Or, if the "bus watchers" were only normally lucky, enough buses would go by for them to try their hand at translating the symbols they saw. If they were sufficiently knowledgeable, they recognized that "PD 4104" meant "Parlor Car, Diesel Powered, 41 Passengers, and the fourth series of this model." They were aware too that "TG 2401" meant "Transit Coach, Gas Powered, 24 Passengers, and the first of the model series." "TDH," they realized, told them that the coach was a "Transit Diesel," with a "Hydraulic Transmission."

A real treat for the "bus watchers" was to see a "sleeper" passing through. These were pioneered by Charles Wren and Pickwick Stages, and were picked up later by Greyhound. Charles began— even while he was President of Pickwick—the Columbia Pacific Nite Coaches Company, which plied between Los Angeles and San Francisco. The three coaches used on this run were named "Alsacia," "Gladys" and fittingly enough, "Morpheus." They were double decker buses, with the top floor used primarily for observation purposes. In time, they became successful enough for Wren to institute additional runs, and soon the "slumber chariots" thundered through the night between L.A. and Chicago. Another Greyhound-affiliated company that ran the sleepers was Great Lake Stages of Ohio, which operated nightly between Cleveland and Buffalo.

T.T. Davis of Alhambra, California, was a driver of an early sleeper. He had to sit over the engine which made his time at the wheel a miserable experience. He was fairly well isolated, however, from his passengers by a glass partition, and he could "smoke up a storm" without getting complaints. On the earliest sleepers, people lay down lengthwise, which made the tough curves difficult for a driver. The later sleepers had the snoozers crosswise, making them quite vulnerable to sudden stops. Many were the people whose dreams were shattered by a tortuous curve or an unexpected stop.[3]

In time, the night coaches were equipped with a crew of three: two drivers, one of whom slept while the other drove, and a porter, usually a black man. The porters were the luckiest bus-men aboard the sleepers, especially on the L.A.—Chicago run. They earned as much money on one of these trips as a driver did in a month. The soft drink and quick food concessions were entirely theirs, and the ice they used was furnished free by the company. At the end of the line, the porter usually tipped the drivers anywhere from five to ten dollars each.[4]

On one of the sleepers that Russell Byrd drove, a telephone system enabled him to listen to the engine when he wished, and also to communicate with the porter, whose "office" was at the back of the bus. During the daytime, Russ reported, the passengers could shift around on the bus as much as they wanted to, as long as the company rule of segregating the sexes was adhered to. Even so, there was one compartment, the lower rear, where young men and women comported with each other, even to the extent sometimes of having amorous affairs. This area of the bus was appropriately nick-named "The Love Nest." The upper rear compartment was the "Political Forum," where the men congregated to smoke cigars and talk politics; the upper front was called "The Old Ladies' Home," for that was where the women gathered to talk over things of importance. "The Musical Den," in the center of the coach, was a place of laughter and gaiety. "The Master Bedroom" referred to the sleeping berths which were kept available during the day for anyone who wanted to relax.[5]

As might be expected, the sleepers were perfect for all the big bands of the Thirties. Russ reminisced at length about some of the famous musicians he transported across the country. Jimmy Dorsey always came up to the driver's cubicle at 4 a.m to chat with Russ to, as Russ put it, get his advice on things, etc. A member of the band told Russ one day that Jimmy had read statistics about early morning accidents because of drivers going to sleep, and was just making sure this did not happen to his boys. Needless to say, Russ's ego was considerably deflated.

Then there was the time Phil Harris' band could not sleep after their concert ended at 1 a.m. Russ stopped the bus, and at 2 a.m. they gave a "concert to God," out in the middle of the desert. Other famed musicians who frequently traveled with Russ were Glen Gray, Rudy Vallee, Benny Goodman, Jan Garber and John Scott Trotter.[6]

Pacific Greyhound Lines began sleeper service in 1930 between San Francisco and Portland. Simultaneously, the Greyhound Corporation in Chicago planned an elaborate debut for their sleepers which they hoped would have nationwide schedules in two or three years. The Greyhound sleeper was to be powered by a 150

HP Waukesha Motor, mounted on a chassis built by the Bender Body Company of Cleveland. A brochure talked about the new sleeper, whose rear-end was to look almost like that of a Pullman Car:

> The coach has berths accommodating nine people .... On one side the berths are single; on the other they are double. The sleeping compartment is in the front of the coach. The rear of the coach is a deluxe club car. A divan extends across the end of the bus and four movable over-stuffed arm-chairs are included in the equipment. A table may be brought in, and the passengers may play bridge or enjoy a light lunch served from the compact kitchenette .... Additional features ... are a built-in radio and victrola ....
> With the berths folded away ... the seating of the coach is 24 passengers. Between the sleeping and the club cars, there is a completely equipped lavatory, even to the extent of a shower bath ...."[7]

Alas, this spectacular coach was extremely short-lived.

On the whole, the sleepers were economic liabilities to the bus industry in general, and to Greyhound affiliates in particular. For one thing, they were highly popular only in the summer-time, and even then, income was not adequate to meet expenses. In a seven month period in 1933, for example, Pacific Greyhound lost $10,000 with its sleeper operation. Another problem was the wide-spread belief by travelers that "buses were not meant to be slept on." A chronic complaint by the berth passengers was that those in seats always made too much noise. Even if this were not the case, the ruts, holes, rocks, curves and ditches along the road-way definitely discouraged sleep. By 1934, the dream of a great fleet of sleepers traversing the length and breadth of this country had fairly well vanished (although in some isolated instances, a few sleepers ran until the 1940s). It was a wonderful idea, but the harsh realities of. the day would not permit its fulfillment.

Greyhound, like most other corporations, was struck a staggering blow by the stock market crash of 1929. It funded its floating debt in '29 by selling $2,500,000 of one-year notes. In 1930 it had to re-fund these notes with a new $4,000,000 issue, good for three years. These measures were only temporary at the best, buying Greyhound a little time in which to save itself.

"By 1932 operating revenues of the Greyhound Lines had dropped 27 per cent from their 1930 figure...."[8], and the

Corporation simply could not pay its debts. In 1932 alone, it lost nearly $127,000. General Motors, with whom the bus company had been linked for many years, came to the rescue by assuming over a $1,000,000 debt to various banks. Again, Greyhound had a breathing space, and Glenn Traer went to work.[9]

"He persuaded the holders of the $4,000,000 worth of gold notes (due in 1933) to redeem the old notes by accepting a new set for an equal amount maturing in 1938," and secured by the stock of several of the more efficient Greyhound operating companies.[10] Only a few of the old note holders objected to this procedure. By March, 1933, over 96 per cent had agreed to Traer's offer.[11] Once more, Greyhound was kept on the road. But the big question for everyone was: "for how long?"

Unquestionably leading a charmed life, Greyhound next benefited and capitalized on an extravagant show staged by the City of Chigago. This was the World's Fair of 1933, celebrating a "century of progress" for the Windy City.

The Fair was situated on 428 acres along Lake Michigan, and its objective was to "tell the story of the great scientific, industrial and cultural achievements wrought in 100 years by a marching civilization."[12] With eighteen nations participating, and a general admission of fifty cents, the fair opened at 9:30 a.m., on May 27, to the blare of factory sirens and automobile horns—all blowing in accordance with a proclamation by Chicago Mayor, Edward Kelly. Postmaster General James Farley was present at the opening as the personal representative of President Franklin Roosevelt.

The fair's sponsors emphasized "pure science"—physics, chemistry, biology and geology. Wonderfully instructive booths were set up to demonstrate all these marvels—so much, in fact, that it took several days for a person to view them all. Technology, "the application of science," was on full, spectacular view as well. The Travel and Transport Building exhibited displays showing the history of transportation in the United States. All major automobiles were represented, but General Motors, celebrating its 25th anniversary, set up a complete assembly line, where it produced twenty to thirty cars a day, all to the astonishment and delight of the visitors.[13]

It was not all science and industry, however. The midway featured Sally Rand in a show called "The Streets of Paris," in which she performed an act, "Birth of Passion." The good citizens of Chicago and the world forgot all about science as they watched Sally's contortions, covered only by white body powder and two large fans. She was finally arrested on a charge of indecency, but was quickly cleared by Chicago's courts. The publicity surrounding her arrest caused even more people to catch her act, and her earnings shot up from $125 a week to $3,000. She explained to a reporter, "I never really made any money until I took off my pants."[14] The fair also inspired *Tribune* sports-writer Arch Ward to have an "All-Star" baseball game played at Comiskey Park between the best players of the National and American Leagues. Babe Ruth hit a two-run homer as the American league won 4-2. The "All-Star" game was so popular that it became a fixture in each year's baseball season.

For some, however, the fair was a springboard for voicing misgivings. Writing in the New York *Times* magazine, R.L. Duffus exclaimed:

> Five years ago the effort [of the fair] would not have been so desperate, nor so magnificent. Science then could have spread its feathers like a peacock and strutted a little as it displayed to the average man the world it had made . . . . Today it must admit that a century of dazzling scientific advancement has culminated in unemployment and misery, in chaos, in dictatorship, in loss of faith in old forms of government and in old political principles for which rivers of valiant blood were shed. Somehow this must make us believe this is the black hour before dawn and that the dawn itself will be more splendid than any we have seen.[15]

For many, the World's Fair in Chicago was indeed a "splendid dawn." It carried over well into the summer and fall, and it saved numerous Chicago businesses from bankruptcy.

The attendance for this five month fair was the greatest ever. In Philadelphia in 1876, about 8.5 million people attended the Centennial Fair. The great Chicago Exposition of 1893 attracted some 21 millions; and the extravaganza of depression-ridden 1933 brought in 22,320,456 paid admissions. Getting these people all over 428 acres, covering a six-mile strip of land required a systematic and efficient transportation facility, and that is where Greyhound came into the picture.

It created World's Fair Greyhound, and put the able Ralph Bogan in charge. He had a fleet of sixty specially designed buses at his disposal, each of which was fifty feet long, with a total capacity of ninety people: fifty sitting and forty standing. He employed 120 drivers who alternated shifts in getting visitors from one place to another over the vast area of the fairgrounds. There was a "high speed" express service, making relatively few stops between one end of the fair and the other; a "midway" service, which kept fourteen drivers constantly at the wheel; and an "island service" which took people to various exhibits. The drivers on these runs no longer had to yell out destinations and stops. Instead, they joyfully demonstrated an electrical announcing system which Bell Telephone had developed for them. A carbon microphone picked up the driver's voice and amplified it throughout the bus.[16] In addition to all the drivers at the fair, the Greyhound Company hired twenty cashiers and a like number of turnstile watchers, and created a ten man maintenance shop.

Obviously, the Greyhound people planned months in advance for Chicago's World Fair. Let's say that you are a citizen of Omaha, and that along about March you decide that you want to go to Chicago in May and see all the wonderful exhibits at the Fair. You go to your local travel agent, or write a hotel in Chicago for reservations. Chances are very good that you will be disappointed. However, you are told, if you will just go down to the Greyhound Station, you'll be "fixed right up" with a "Greyhound Tour Package." Its price includes round-trip transportation, hotel lodgings in Chicago, and the rides on Greyhound vehicles at the fairgrounds. The truth, you discover, is that Greyhound has reserved entire blocks of rooms from all of Chicago's finest hotels. Therefore, if you are going to see the fair at all, you definitely have to "Go Greyhound." The big concerns in America, including Greyhound, had always argued that by its very nature the bus business was monopolistic. Greyhound most adequately fulfilled this premise in 1933 at Chicago's World Fair.

Despite the element of hidden coercion, the Greyhound fair tours fit the traveling needs of thousands of people. The operation, in fact, went over so well that it put Greyhound permanently into the highway tour business. Even before the fair ended, Greyhound was planning charter tours to numerous national parks in the northeast, not the least of which was Niagara Falls. The fair also inspired Greyhound to establish its own travel agencies—not just in the United States but in Europe and South America as well. It wanted to bring Europeans and Latinos to this country by boat or air, and then have them take the bus once they were here.[17]

World's Fair Greyhound netted the Corporation $500,000 (this did not include the round-trip package tours), which helped considerably to bring it out of its financial slump. Greyhound, of course, had every intention of continuing its fairground operation on into 1934. The officers of the fair, however, noting Bogan's huge successes, "clamped far more severe terms" on Greyhound's concessions, and as a result, it earned little.[18] Nevertheless, the 1933 operation gave a much needed stimulus to Greyhound's economic growth. Definitely up from the previous year, Greyhound's net profit for 1933 was approximately $1.6 millions. World's Fair Greyhound played a decisive role in this upward swing.

Another event that caused Greyhound to wag its tail was the nationwide showing of 1935's "best movie," *It Happened One Night*. In it, Claudette Colbert played a society girl who fled the restraints of her wealthy, over-powering family, primarily her father, by crossing the country from Florida to New York City by bus. Many of the film's scenes were shot inside the coach, showing audiences everywhere the cross-sections of American travelers, and instilling the idea that all classes are assimilated on buses. Frank Capra directed the movie, and he focused on Miss Colbert and Clark Gable (who played a journalist) only after he had put them into the mainstream of America symbolized by the bus travelers. His idea was to show that a bus could be "home" to a wealthy socialite just as much as to a rugged hard-nosed newspaper reporter. And both could fit very well into the broader social spectrum, in which the bus came to indicate a unified American value system. Of course, the socialite and the newspaperman fell in love with each other, and soon thousands of people all over the country were "hopping a Greyhound," looking for similar experiences. Alas, they mostly proved the old adage that "life should be more like the movies."[19]

Greyhound, of course, was overjoyed at the film's popularity, and gleefully sold tickets to theatre buffs who now wanted to take a bus trip. Cinemas and buses became the focal points of escapism, so much desired by that generation of depression-ridden citizens.

Another film that considerably helped Greyhound was *Cross Country Cruise*. It started out in Denver when a husband shot his wife in a department store with a bow and arrow. He planted the body in a display for drawing room furniture where three mannikins were playing bridge. The murdered woman, of course, became the fourth partner. The man then took a bus for Seattle, and on it he met Lew Ayres and assorted other footloose people trying to make a new start in the west after several failures in the east. The bus in this film was not nearly as central to the "plot" as it had been in *It Happened One Night*. Its value primarily was in introducing "many moviegoers to the modern marvels of bus transportation."[20] It served as the central meeting place for the movie's various characters, and it showed the viewers a lot of beautiful scenery between San Francisco and Seattle.

Again, Greyhound was pleased with the publicity that accrued from *Cross Country Cruise*. No matter that such a base murderer could be one of its paying passengers; after all, he was ultimately apprehended and brought to justice. The film played for quite some time at the Orpheum Cinema in San Francisco. Greyhound parked a huge sleeper on the street just outside the theatre to give the fans an idea of what they would see inside.

Still another plotless wonder that benefited the Hound was *Fugitive Lovers*. Robert Montgomery played a convict falsely convicted of a crime. He escaped from the penitentiary and boarded a bus which just happened to be passing by. It also "just happened" that two of the other passengers were a mobster (Legs Coffee) and a beautiful woman (Madge Evans) trying to escape his evil influences. So ... guess what? Robert Montgomery dressed in another man's clothes to put the police off his scent, and at the same time, rescued the fair damsel. The bus formed a nice, tight environment for the fragile plot line, and again it showed America's movie-goers some marvelous scenery, and made them yearn for something other than vicarious experiences.

The following year, 1935, *Thanks a Million* appeared, which was a political-musical movie. (Musicals always seem to be very popular during depressions.) A successful gubernatorial candidate (a Democrat, naturally, in FDR's America) decided that he would rather have the woman he loved than be governor of Pennsylvania. He therefore refused to assume his office; instead going after his sweetheart on a bus. Naturally, he found her in about ninety minutes, and Greyhound could add some more friends to its steadily growing roster.

"If you want to beat the depression, get yourself some good bus movies," could very well have been Greyhound's refrain of the mid-thirties. Almost doubling the previous year, in 1934 Greyhound profits were $3,150,000. In 1935, the net intake was $4,670,000, and for the first time in history, more people rode buses than trains.[21]

This overtaking of trains by buses, however, did not necessarily mean that the rails lagged economically. Historically, bus fares were two-thirds of the rail rates. in 1933, it cost about three cents a mile to travel by train; subsequently, the bus rate was roughly two and a half cents. In the most dismal days of the depression, however, some bus lines dropped this arrangement in the interest of volume.

For the trip from New York to Chicago, for example, Greyhound sold
tickets for $8.00, causing some other lines to give away the 900 mile
trip for $1.00.[22] Railroads obviously could not compete with these
inanities, and, as it turned out, neither could the buses.[23] In one area,
at least, in the South, an attempt was made to rectify the killing
competition that had developed between buses and trains. In April
1934 there occurred the so-called "New Orleans Agreement." This
provided that both trains and buses charge a flat two cents a mile,
with the understanding that after 175 miles, the bus rates would
gradually be lowered.[24] Southern Railroad, however, objected to this
arrangement, wanting to hold its fares at a constant one and a half
cents. The ICC concurred in Southern's desire; the "New Orleans
Agreement" was scuttled, and ruinous competition continued
apace.

All of these developments pointed anew to the need for federal
regulation of the bus industry. It had been talked about since 1914
when Pennsylvania enacted a law regulating safety conditions on
buses, and Minnesota decreed that "the operator of a motor vehicle
shall on signal of raising ... the hand or by request of a person
leading, riding, or driving, a horse bring such motor vehicle to a
stop." Inter-city bus regulation was simply too big a task for the
states to handle. In one state, safety of passengers would be the
paramount consideration, while in another, road and bridge
conditions would be emphasized. Many states tried to dictate the
routes for inter-city buses, and some wanted to regulate fares. In
addition to all these differences, it was quite possible for some large
border metropolis like Kansas City to allow certain types of buses
within its boundaries while the state of Missouri itself refused them
altogether. This confusion reigned for many years, and definitely
caused the bigger companies, Greyhound in the lead, to lobby for
federal regulation.

In 1925 Minnesota passed a Bus Regulatory Act, which required
new companies to secure "certificates of convenience and necessity"
before starting operations. Michigan followed suit, and it appeared
that some semblance of uniformity was to be achieved through
cooperative efforts by the states. The federal Supreme Court,
however, in Michigan Public Utilities vs. Duke, ruled that an
individual state could express itself only in matters of interstate bus
safety: it could not delve into routes, fares, "convenience" or
"necessity."

It became very clear now that if buses (and along with them, trucks) were ever going to be regulated, it would have to be done on a federal level. A bill to that effect was introduced into Congress in 1925. It passed the Senate but failed in the House, a procedure that occurred at every session of Congress for the next decade. Railroads increasingly favored federal regulation of buses, for that would control the competition between the two types of carriers.[25] The trucking industry, however, steadfastly fought regulation: "Operating ... with individual trucks or in very small companies ... charging almost any rate that comes to mind, the truckmen hear nothing in the I.C.C. but the hissing sound of Stalin."[26] Trucking opposition was one big reason for the long delay in attaining federal legislation.

But a regulatory bill was on the "must" list of President Franklin Roosevelt, and he usually got what he wanted. He wished to create a coordinated system of transportation by rail, highway, water and air, and a federal regulatory bill was an important step in that direction.[27]

The Motor Carrier Act of 1935 was authored by Congressman James S. Parker of New York, one-time chairman of the Committee on Interstate and Foreign Commerce. Its final version was introduced into the House by George Huddleston of Alabama, and in the Senate by Montana's Burton K. Wheeler. It swept handily through both houses at the behest of the reform-minded President, and he signed it in early October.

Basically, the Motor Carrier Act (MCA) put trucks and buses under the jurisdiction of the Interstate Commerce Commission, in the way railroads had been for years. The ICC now granted or refused the certificates of necessity and convenience that Minnesota, Michigan and a few other states had attempted in an earlier period. Under a "Grandfather Clause," bona fide companies that had been in existence on June 1, 1935, were automatically approved by the ICC for continued operations. After that date, however, a bus company had to present its credentials and prove its case before the federal regulatory agency.

Among the ultimate objectives of the MCA was the prevention of an over-supply of transportation for America's citizens who wanted to go somewhere. This in turn would deter wasteful and destructive competition.

It soon became a question, however, among all interested parties, of just how great was the authority now thrust upon the ICC by this Act. Quite extensive, came back the answer. The ICC imposed strict rules of accounting on the inter-city buses, and it forbade the companies to borrow beyond certain limits. Not the least of the ICC's new-found power was to regulate rates, and to impose a sixteen hour per day limit on drivers being on duty, and restricting their actual driving time during that period to ten hours. As time passed, the ICC proved that it was quite similar to most other government bureaucracies: it took on powers that had not been specifically spelled out by Congress. For example, when the MCA was first passed, only drivers came under ICC's control. Soon, however, the commissioners ruled that their authority extended to all other employees as well. This included, of course, the ticket agents, porters, janitors and, later on, the cooks and waitresses in terminal cafes and restaurants. Greyhound rather quickly, in fact, began to have misgivings about this federal control that it had wanted so long, for such control ultimately proved as much a curse as a blessing.[28]

Another "curse," or at least a serious disadvantage—from Greyhound's viewpoint—was the rousing of the labor movement in the late 1930s. The National Recovery Administration exempted labor from anti-trust and monopoly activities, a condition that greatly encouraged union organizing. Also, the Wagner-Connery Act, setting up a National Labor Relations Board, provided for federal mediation in disputes between employees and management, and allowed workers to choose their own unions.

Greyhound's first major exposure to labor problems came on the west coast. Employees of Pacific Greyhound complained that company officials had used threats, intimidation, discharges and wage rises and decreases in an effort to stop unionization. Naturally, Greyhound management denied the charges. Early in 1937, however, that same management announced that its "company unions" would no longer be used for collective bargaining and that Pacific Greyhound employees could choose their own affiliate. This company decision was considerably encouraged by a recent U.S. Supreme Court ruling that the Wagner Act was constitutional. The gist of the Court's action was that no employee could be fired for joining a union. As a result, in addition to Pacific Greyhound's sweeping affirmation of union affiliation, it also re-instated five employees who had been fired for union agitation.[29] Most Greyhound people voted to join the Amalgamated Association of Street Electric Railway and Motor Coach Employees, a part of the American Federation of Labor. The AASERMCE (now shorted to Amalgamated Transit Union, or ATU), thus became the chief bargaining agent for Greyhound employees in 1937, and remains so to this day. A few drivers around the country, however, affiliated with the Teamsters and some with the Brotherhood of Railway Trainmen, BRT (because of the large railroad investments in Greyhound Lines, especially in the east). It was this latter organization that called for, and got, what was the first major strike against Greyhound.

The trouble began in late November, 1937. Though Greyhound drivers' pay, at 3.61 cents a mile, was reckoned the highest in the industry, they still felt put upon by their management. In the east, therefore, on November 25, over 1,300 members of the BRT walked out on eight different Greyhound affiliates: Ohio, Pennsylvania, Capital, Canadian, Illinois Eastern, New England and Central. The drivers wanted 5.5 cents a mile for their services, and a minimum daily distance of 200 miles. Even more importantly, they demanded a closed shop in which no one but BRT members could work for Greyhound. From mid-night on the 25th, drivers stopped their buses at the nearest station, where passengers with onward tickets were given a refund.

There was violence, as the strike spread to sixteen states. Greyhound service between New York and Philadelphia was cut off altogether, and police officers accompanied drivers and passengers wherever it continued. The union charged the company with using "inexperienced" drivers, and not giving them enough rest on the runs. Of course, Greyhound denied these accusations.

Maryland state troopers arrested eleven men charged with halting a bus and beating the driver. Five men disabled a Greyhound in Brookline, Massachusetts, and were charged with destruction of private property. A bus loaded with thirty-six passengers pulled into Rochester, New York, with slashed tires. A crowd of about 500 further assailed the bus, throwing rocks at it, breaking the windshield and most of the windows. At Olean, New York, an outbound bus stalled. Large quantities of sugar were found in its gas tank. In Virginia, a driver was beaten, and required hospitalization, and a bloody melee broke out in West Roxbury, Massachusetts, when striking drivers charged with baseball bats and billiard cues into a group of policemen trying to protect non-union operators. The Greyhound strike proved to be every bit as violent as those affecting the automobile industry at the time, particularly the one at Ford Motor Company.[30]

All during these violent outbursts, a federal mediator, John L.

Conner, worked hard to bring the two sides together. On December 1, he succeeded. The strike ended on that day, and it could hardly be called a victory for the drivers. They agreed to one-fourth of a cent per mile pay increase (far from their demanded 1.89!), and they got nowhere with their closed shop bid. Nor was there any minimum mileage agreement reached; in fact, it was widely reported that the union accepted a settlement that had been offered by the company even before the strike began.[31]

Depressions and strikes notwithstanding, Greyhound continued into the 1930s what it could do best: grow by gobbling up the competition. On December 19, 1936, the Atlantic Greyhound Lines, headed by A.M. Hill, merged with Atlantic Greyhound Lines, East Coast Stages and Safeway Transit. Capital Greyhound Lines of Virginia, Central of Michigan and Northland of Illinois, all were assimilated by their parent corporations. In the southwest, the Golden Eagle Southern Lines melded into the Southwestern Greyhound. Pacific Greyhound Corporation had a banner year, too, as it consumed eight independents: Kern County Transportation; Peninsula Rapid Transit; Union, Pacific and Pickwick Stages; Southern Pacific and Pacific Lines. Pennsylvania Greyhound took over Buffalo Inter-Urban, Montgomery Bus Company, People's Rapid Transit, Pennsylvania-Virginia General Transit and Pennsylvania Transit. By the late Thirties, the combined Greyhound concerns in the United States operated nearly 2,000 buses in forty different states.[32]

With its policy of constant expansion, it was natural for Greyhound to experiment with new types and models of buses. As early as 1934, Greyhound made a deal with General Motors for a "super-coach." The "719" made its debut two years later. With a seating capacity of 36, the "super-coach" was constructed of steel and aluminum, and its engine mounted in the rear eliminated most of the obnoxious fumes and odors that had drifted up to passengers in earlier days. In 1937 a similar model, the "743," rolled off the assembly line at General Motors; it could seat 37 people.[33] In the years ahead, Greyhound continued its efforts to increase seating capacity and achieve lighter buses at the same time.

Greyhound negotiated in the Thirties with Eckland Brothers about building a four-wheel drive bus. The Brothers' new bus had two engines. One powered the back wheels, and the other the front. It was said to have been excellent mechanically, but it was extremely heavy, and thus too costly for the depressions days. The "dual coach," as it was called, never was put into actual service.[34]

Also in the Thirties came the first hot water heater, created by Greyhound vice-president Orville Caesar, who very rapidly was becoming the man most closely identified with Corporation activities. He also suggested long "picture windows" for his vehicles, and began experimenting even in those long-ago days with "air-suspension." In 1936 diesel fuel was introduced, and it resulted in a forty percent savings in operating costs. (In 1936 the average gasoline bus, "written off" every eight years, cost Greyhound about $10,000 each. If a private citizen wanted to purchase one, the price shot up to $13,500).

Greyhound did not buy any of its tires, each when fully inflated weighed around 300 pounds. Instead, it rented complete sets from Goodyear and Firestone. The tires were regularly inspected, and a rather complicated "bonus system" was inaugurated by which varying degrees of care would produce a bill to Greyhound from eight tenths of a cent per mile to one and a fourth. Generally, brand new sets of tires were installed every 25,000 miles (later, this figure rose to 100,000).

Stringent rules (some 300 of them) for drivers were adopted by the mid-Thirties, and Greyhound seemed to take pride in telling the country that two-thirds of the applicants were turned down. One rule was "Make the Horn Say Please." Just as corny was "Remember, a man on the street today may be a passenger tomorrow." The driver had to be at least five feet, eight inches tall, weigh no more than 165 pounds, and preferably be between 23 and 30 years of age, and he had to know how to ride a bicycle.[35] Greyhound put out a "profile" of its driver: he owned his own home or was buying it and was a good provider for his wife and three children (in 1936 he made $180.00 a month). He loved to travel (obviously) and he liked people (a debatable statement sometimes). He attended church regularly and encouraged his children to participate in boy and girl scouts.

A combination of driver and equipment efficiency gave Greyhound what it considered an enviable safety record. The very first of the driver's rules was, "to be on time is never as important as to arrive safely." (Greyhound drivers had to pay any speeding fines they got from their own paycheck.) A person riding in a private automobile, it was asserted, was fourteen times more likely to be involved in an accident than when he was on an inter-city bus.[36] This claim seemed to be reinforced as the ratio between cars and buses continued to broaden. In 1916, there had been 3,300,000 private automobiles in the United States; by 1930, the number had grown to well over 20 million.[37] The American public was obviously willing to allow the car to dominate its life—even if that dominance meant a dreadful annual toll in dead and injured. By 1939, the Greyhound system averaged one accident (not necessarily producing any casualties) per 65,000 miles, a far better record than automobiles, singly or collectively, could claim.[38] As far back as 1929, Greyhound hired a safety director, Marcus Dow, to give lectures and seminars on good working habits to all its employees.[39]

Perhaps the safety record was enhanced by the rather elaborate system of communication that drivers on the road worked out to inform each other of conditions along the way. One flick of the lights was simply a salutation; two flicks meant "all clear" ahead. Three flicks, however, meant that the road was blocked ahead, or that some dangerous situation existed. If a driver flicked three times, and then pulled off the road, that meant, unequivocably, stop! Sometimes—in the daytime—drivers gave hand signals. Two fingers meant that the highway patrol was near-by, looking for speeders. Three fingers signified a congested and dangerous road on up the way. The driver receiving all this "information" flicked his lights once in return. The flick simply meant "thanks."[40]

Increasingly, the driver would stop at a specially built Greyhound terminal when he got into a sizeable town. These terminals had not yet earned their unsavory reputation and were considered, in fact, better than the restaurants, filling stations, drug stores, etc., with whom Greyhound had contracted earlier to handle its business. The first generally acknowledged terminal in the country, as such, was in San Diego, owned by Pickwick Stages. It operated as early as 1922.[41] Throughout the Twenties, Greyhound built terminals in most of the larger cities: Los Angeles, San Francisco, New York, Philadelphia, Chicago, Baltimore, etc. It was not until the Thirties, however, that Greyhound—inspired largely by the depression—realized that it was definitely the "common man's carrier" in the United States. It had 46,000 miles of route, for example, in 1936, and it served tens of thousands of little towns and hamlets overlooked by trains and airplanes. The terminals Greyhound built eliminated curb side loading and unloading; instead, passengers were accommodated by large waiting rooms, often adjoined by eating facilities. The terminal that opened in May, 1932, in Albany, New York, had two waiting rooms, the larger one in the rear.[42] Many new terminals in the South also had two waiting rooms; not for convenience as in Albany but to comply with state segregation laws. Perhaps it is not entirely coincidental that publicity photographs of the time seem to emphasize the interior (waiting rooms and lunch counters) of northern terminals, while the southern establishments demonstrated how solid their outside architecture could be. The nation's racial problems would ultimately affect Greyhound very deeply—as indeed they did the majority of institutions and citizens.

Another experience for Greyhound, in 1935, was that its stock listing was transferred from Chicago to the New York Stock Exchange. The Corporation reported that it owned stock in thirteen operating bus companies. It listed its assets at $1,176,432. That was good enough for the governing committee of the New York Stock Exchange—and it bade Greyhound a welcome aboard.[43]

Still another event, this one in 1936, that ultimately affected Greyhound—though it did not know it at the time—was the creation of a new bus system. This was National Trailways, inaugurated by three railroads—the Santa Fe, Missouri-Pacific and Burlington—with the avowed intention of duplicating Greyhound's "through" systems, and competing with it wherever possible.

As the decade drew to a close, Greyhound benefited once more from a World's Fair. This was the New York presentation of 1939, and to get visitors from one place to another, Exposition Greyhound Lines was formed—again with the indomitable Irishman, Ralph Bogan, in charge. The buses used at this fair, built by General Motors, were forty-five feet long and nine feet wide. Each seated 160 passengers. Though Exposition Greyhound was obviously helpful to the Corporation as a whole, its importance and significance came nowhere near the benefits of World Fair Greyhound in Chicago six years before. The economic urgency was not present in 1939 that had been there in 1933. Also in 1939, there occurred the "Golden Gate Exposition" in San Francisco. Here, Greyhound presented a large display of the 743 "super-coaches." On both sides of the continent, therefore, Greyhound caught the imagination of Americans, showing them how far bus transportation had progressed in the past quarter century; but more importantly, demonstrating the vast and fascinating possibilities that lay ahead. Neither the public nor the Corporation, however, could know that a horrible war was in the offing, a war that would indeed change many lives.

The Thirties marked the first full decade of Greyhound as a distinct corporate entity. Its existence during these ten years was marked essentially by the survival instinct, which was activated by sound, clever, business decisions (Glenn Traer) in one respect, and by sheer, unpredictable luck (the movies and world fair) in another. Most of the founders of the bus lines that ultimately became Greyhound—Eric Wickman, Arvid Heed, Andrew Anderson, Buck Travis—faded somewhat into the background as specialists responded to the ups and downs of the economically depressed years of the 1930s. As we have seen, however, this statement did not apply to Ralph Bogan who piloted, first, World Fair's Greyhound, and then, Exposition Greyhound into the Corporation's coffers. And, most assuredly the statement did not include Orville Swann Caesar, who had remained strenuously active throughout the period. In fact, his greatest days were still in front of him.

"Greyhound Stories"—Notes and Quotes

A woman with an infant sat just behind the driver. The baby refused to take the food offered to it by the mother. Finally, exasperated, the woman said, "Baby, if you don't take this titty, I'm going to give it to the driver."—A universal bus drivers' story.

Just prior to World War II, I was promoted to the position of ticket agent in the Pacific Greyhound depot in Hollywood, California. Several local bus carriers operated out of the terminal and it was common practice to respond to phone calls with 'Hollywood Bus Terminal' to avoid confusion. Responding to several hundred phone calls a day made the response virtually automatic.

"Shortly after Pearl Harbor I enlisted in the Marine Corps.___ One day I was assigned to work the rifle range ___ where targets were raised and lowered after each firing sequence. [There was] a field telephone over which the Gunnery Sergeant would give [commands]. On one occasion, when my mind was on other things, the telephone rang sharply. I lifted the receiver and immediately responded, purely out of habit, 'Hollywood Bus Depot.' The response from the Sergeant was unprintable. Scrubbing the floor of my squad tent with a toothbrush was unforgettable."—Charles Kirkpatrick, Phoenix, Arizona.

One day, before buses had lavatories, a passenger rushed to the driver and said it was an emergency. As luck had it, the bus was passing by a farm which had an outhouse on it. The man ran frenziedly to it, went inside and closed the door. The bus waited, and it waited, and it waited. After twenty minutes, the driver knocked on the outhouse door. The man was inside staring intently down the hole. "What are you doing?" the driver asked. "Well," the man stammered, "I dropped two dimes down there, and I'm just debating whether or not to reach and get them."

The driver responded, "Well, do something, please. I've got a schedule to keep."

All of a sudden, the man took a twenty dollar bill and threw it down the toilet hole. Amazed, the driver exclaimed, "What in hell are you doing? Are you crazy?"

The man answered, "You don't think I'm stupid enough to put

my hand down there just for twenty cents, do you?"—Another
universal bus-drivers' story.

"A Load in the Rear"
"We were waiting in line
for the driver to appear
when over the speaker
comes 'load in the rear.'
We look at each other
trying to find out
just what this gruff voice
is talking about.

I rush to the door at the rear of the bus;
dodging others without any fuss;
The others are asking and shaking with fear,
wondering just where may be the rear.
I take out my ticket to check on my route
Then turn to see a bus pulling out,
That was my bus pulling out in the rear."—
Exhaust *(Florida Greyhound), June, 1945, p. 27*

"It's just like him to hang around a bus station. He probably
likes to watch those Scenicruiser horrors arrive and depart. In his
worldview the bus is apparently a good thing. That shows how
retarded he is."

"The Greyhound Bus Line is sufficiently menacing to make me
accept my status quo. I wish that those Scenicruisers would be
discontinued; it would seem to me that their height violates some
interstate highway statute regarding clearances in tunnels ....
Those things really must be removed. Simply knowing that they are
hurtling somewhere on this dark night makes me most
apprehensive."—Ignatius P. Reilly in John Kennedy Toole, A
Confederacy of Dunces. *Baton Rouge: Louisiana State University*
Press, 1980. Used by Permission.

Chapter Three
Caesar's Empire

Eric Wickman may have been the President of the Greyhound Corporation but Orville Caesar ran it. In 1940 Greyhound was composed of fourteen different operating units, each with its own organization. Financial control was exercised by the Corporation at its offices in Chicago.[1] Maintaining systematic order in an organization that had now grown so large required business acumen (some accounts indicated that Wickman never did learn to read a financial report correctly) and a willingness and capability constantly to be on the road checking the "provinces" in the far-flung Greyhound Empire.[2]

One of Caesar's multiple business talents was to make oft-correct predictions about the future.[3] For example, unlike certain politicians and diplomats, Caesar took the deteriorating situation in Europe to foretoken soon a state of war, and he knew the event would literally transform the bus industry. In October, 1939, he wrote to the heads of all Greyhound operating units informing them that General Motors wanted their supply needs up to eight months in advance because of an expected parts shortage. Caesar showed some pique when various affiliates ordered "incorrectly," that is, not supplying equipment for at least a half year's supply. He wrote testy follow-up letters to the errant children, and finally got the job done.[4] Unfortunately, Caesar's prediction of war was correct, as was his conviction that the conflict would have serious repercussions for Greyhound.

As a start, it meant a greater number of riders than ever before. Trains were used primarily for major troop movements from one camp to another, and to carry war materiel. The buses, however, hauled many soldiers to their embarkation points from bases on the east and west coasts, and carried inductees from the places of swearing in to their assignments. They were also the main carriers for getting factory workers to and from their jobs. For the Army, Greyhound operated a fleet of special "silversides" (diesel powered, seating capacity of 40) over 1,600 miles of the Alcan Highway. In addition to military necessities, Greyhound tried to maintain

61

reasonable civilian service in a country where gas rationing for private automobiles quickly became a reality. Greyhound publicized the slogans, "Don't Travel Unless Your Trip is Essential," and "Serve America Now so That You Can See America Later." It was difficult, if not impossible, for Greyhound and all the other bus lines to adjust to the new demands suddenly thrust upon them, and at the same time comply with a rash of recently conceived governmental directives.

To begin with, there was a serious parts problem. Greyhound's policy of preventive maintenance and stockpiling of parts simply did not meet the needs of its expanded operations. As early as January, 1941, Caesar appointed a parts analyst for Greyhound; he also wanted General Motors to assign someone to work exclusively with Greyhound on the parts problem. This GMC would not do, a fact that helped during the war years to considerably alienate the two companies from each other. The problem was compounded, too, by Greyhound's increase of mileage in 1941 by twenty-five percent, bringing its total annual miles to 258 million. At the time of Pearl Harbor, December 7, 1941, there were approximately 20,000 inter-city buses on the nation's highways; Greyhound owned 4,000 of them.

In 1942 the manpower shortage most forcefully asserted itself. Several important GMC suppliers worked well below their possible capacities, and this aggravated the parts problem at Greyhound. For example, the Ferro Foundry and Machine Company in Cleveland operated at sixty per cent; the Standard Foundry in Racine at fifty per cent; Gell Manufacturing Company of Albion, Michigan, at sixty per cent; and United Brass and Aluminum, in Port Huron, Michigan, sixty per cent.[5] On top of this drastically reduced output, these suppliers, like businesses everywhere, were under government instructions, through the War Production Board, to supply parts to civilian concerns only after military needs had been met. Even so, Greyhound increasingly gathered the opinion that parts orders from GMC were held up as much by inefficiency as by the war.

The greatest shortages were gasoline engine valves, differential pinion gears, transmissions and connecting rod bearings. The wheel situation, however, was almost impossible. A Greyhound executive wrote: "We are now operating many buses on long runs without a spare wheel because of the necessity of removing [it] in order to keep other buses in operation. Buses in shops for repairs have been robbed of all wheels . . . to replace broken wheels on other buses. All wheels are repaired to the fullest extent possible, but after many thousands of miles of operation, the older wheels eventually must be junked."[6]

Perhaps the greatest blow came in June, 1943, when GMC informed Greyhound that all orders prior to January 1 were being canceled.[7] A Greyhound memorandum in August summed up the Corporation's frustrations: "Other companies with whom we deal [give] definite reasons regarding inability to furnish certain materials and advise us what steps they are taking with the War Production Board to get us out of difficulty. GMC gives us no information of this kind, and we are in doubt as to whether delays are due to war demands or lack of follow-up by GMC." The memo said further that GMC's delivery promises were "entirely unreliable," and that GMC changed its order procedures "without advance notice."[8]

Greyhound's continued threat to go to the War Production Board with its parts problems caused GMC to call a general conference of the two corporations. Caesar headed the Greyhound delegation, while I.B. Babcock was GMC's chief spokesman. The meeting really did not solve problems. Caesar hammered away at the point that service at other places was better than at GMC. (Unfortunately, however, those "other places" could produce only a fraction of the parts that Greyhound needed. Even with all the difficulties, GMC remained Greyhound's principal supplier.) He also spoke out forcefully for *direct delivery*; instead of the foundries sending materials to GMC and then GMC sending them to Greyhound, a direct delivery would save much time and money. Babcock, however, wanted to keep a closer watch on things than this plan would allow; thus, he refused the idea. He also accused Greyhound of creating many of its own problems—by ordering in ways that did not comply with GMC's official order form. Caesar retorted to this claim that GMC's constant change of policy— without advance notice—made proper ordering difficult, if not impossible.[9]

There were, however, two positive suggestions that came from the meeting. One was that parts should be delivered to Greyhound "in the rough," and Greyhound should finish the work. Nothing, however, subsequently came from this proposal. The other suggestion—which Babcock did accept—was for GMC to appoint a committee of five to deal with bus problems. Greyhound did not get the individual treatment it sought; it had to be "bunched in" with all the other bus companies that depended on GMC—but at least a beginning had been made toward dealing with the parts dilemma.[10]

In early 1944 the War Production Board adopted a rule by which manufacturers could divert five per cent of their output for civilian requirements. This did not herald a solution to Greyhound's parts problems, however, because the WPB directive was permissive rather than mandatory.

In fact the situation grew worse. A bedraggled Babcock wrote to Caesar in February (after another threat by the Greyhound executive to take his problems to the WPB) that "the manpower shortage in foundries has been so serious during the past four months that military service parts deficiences have been created. Licenses have been paid on a number of buses that, for various reasons, could not be put into service."[11] N.C. Neph of Greyhound responded to this and other letters by telling the WPB in full about parts hold-ups, and asking the government agency to do something about them. He went into detail about the necessary war-time operations of buses.[12] His plea, however, made little impact. Caesar complained again to Babcock that even when parts did become available, "we have great difficulty in getting our share of them." He blamed this non-delivery on GMC's policy of prohibiting direct orders to its various suppliers, a procedure that held out Greyhound's buses "just so many additional days."[13]

In April Babcock repeated GMC's distribution method to Caesar:

GMC first fills all "down" orders (i.e., inoperable vehicles.)

GMC holds in its stock a limited supply of parts for future emergencies, to be issued only upon vehicle down certificates.

The parts issued after the emergencies were distributed on a ratio basis, with oldest orders first.

Greyhound reacted to this distribution method by pointing to the large number of orders that GMC had lost, or canceled because of such large quantities being ordered so far in advance of delivery possibilities.[14]

Also in April, however, Babcock held out a ray of hope when he told Caesar that GMC was nearing the end of its army drive and that things should improve considerably in the civilian sector.[15] He followed up this promise by asserting that Greyhound received fifty per cent more material in the first five months of 1944 than in the last five of 1943.[16]

On May Day, 1944, Babcock continued to rub soothing balm into Greyhound's countenance. He wrote this lengthy letter to Caesar, which at once explained most troubles and pointed to a brighter future:

> We have endeavored several times in the past to explain to people not thoroughly acquainted with our operation, including your personnel, that with handling as many as 3,600 back orders, as in the case of Greyhound, there are always back orders out of file for disbursing material. Consequently, there is no time when preparing a list of such back orders that the file is complete. Therefore, when such a list is prepared, same will not coincide with Greyhound's records. The only way that we could get a complete list would be to stop all disbursements of back orders until [they] . . . were returned for file. This would mean a tie-up of the handling of back orders for several days.
>
> . . . We realize that it is extremely important to Greyhound to keep all their equipment operating, with the amount of traffic which you are forced to handle because of wartime conditions. We think Greyhound is doing a terrific job, and have the utmost admiration for the way it is being done in the face of so much difficulty. We . . . are making every effort to be of as much service as we can under similar wartime difficulties.[17]

The situation for Greyhound continued to improve as the military operations began to wind down in late '44 and early '45. Greyhound and GMC never did quite "make up" with each other. The parts matter, the question of who would design Greyhound's post-war buses, and a Justice Department "request" ultimately caused the two companies to divorce each other.

Another problem for Greyhound during World War II was the government's imposition in 1942 of a thirty-five miles per hour speed limit on all motorized vehicles—this in an effort to conserve rubber. Publicly, Greyhound accepted this restriction, in the name of patriotism, but privately it fumed. Caesar and his Corporation believed that the speed limit did not really save tires, as the government claimed. Even if it did, the savings would be more than offset by the injuries to gears, valves and transmissions. His buses, Caesar maintained, were built specifically to cruise at forty-five to fifty MPH. They went into high gear at thirty-seven MPH; thus, at thirty-five they were indeed taking a beating.[18]

There was some labor strife for Greyhound during the war years, but not enough to affect it materially. In October, 1940, before our official entry into the hostilities, Greyhound discontinued several short runs between New York and Boston, on grounds of unprofitability. With this discontinuance, a half dozen drivers were laid off, causing Local 1202 in New York and Local 1205 in Boston, of the Amalgamated Association of Street, Electric Railway and Motor Coach Employees to strike. Before the trouble was settled (with Greyhound's promise to reinstate the drivers and restore some of the routes) on November 1, about 300 Greyhound employees had become idle.[19]

Still before Pearl Harbor, May, 1941, Pennsylvania Greyhound was stymied by a strike. Again represented by Amalgamated, the drivers demanded a closed shop, wage increases, and a forty hour work week. Ultimately affecting some 1,400 workers, Greyhound traffic practically ceased for a time in several major cities.[20] Secretary of Labor Frances Perkins stepped into the fray, and ordered federal mediation. Wage increases resulted, and to a considerable extent so did the closed shop. The strike ended on May 9.

Just days before the Japanese attack, a strike hit Central Greyhound, stranding 4,000 commuters in Cleveland, and additional thousands in other cities. The Union charged Central with hiring eight women to clean buses at forty cents an hour, when the contract stipulated a minimum of sixty cents. In New York, 125 drivers and seventy mechanics walked out, and 100 operators followed suit in Boston. By late December, this strike was still in progress, and Amalgamated ordered 1,200 more Central employees off the job to make an impact on the entire system from Chicago to Boston. The widening of the strike, of course, brought in federal mediators. On the 28th, the problems were apparently solved, only to resume the next day. The Union accused Greyhound of reneging on a promise to submit to arbitration. Greyhound demanded that the Union present a list of points to be arbitrated. (Apparently, both sides had now forgotten the poor cleaning women, and the Union was, as one of its officials, Samuel Berrong, said, "striking for a new contract.") This new conflict broadened the strike to 1,800 Greyhound workers. The government ordered intensive negotiations by the two sides, and on December 31, John R. Steelman, Chief of Federal Conciliation, squeezed out another agreement. It was to get all the idle buses back into immediate operation, because of war-time necessities, and then to submit all disputes to a three-man arbitration committee.[21]

Probably the most serious dispute in the war involved Pacific Greyhound. During negotiations for a new contract, the drivers decided to enforce certain company regulations to the letter.

Claiming that the ICC allowed them, in the interest of safety, to limit the number of passengers they permitted to board, the drivers prohibited anyone from standing while the coach was in motion. This action stranded hundreds of ship-yard workers in northern California, resulting in thousands of lost man-hours of work. The "standee" controversy caused the navy, in some instances, to commandeer the buses. And it brought a statement from the feisty President of Pacific Greyhound, Frederick W. Ackerman (later the Corporation Chairman): "... It is apparent that the drivers, through their Union, are taking the ridiculous position that they should not be held responsible for the operation of their bus should they be carrying one 'standee,' [or] for violating city, state or company regulations."

The conflict produced a hurried reaction from the National War Labor Board, which told the drivers that any grievances they had against Greyhound would not be considered until the "standee" ban was lifted. The operators held a hastily called meeting and decided to comply with the Board's "suggestion."[22]

There were numerous other labor problems while we were at war. Several "wildcat" strikes hit Greyhound, and sometimes resulted in better pay and pensions. Generally, they lasted only a day or two at a time. War-minded government boards were definitely disinclined to allow strikes to interfere seriously with the military effort.

Despite Greyhound's complaints about scarce parts, restrictive speed limits and labor controversies, it nevertheless fared well during the war years. In fact, like many other corporations of the day, it had to pay excess profits taxes. In 1941, before taxes its net income was $16,600,000; after taxes, $9,250,000. The next year, before tax income was $41,700,000 and $11,500,000 afterward.

In 1943 Greyhound actually began a new expansion program in the south and southeast by acquiring minority interests in a number of independent lines. Also in 1943, it formed Greyhound Skyways, a helicopter service to work in conjunction with its routes and to experiment with air-mail pickup in the New York area. The ICC looked somewhat askance at this venture (despite favorable testimony for it by helicopter pioneer Igor Sigorsky), so Greyhound did not agitate for it. It continued, however, to expand on the ground: by mid-1944, Greyhound had 64,700 miles of route, serving over 6,000 cities and towns throughout the United States. This was five times greater than any single railroad in the country, and one-fourth of the entire train mileage.[23]

As might be expected, the Greyhounds during the war years were, to say the least, crowded. Service men and women loaded first, and then women with children. Many times a single woman passenger made a deal with a soldier, whereby the woman was claimed as a wife or a sister, and got preferential treatment. According to Russell Byrd, when a bus was loaded and a woman wanted to board, the driver's customary remark was, "the only place left is my right knee." Other stock *dicta* were, "O.K. sardine; step into your little can," and "wiggle back a little further in the aisle, sardine."[24]

One example of buses and the military, *on the whole*, cooperating with each other was Division Nine, established by Pacific Greyhound. At the Mare Island Station in Vellejo, Commander William Peters laid out twenty-six inter-urban and eight local routes to create a bus service into the naval yards. The routes covered every town and city within a radius of fifty miles. Said to be the largest contract bus operation in the world, it started on March 1, 1942.

The buses were austere, and painted navy gray. There was an average of 450 drivers at all times. When manpower became scarce, women were used. By 1944, half the drivers for Greyhound's Mare Island operation were female.[25] The fare for all these runs into Vellejo was ten cents. In Greyhound jargon, they were known as the "Dime-Catcher Runs."

At one community, Rodeo, an all-day shopper was inaugurated. It ran between the main shopping area and a government housing project. The public could ride free on this bus, and it proved a perfect outlet for mothers looking for baby-sitters. They simply let their children ride around on the bus until they finished their shopping or visiting. Finally, officials caught on to this ruse, and rescued the hapless Greyhound driver from being an un-paid baby-sitter.[26]

Well before the conflict ended, Caesar and his entourage had ambitious post-war expansion plans. Greyhound contracted with a group of financiers headed by the National City Bank of New York for $35 millions in credit for new equipment purchases. Also, it planned to issue about $15 millions in stocks and debentures for future projects.[27]

The Greyhound planners postulated in January, 1943, that the future held interstate highways, increased civilian patronage, new bus depots and perhaps a helicopter service with downtown landing facilities. Clearly the bus transportation enterprise that looked ahead would reap bountiful rewards, and Caesar meant to be the first in this regard.

An internally prepared report in June, 1944, predicted a price war after hostilities ceased. A fifty passenger bus with no standees allowed was highly desirable, with the great emphasis on comfort. What Greyhound wanted was a "Scenicruiser," a "split-level" double decker bus. This desire was primarily in the mind of Raymond Loewy, a New York industrial designer, who became a consultant for Greyhound in 1935.

Caesar's men considered several companies to build the Scenicruiser. Douglas and Curtis-Wright received passing attention, while most concern was directed toward GMC and Consolidated Vultee. Many people within the Greyhound organization opposed GMC for the job, and strongly favored Consolidated. For one thing, GMC rejected several features that Greyhound designers wanted. The new bus, said Greyhound, should have a toilet. GMC turned down the idea, even though a toilet appeared—to Greyhound—"most essential for a bus carrying so many passengers." GMC specifications also called for much smaller windows than those desired by the bus company.[28]

With respect to body construction, Greyhound engineers said that GMC was "months if not years" behind Consolidated with the tubular style that Greyhound wanted. Also, GMC refused to use parts or accessories in the new bus that came from companies competitive with its subsidiaries. As time went on, GMC even withheld from Greyhound the right to specify the *types of parts* to be used in the new Scenicruiser. One might ask, then, why Greyhound even chose to consider GMC at all for this job. Perhaps it was the long affiliation between the two companies—after all, GMC had supplied the Yellow Coach to Greyhound for many years—that caused this continuation of relations. But relations between the two were not placid during the war, and there was plenty of sentiment at Greyhound in the late forties to dump GMC altogether.[29]

Greyhound proceeded quite far with Consolidated Vultee to build the new Scenicruiser. Rather abruptly, however, and without explanation, Consolidated canceled its contract with Greyhound. Consolidated agreed to deliver, *gratis*, to Greyhound all the tooling dyes, templates, drawings, engineeer data and other works in progress on the Scenicruiser. All work was transferred to the Tropic-Aire plant owned by an old associate of Wickman's, Carl Will. Caesar expected the first of the experimental units from Tropic-Aire within a year's time.[30] Plans changed again, however, because by early '46 a Chicago based subsidiary of the Greyhound Corporation, Greyhound Motors and Supply Company, was working on the new model. It completed its labors and announced the Scenicruiser to the public on July 1, 1949.[31] (Even before this, however, there had been, in 1944, a two-level Greyhound, known as the "Highway Traveler.") After this initial model, production was turned over to GMC, which supplied Greyhound with Scenicruisers for the next several years.

Another important post-war event for Greyhound was the retirement of Wickman to the chairmanship of the Board. This action elevated Caesar to the presidency. He had been the President in everything but name for the past ten years, so his promotion was mostly a formality.

Wickman seemed now to attract more attention than before he retired as President. He decided to go back to his native Sweden—his first visit since that long ago day in 1903 when he sailed for the "promised land." He left New York on October 4, 1946, aboard the Motor Ship *Gripsholm*. Near Aberdeen, Scotland, Wickman suffered an extensive heart attack. The ship's captain radioed the authorities about Wickman's condition, and noted that a drug, heparin, was badly needed. A Royal Air Force plane flew twenty feet over the *Gripsholm*, and its pilot—true to RAF precision—dropped the heparin directly onto its bow. The drug was administered by the ship's doctor and Wickman's life was saved. He traveled on to Sweden, where he was hailed as a hero—not only for starting the world's most famous bus line, but also for coming through such a dramatic experience out in the ocean. The King of Sweden, Gustaf V, knighted Wickman for living up to the Monarch's motto of "Service for the Unserved."[32]

From 1945 to the end of the decade, Caesar conducted a strenuous campaign to get certain benefits for his Corporation. To do this, he put agents out in the field, and had them lobby before the Federal Congress and the state legislatures. He was only partially successful.

For one thing, Caesar wanted to stretch the width of his coaches from 96 to 102 inches. Those six inches are probably the most controversial half foot in the entire history of American transportation.

An incentive for the 102 bus was expressed in a letter to Caesar in early 1946, which spoke of the "large and extensive" highway building program just about to get under way. The federal and state governments wanted an "integrated, national highway system," with the elimination of "bottlenecks near large metropolitan centers."[33]

The letter predicted that the authorities would be more opposed to excessive weight than to greater lengths and widths, because the former would mean larger expenditures in paving, and in bridge-building than the latter. The inter-city bus industry, Caesar and his subjects believed, was in an excellent position to capitalize on the highway systems that lay just ahead. Bus needs were modest and reasonable, he felt, especially by comparison with trucking demands, and by the subsidies he reckoned to be handed out to the railroads.

Those conceptions made it particularly difficult for Caesar to comprehend New York Governor Thomas Dewey's veto of the Rapp Bill, which would have authorized a 102-inch width. The Governor said, "There are many [New York] state highways within the limits of villages which are too narrow to accommodate safely buses of a greater width than those presently allowed by law. And it will be a long time before such highways can be widened. I believe it would be dangerous to allow wider vehicles to be operated on these highways."[34]

Caesar had said all along that the 102 inch Greyhounds were still quite a way in the future, and that they would operate only on big city highways, rather than on routes through towns and villages. Thus, he doubly lamented Dewey's veto, and the possible influence it might have on governors of other states. He continued his plea that the 102's would be few in number, and that their use would be in the interest of public safety (though he did not say how).[35]

So intent was Caesar on getting the 102's that, within his own domain, he would brook no opposition whatever. Apparently, some members of the Ohio Motor Bus Association, operators of small, independent lines, objected to the 102, and Caesar dressed them down. An Association spokesman, C.J. Randall, pacified Caesar by telling him that even though the 102 program benefited only a few bus companies, the Ohio group was supportive of the theory that "what is good for the large companies is good for all."[36]

Caesar might have been able to intimidate bus people; not so, however, with politicians and engineers, many of whom had special interests more important to them than Greyhound. In New York, following Dewey's veto, the milk haulers let it be known that if buses ever got 102 inches, they wanted them too. And right behind them came the petroleum transporters.[37] The New York Governor and many legislators thought they could foresee a time when monstrous eight and a half foot trucks and buses would be lumbering through the peaceful by-ways of their state, endangering the property and lives of innocent people. They would yield, therefore, neither to the trucks nor the buses on this matter.

The chief engineer in Montana maintained that increased width would constitute an additional hazard on his state's highways. For one thing, all the bridges were too narrow safely to accommodate this width. The engineer designated all roads in Montana as inaccessible to 102 inch buses. He convinced the state legislature that his judgment was sound.[38] A Nevada law stipulated that any vehicle wider than eight feet could not travel at a speed greater than eight miles an hour. Caeser wrote to Ackerman, suggesting that the Pacific Greyhound President foment plans by which to get this obnoxious Nevada law repealed.[39] Caesar also wrote to every stockholder of the Greyhound Corporation, which included his wife, to write to their congressmen and state legislators, and tell them how badly the country needed 102-inch wide buses. He suggested constant comparisons in weight, length and width of buses and trucks. The Greyhounds, he believed, would come out most favorably in the contrast. Even these intensified pressures did not achieve the 102's which he whole-heartedly cherished.[40]

Another thing Caesar wanted, and he was a bit more successful here than with the 102's, was a bus that was forty feet long instead of the usual thirty-five. He got it in 1949, with the Scenicruiser, but only after one state legislature at a time allowed it. (The prototype of the Scenicruiser was taken around the country, primarily to state capitals, as a lobbying tool for the forty foot bus.) This time-consuming process meant that the forty-footers (including the Scenicruiser) could be used only in certain states, and even then sometimes along restricted routes. Demonstrative of the confusion in 1949, St. Louis allowed the forty-foot bus; the state of Missouri did not. Indiana passed a forty-foot bill, but Pennsylvania refused it for some time, making routes between these states for the longer buses an impossibility.

Greyhound bared its teeth again as New York passed a forty-foot bill (the Van Cleef Bill), only to have it fall before another Dewey veto. The states that had enacted such a law, the Governor said, "for the most part ... are ... in the newer sections of the country with safer roads." He went on to note that numerous New York state agencies were divided in their opinion of the forty-foot bus. These divisions, plus the opposition of the American Automobile Association, were sufficient to produce Dewey's rejection of the proposed legislation.[44]

Needless to say, the veto sparked Caesar's anger, and encouraged him to step up his campaign. He blamed the truck industry for much of Greyhound's problems. Every time a forty foot bill came before a state legislature, the truckers immediately clamored for longer lengths themselves. They already had vehicles forty and forty-five feet long in use in many of the same states that refused a forty-foot bus! Clearly the trucking industry had a louder voice in Washington, and in state capitals, than the bus lines did. Caesar's oft-repeated suggestion that the transportation of people should receive a more sympathetic consideration than the hauling of logs, cattle and commodities generally fell on deaf ears. Ultimately, however, opinions changed, and the forty-foot bus became a reality.[42]

By 1948 the word "greyhound" connoted "bus" to most Americans, rather than "dog." No wonder: in that year, the running dog emblem was on 5,800 buses, which carried 211 million passengers. Greyhound, by now, had indeed become a permanent fixture in American life—even American folklore. This latter quality was pointed out in a *Reader's Digest* story, told by William T. McFadden of Decatur, Illinois:

> "Sitting next to me in the bus station . . . was a man so old . . . that I wondered that he was traveling. Before long he turned to me and said, 'Where you bound for son?'
> " 'Chicago,' I replied, 'Where you going?'
> " 'Shucks, boy, I ain't goin' nary a place. A fellow can see more sights, pantomimes, and melodramer just 'a sittin' in this waiting room than you could see at any of your moving pictures, and it don't cost you a cent'."[43]

Also, the story about the "driver who couldn't sew" made the rounds. A male passenger tore his pants getting off a Mac bus in Bothell, Washington. The driver tried to sew up the tear and jabbed the man's rear end with the needle. The authorities spent some time wondering whether to classify the event as an accident or a casualty.[44]

Greyhound had now begun giving colorful names to its coaches. The *Sun King*, for example, traveled between Cincinnati and Jacksonville, and the *Sun Maid* ran out of Birmingham. To the west were the *Sewanee Ltd.* and the *Bayou Ltd.*, both belonging to Teche Greyhound. It became a part of travel jargon for a customer to buy tickets for transportation on a specifically named bus.

Two-way radio equipment was installed in 1948 and '49 in the buses on routes between Chicago and Detroit, and plans were made to extend this communication system to all Greyhound operatives. (This plan, however, was never fulfilled.) In the late '40s, new terminals were completed at Cleveland, Salt Lake City, Omaha, Lexington (Kentucky), Akron, Orlando and Daytona. Terminal projects under way included Chicago, Toledo, Grand Rapids (Michigan) and Fort Worth. Even a quartet was started for a time by a driver named R. Schonover. The musical group was called the "Greyhound Syncopaters," and it made numerous tours of large metropolitan areas. Many references during the time mentioned the Greyhound Orchestra, which also made limited appearances, playing, on numerous occasions, "The Greyhound March."

Caesar's Empire was indeed far flung as the second half of the twentieth century made its debut. It was run paternalistically, but most Greyhound employees said it was a good place to work. Caesar had been with the Corporation now for a quarter century, and he had witnessed all the set-backs and triumphs of the period. An intensely innovative man, Caesar never stopped trying to improve the product—travel—that he offered to the American public. He saw something new in the bus business almost every day, and he continued the grueling pace of being the top bus man in the country. On into the '50s he directed Greyhound, and expanded its holdings even more. His position was, he believed, the most exciting job in the world. No wonder he loved buses so much.

"Greyhound Stories"—From the Sublime to the Ridiculous

In the Vietnam conflict, the men of the 240th Assault Helicopter Company 214th Combat Aviation Battalion, adopted the Greyhound symbol for their helicopters. One of their members wrote a poem, "The Greyhound," and sent it to the bus company's headquarters in Chicago. Here is a part of that poem:

Knife through the skies proud canine
fleet image of a carrier command,
A once familiar symbol of a peaceful road,
in a far distant land.
Leap to the stars brave greyhounds,
dogs of battle;
you veteran courser of the earth,
now seek the fire-streaked sky
and join the legions of our air-born company

*   *   *

Now gently hover lest in your thirsting haste
A wound is freshened in that poor head
in this brave heart
Wing homeward then
And set your graceful form to rest
on friendly earth once more.—Go With Greyhound: *No. 1, Vol. 3;*
1968. Used by permission.

"*I began my Greyhound career by renting pillows aboard the buses ___ The bus drivers all affectionately called me the 'feather merchant.' A little old 70 year old lady slapped me once for 'attempting to cop a feel' while I was trying to recline her seat to place her rented pillow behind her.*" —*Charles Kirkpatrick, Phoenix, Arizona.*

"*Just after World War II, General Motors built a bus to 'bridge the gap' until the Scenicruiser could be produced. Drivers referred to this 'substitute bus' as the 'Henry J' (after the car built by Kaiser). This displeased H. Vance Greenslit, so he told a supervisor: 'I'm going to stop the drivers from calling that bus a 'Henry J.' The supervisor responded: 'Mr. Greenslit, those drivers have been calling me 'that old son-of-a-bitch for thirty years! And I doubt you will have any success at stopping them from calling those buses Henry J.' The supervisor was right!"—George Walker, Lousiville, Kentucky.*

A driver was passing a car one time, and got up to 75 MPH. All of a sudden, he remembered a railroad track, where he was supposed to stop. He was going too fast to stop. Out of habit, though, he opened the door as he crossed the tracks. This brought in a huge gust of wind which blew everything all over the coach.—Greyhound story.

There was once a ticket agent in San Francisco named William Butler. His principal job was to sell tickets for Greyhound's special runs to the race-track. He always stood just in one spot behind the ticket-counter. He finally wore a hole through the linoleum, and then a sizeable dent in the floor. When he retired, his buddies cut out the area where he had stood for so long, bronzed it, and gave it to him as a retirement present.—Harry Freedman, Portland, Oregon.

"Seven miles east of Rockford (Illinois), I made my turn into the Illinois toll road, interstate 90. As I approached the toll gate ___ my [Swedish] passenger in the right front seat said, 'Driver, how do they determine your toll for this road—must you tell them the number of passengers on board?'

"I replied, '___ in Illinois we only have to tell them how many axles we have.'

He jumped up and shouted, 'Oh my God—We have five of them on this coach!'

"And so we did! There was Axel Petersen, Axel Johnson, Axel Swenson, Axel Henson and Axel Anderson!"—Bernard L. Murphy, Rockford, Illinois

"Once many years ago while working in the San Mateo depot, I noticed two teenagers in the waiting room. Soon Bing Crosby appeared and purchased two tickets for them to Santa Clara, where the twins were going to college. When Bing left, the twins asked me to refund the ticket price to them as they were going to hitchhike to Santa Clara."—Harry Freedman, Portland, Oregon

There is a cartoon by Wally Falk showing a man on a bus naked, and he's telling a woman next to him: "My Doctor suggested a long bus trip to forget everything, and that's exactly what I did."— Rearview Mirror, *December, 1955.*

Two fleas wanted to go out to dinner one night. As they were leaving, one said to the other: "Do you want to walk or hop a greyhound?" Anonymous (Thank God).

Chapter Four
Toils and Troubles

Greyhound began the new decade with a somewhat tarnished image. For one thing, it received a great deal of unwanted publicity from an incident in Chattanooga, Tennessee, involving Southeastern Greyhound.

It was generally known throughout the industry that drivers collected cash fares and that frequently this money was not turned into the company treasury. In May of 1950, Southeastern's officials decided to put a stop to this illegal practice. It was the method Greyhound employed to detect the culpable that brought it to such grief.

Special bus agents were hired, who instructed twenty-seven suspect drivers to come to a certain hotel in downtown Chattanooga. Upon arrival, they were locked into one large room, and interrogated, one by one, they said in a "Nazi-like manner." (One interview lasted almost five hours.) Whenever they were asked questions, they alleged, a man with a pistol in his hand always stood behind them. The drivers were confronted by "passengers" who had paid cash fares for their trips; cash that the company said never got to its proper destination. (The spotters in some instances had taken photos and movies of drivers over a space of several weeks. The film did, indeed, incriminate numerous people.) Eight drivers finally convinced the company officials of their innocence, and they were allowed to leave. The other nineteen, however, were kept from Monday morning to the following Tuesday night. They were not allowed to contact their families, and during the night only nine cots were brought in for them to sleep on. Altogether, they were held hostage for thirty-six hours.[1]

The released drivers lost no time in informing their colleagues and the press about their imprisoned brethren. Hundreds of travelers were suddenly stranded as operators from Lexington, Kentucky, all the way to Jacksonville, Florida, walked away from their buses. This action stopped 175 buses operating through Chattanooga alone. Very shortly, sympathy strikes appeared, and

78

all bus lines radiating out of Chicago came to a complete halt. Attendance at the Kentucky Derby was dealt a blow, as seventy-five charters to Louisville were canceled as a result of the work stoppage. Guy Huguelet, President of Southeastern, angrily called the walkouts a "wildcat strike."

Whatever it was, it got results. The nineteen remaining captives were released. All the drivers involved were fired, but the company pledged its non-use of kangaroo courts in the future.[2] The Union, Amalgamated Transit, charged Greyhound with harassment in the case, saying that all the detained men were experienced union-drivers, and that the company was simply trying to destroy their labor organization.[3] The drivers who had been detained subsequently went to court, charging entrapment. Though only one had his job restored, they each collected $5,000 in damages from Southeastern Greyhound.

In the public's mind, by 1950, there was just one "Greyhound." Little attention was paid to the fact that Southeastern was only a subsidiary of the larger Corporation, and that actually the latter had little to do with the events at Chattanooga. "Greyhound is Greyhound," said the traveling public. Therefore, a bad image for one affiliate created similar reputations for the entire concern.[4]

Another unseemly image for Greyhound in the early '50s was that it and the other bus lines were apparently excused from obeying speed laws. The Chicago *Daily Tribune*, October 7, 1953, wrote a scathing editorial on the subject, titled "Who Gets the Bus Pay-Off?" The newspaper's travel editor had reported that on one of his trips aboard a Greyhound, it hit "68 MPH" (45 MPH was the speed limit) "on truck-crowded, man-killing Route 66 between St. Louis and Chicago."

The editorial went on to assert that "any driver who travels the rural highways to any extent knows that bus drivers are habitual violators of the speed laws..; yet seldom appear in court to answer for their offenses. That spells a pay-off, clearly."

The paper claimed that bus immunity to prosecution for speeding and overweight violations "has become notorious." During the governorship of Adlai Stevenson, the *Tribune* alleged, one downstate Illinois police captain was grounded for ticketing speeding bus-drivers. The paper closed its editorial by asserting that "the fact that they [the buses] will lose money if they obey the law cannot possibly excuse ... [speeding] by the operators."[5]

Still another tail-tucking event for Greyhound in the '50s came out of a small town in Florida, named Manalpan. The incident involved Florida Greyhound Lines, but, again, to the public, sectional designations were not important—it was *Greyhound*, period!

The Manalpan city fathers passed an ordinance in January, 1951, making it illegal to operate any commercial or sight-seeing buses along Ocean Boulevard. Greyhound, for a time, did not observe this law. The good mayor of Manalpan, J.D. Getny, wrote to the manager of Florida Greyhound that "recently I have received complaints that ... buses have been operating in violation of this ordinance, and I have given instruction to our police officer to make arrests if there is any further violation thereof. Please be governed accordingly." Not only Greyhound but also all the other bus lines operating through Manalpan were most assuredly "governed accordingly."[6] Obviously, Greyhound's influence in Manalpan was not what it was in Chicago.

An important event for Greyhound came in 1955, when Caesar decided to relinquish his presidency and become Chairman of the Board. He had now been associated with the bus business for nearly forty years. His contributions to Greyhound were manifold, not the least of which was the Scenicruiser. His health had begun to fail, and he believed the Corporation should be passed to younger hands.[8]

The new head of Greyhound was forty-seven year old Arthur Genet, who had been the Vice-President for Traffic of the Chesapeake and Ohio Railway Company. He was the first "outsider" to take over the Greyhound buses, and many people blamed this condition for the fact that his presidency was not very successful.

In September, 1956, Genet gave a speech entitled "The Road Ahead," to the National Association of Motor Bus Operators. He predicted that within a decade, railroads "will have virtually abandoned the business of carrying passengers." (How right he was!) He also stated that the Interstate Highways would be a reality.[9]

Genet firmly believed that those passengers deserted by the trains would move to the buses. He began, therefore, "tooling up" for what he considered to be a "sure thing." He, along with other bus-men, believed that the combination of passenger train discontinuance and the completion of the Interstates would bring the great "breakthrough" for which they had waited so long.[10]

Alas, the traveling public acted differently this time from the way Greyhound expected. The Interstates drove them to their own automobiles, and to the airplanes.[11] Largely because of these factors, Genet believed that Greyhound should get into the car rental business. There was no reason, he believed, why Greyhound should not have a car waiting at airports for plane passengers who wanted one. Also, a car could work neatly in conjunction with big city bus terminals. The Rent-A-Car operation, he felt was "logical for Greyhound because of its years of experience in ... maintenance, transportation, and public service."[12]

The only problem was that Greyhound's Rent-A-Car program grew too fast. "It was like a brush fire without any controls."[13] Genet bought scores of new automobiles and placed them at airports and bus terminals, at "U-Drive-It" stations, where he thought the traveling public would hire them. His hopes did not materialize, because bus travelers were simply not the kind of people who rent cars, and because Greyhound could not compete with Hertz, National and the other car-renters at major airports. The Rent-A-Car program caused Greyhound immense financial difficulties in the late '50s, and almost bankrupted the Corporation. The program ws discontinued in 1958, and along with it, Genet's presidency. He left Greyhound and joined the Brinks Organization. Hardly did it need to be added that Greyhound was the laughing stock of America's corporate world.[14]

To replace Genet, the Corporation brought in the colorful and forceful Frederick W. Ackerman, who had been a protege of the famed Buck Travis. Ackerman had been the President of Pacific Greyhound for many years, and he had the profound respect of busmen everywhere. He was a "slender, bespectacled man with questioning eyes and thinning gray hair."[15] An accountant by profession, he was an "incredibly fast reader," who liked to "see things on paper."[16] An avid sports fan (San Francisco Giants), Ackerman was short-tempered ("intolerant of incompetence," was the way one of his colleagues put it), and "hollered and shouted a little bit," and occasionally "banged on his desk" to get his points across.[17] He was definitely a "go-ahead" person, showing this characteristic even in the way he walked—always several paces ahead of everybody else. He wrote his own memos—on a typewriter—and signed them with either his initials or his signature.

Ackerman was exactly what Greyhound needed at the time. He came in when the company was nearing bankruptcy, and he saved it. He immediately got Greyhound out of the car-rental business,[18] and instituted a severe austerity program. It was through his "bullet-biting" that Greyhound recouped its losses.

Many bus-men will say that Ackerman made the Greyhound buses what they are today. Here is what James Kerrigan, who has figured prominently in the bus line's history himself, has to say about Ackerman:

> Greyhound could have been one of the great corporations of all time had Ackerman been younger, or had stayed active .... He took a company that was in terrible condition and made it a financial giant. When Ackerman left active management, a national magazine ran a photo of him, and said, 'the problem with Greyhound is what to do with the cash.' By 1960, there was no debt to speak of for Greyhound, and the foundation had been laid for what could have been an absolutely great corporation. Caesar and all those guys—I mean, it was great what they put together, but the times helped them. When Ackerman came in ... it took special management skills, and he was very cost effective .... You know, it's easy to go out and make speeches; something else to take the hard position for being fiscally responsible. Ackerman understood the [bus] business. He was an outstanding guy.[19]

It does seem logical, therefore, that if anyone in the past thirty years deserves the sobriquet "Mr. Greyhound," that person is Frederick W. Ackerman.[20]

One problem that Ackerman had to deal with was the spectacle Greyhound made of itself in 1958 when it tried to get a new terminal building in New York City. It wanted to consolidate its 34th Street, 50th Street, 45th Street and Long Island City operations into one ten million dollar building on 34th Street.

The New York Port Authority strenuously opposed the plan. First the P.A. maintained that all bus lines who had previously agreed to use the P.A. terminal at 41st Street and 8th Avenue did so on condition that the city not authorize any new terminals east of 8th Avenue. The Greyhound plan would negate this prior arrangement. If it got its way in this matter, Trailways, and every other bus line in the area would clamor for similar benefits. There would be no end of it, once the exception was made. The Port Authority, therefore, steadfastly held its ground.

Greyhound mounted a massive public relations program to win

support for its terminal consolidation plan. It took out advertisements in newspapers and trade journals, and pointed to the following factors it deemed in its favor:

*Greyhound's terminal project had the approval of the Mid-Town Realty Association, representing some $180 millions in city property.

*The new terminal would reduce Greyhound's present mid-town Manhattan miles by seventy-seven per cent.

*A nine foot recess in the curb line on 34th Street, and a similar setback at the main passenger entrance would provide a taxi area without impinging on the flow of east bound traffic. Nor would the sidewalk area be hampered; ample room would still be available for pedestrians.

*The new terminal would have twenty-two passenger platforms. The buses would enter by 34th Street and leave via 33rd.

As Greyhound stepped up its campaign (only a public relations blurb would be silly enough to call the terminal project "Greyhound's Miracle on 34th Street"), the Port Authority became increasingly adamant. Finally, Greyhound lost its humor on the matter, and accused the Port Authority, in the name of profit, of trying to force the Hound to the P.A. facility. It accused the P.A. of operating at a huge annual deficit, and it obviously hoped that Greyhound would rescue it.[21]

Whatever the Port Authority's motives, this was one battle it won. Greyhound did not get the new facilities it wanted on 34th Street. Instead, it got a lot of publicity that caused people to believe that it was 'seeking an unfair exception to Port Authority rules and New York City ordinances. After a few years, Greyhound begrudgingly moved its operations in New York to the Port Authority Building.

(Greyhound was, however, given the premier position in the facility. It had the first set of ticket selling spaces as one entered the terminal from 8th Avenue. In more recent times, an annex was built to the P.A. Building, with *all* of the arrival and departure bays for the exclusive use of Greyhound.)

In reference to terminals, generally, in the '50s and '60s, they did indeed have an unsavory reputation in the eye of the public. Often they were located in the most derelict parts of towns and cities, and became a gathering place for hoodlums, pick-pockets and perverts. Police records were filled with incidents that happened in and around bus terminals and depots. Writer Stephen J. Sansweet, who traveled coast to coast on a Greyhound, described the Columbus,

Ohio, terminal as typical. He said quite bluntly that it was a slum. "Two dozen people sat aimlessly in orange and plastic chairs surrounded by faded green walls, filthy drapes and coffee-stained counters .... Police chief Robert M. Bans said 'pickpockets, con men, perverts—they all come there [to the terminal] to prey on the travelers. We give the terminal quite a bit of attention'."[22]

Bus-men, however, defend the terminals. In many instances, when they were first built, they were in desirable locations. But then the city literally moved away, as its center deteriorated, thus attracting the idle, trouble-making elements. Transportation Director E.W. Simmons says it must be remembered that Greyhound has only 132 distinct terminals of its own. The balance of its stations are commission agencies, and there are over 3,000 of these. A commission agency can be a filling station, a grocery, a drug store, or any enterprise willing to sign a contract with Greyhound. The company obviously has little control over what happens at these agencies. At the company terminals, he said, Greyhound hires its own security force. Sometimes, however, a city will assign regular police beats at the terminals. In some places, Greyhound and other bus companies hire off-duty policemen.[23]

Another Greyhound official stated that the negative image of terminals was vastly overplayed. Terminals have a tendency, he said, "to attract those people who are looking for something that is open twenty-four hours a day." He asserted further that "we do everything we can within the law to see that vagrants are not permitted to stay around. There are certain limitations—we can't shoot them. They can buy a ticket, you know, and just sit there."[24]

Kerrigan, under whom more terminals were built than during any past or succeeding presidency, said that the lay person does not understand that airports are built with public funds, and that bus terminals are not. "There's no way a bus company ... can do the job adequately .... I am an advocate of transportation centers that are publicly funded, because they are for the convenience of the public ...."[25] If all inter-city buses used just one tax-supported facility (as largely is the case of New York's Port Authority) instead of separate units, bus travel would be more cost effective. Kerrigan believes that the bus companies have as much legitimacy as the airlines and the railroads in warranting public assistance. He emphatically does not believe in subsidies for tickets; only for transportation centers.[26]

The question of terminal quality will probably continue as long as there are buses. Each individual traveler forms his own judgment in accordance with the experience—good or bad—that he has had on his trips. Some travelers view the terminals as scenes of intense excitement, where every emotion is played to the hilt as people come and go; dozens of human interest stories occur every day at the major terminals. Other individuals, however, regard terminals as places to get away from as quickly as possible, lest they be attacked by someone, or catch a dreadful disease.

In reference to buses themselves, during the '60s, Greyhound had to start building it own. The reason was largely the Scenicruiser which, after the prototype was developed, General Motors contracted to build. The only problem with this arrangement was its exclusiveness. It eliminated most of GMC's competitors who might also wish to build buses for Greyhound. The U.S. Justice Department frowned on the situation, for it was in restraint of trade. The government, therefore, "suggested" that Greyhound find additional sources for the Scenicruisers.

Greyhound turned to Motor Coach Industries, a subsidiary at the time (mid '60s) of Canadian Greyhound Lines. Bus bodies were constructed at Winnipeg, Canada, and then trucked across the border to Pembina, North Dakota, where all the running equipment was installed. This new arrangement for buses ended the historic connection between Greyhound and General Motors.[27]

Another major adjustment that Greyhound had to make during the period was to the Civil Rights Revolution. In the past, when a bus crossed the border from an integrated to a segregated state, the driver had to stop and order all the black passengers to the rear. Frequently about two-thirds back, a plastic divider was installed. In front of it, the whites sat and behind, the blacks, or "colored."

There had been at least one instance, however, when a black passenger refused to yield. In 1944, Maggie Mack was on a Greyhound that crossed from Missouri into Arkansas. The bus stopped and the driver commanded her to the rear, in compliance with Arkansas law. When she refused, the driver called a policeman. Miss Mack claimed that the policeman slapped her as he forced her to the back section. She filed charges against Dixie Greyhound, and a federal court in St. Louis awarded her a $1,500 judgment.[28]

Greyhound's policy was to take no strong philosophical stand on the civil rights movement; rather, to obey the laws of the states in which it did business. It was put into the unenviable position, however, of being caught in the middle as the "Freedom Riders" (sponsored by the Congress of Racial Equality) traveled into the South.

In May and June, 1961, trouble flared all over the South, as efforts were made to desegregate terminals, Post-House restaurants, and the buses themselves. Incidents occurred in Rock Hill, South Carolina, Jackson, Mississippi, and Montgomery and Birmingham, Alabama. A Greyhound bus carrying "Freedom Riders" was attacked and burned in May, 1961, near Anniston, Alabama. (Governor John Patterson refused police protection to the "Freedom Riders," saying that they were made up of "rabble-rousers." That the extremists who burned the bus belonged to the same "rabble-rousing" element apparently never occurred to the Governor.) The event in Anniston was the most serious injury suffered by Greyhound during the entire "Freedom Rider" movement.

In late May, Attorney-General Robert Kennedy sent U.S. Marshals into Alabama, and other southern states to protect the "Freedom Riders." The ICC also banned segregation on buses. By early summer, 1961, these federal offensives had their effect, and the bus lines became fully integrated throughout the United States.

The bus officials themselves generally were pleased with the Federal government's desegregation orders. For one thing, not having to provide dual facilities at southern terminals resulted in great savings. Too, it was simply a waste of precious scheduling time, and also downright stupid to have to stop at integrated-segregated borders.[29]

Aside from responding to governmental decrees in reference to GMC and civil rights, Greyhound began several internal practices that were to have important results.

One was a new plan of diversification. When Ackerman became Chairman of the Board in 1961, he announced that "possible acquisitions" were in the wind. This time, however, all the safeguards that Genet had apparently neglected would be installed. Thus, Ackerman put the company on a course in which the Greyhound Corporation would ultimately own about a hundred other entities, as far apart from one another as hamburger joints (Burger King, which in many terminals replaced the "Post-Houses") and soap factories (Dial).

The person who capitalized on this new spirit of acquisition, however, was Gerald H. Trautman. He became the President and Chief Executive Officer in November, 1965, when seventy year old Ackerman sharply curtailed his activities in the Greyhound Corporation, though he did continue as Chairman. Trautman was Ackerman's personal lawyer, and had served as a Greyhound attorney for the past twenty years; in many respects, he was Ackerman's protege. In time, Trautman became himself the Chairman of the Board and continued apace the practice of collecting companies. Just as Greyhound used to be adept at gobbling up smaller bus lines, it ultimately became just as effective in fields of non-transportation.[30]

Another new plan was to put "Golden Scenicruisers" on the road, and this activated Greyhound's Public Relations Department. Verne F. Kelley was the person in charge, and he solicited names from each operating division. Some of the more colorful suggestions that came back were: Gold Arrow, Flying Clipper, Pacemaker, Red Carpet Service, Flamingo Flight, Royal Poinsettia, Silver Seminole, Miami Pride, Ponce de Leon, Ltd., Conquistador 26, Sovereign Service, Paramount Service, Big-O Service, Golden Highway, Green Stripe, King Robert, All Star, The General, Falstaff, Banner, Lord and Lady Greyhound Cruiser, and All Star Scenicruiser.[31] This was fulfilling with a vengeance some of the plans in the '40s to name buses.

Perhaps it was just as well that the naming program never really got started, and that very few of those names were ever actually applied. They would give Greyhounds, it was feared, too fancy an image, and this might change the "common" reputation they had always enjoyed. If the naming trend continued, the next step could very well be hostesses and food services aboard (though Greyhound in the past had had both).[32] Greyhound promised only to "take their riders where they want to go," without too much embellishment.[33]

This theme of commonality was especially stressed in all of Greyhound's advertising. In the late '50s Greyhound went into radio and television in a big way. First, there was "Operation Momentum," which ran from September to December, 1958. Part of "Momentum's" thrust was to show buses in bad weather, and capitalize on the advantages of letting a professional driver, with modern equipment, contend with the rain, snow, ice and fog. The meaning was clear that under these circumstances, the bus was much safer than a private automobile or airplane.

Then came "Operation Orbit," January-February, 1959. These were the lean times of year, when travel was at a minimum; thus Greyhound must secure a holding pattern; i.e., "stay in orbit." From March to June, 1959, it was "Operation Impact," in which massive advertising campaigns were launched on radio and television, and in newspapers and magazines, to get people out on the road—in buses. After "Impact" came "Operation Payload," covering the summer months, in which Greyhound hoped to reap bountiful profits from all its labors.

On NBC Monitor Radio, the company used the "Go Greyhound" theme as it had Bob and Ray and Fibber McGee and Molly to tell all about the virtues of bus travel. There was a woman who "wrote" to Bob wanting to know how to protect her chassis as she drove across the desert. Bob told her to wear an overcoat—or better yet, take a Greyhound. Ray frequently informed their listeners that on a Greyhound, "It's what's up front that counts." One day Bob asked Ray about the ticket sticking out of his pocket. Ray had heard that it was relaxing to buy a Greyhound ticket, and he was giving it a try. The two frequently talked about an anthropologist, Clayton T. Brittlebone, who said that man's arms and legs were getting shorter from non-use. This worried Bob, for he had just received a letter from a man who "didn't lift a finger" on a recent Greyhound tour. The man's name was "Stubby."[34]

Fibber and Molly one time were planning a vacation in their automobile. Looking at a map, Fibber deduced that they would get to "Motor Oil" the first night. Molly, wanting to know the location of this place, was told that it was right next to another little town called "Change." She decided then and there that they would take a Greyhound. One time Molly told an old-timer that she always took a Greyhound on her vacation, because her car was too hot. She never did convince him that she had not stolen her automobile. Molly one day mentioned Greyhound's air-suspension ride to a little girl. The little girl then found McGee and asked him what air-suspension was. He said, "It's when you quit talking." Radio audiences chuckled, too, at all of McGee's antics to keep "Uncle Whipple" from paying them a visit. This was yet another reason why he and Molly should be on an air-conditioned Greyhound speeding down a road to some romantic destination.[35]

Radio was effective for Greyhound, but its influence was as nought compared to the relatively recent medium of television. Art Linkletter's show, "People are Funny," featured "Miss Alice Quimby," President of the "Westbrook Bird Watcher's Club," who told viewers all about the comforts of Greyhound. The Steve Allen Show, in a "toe to toe" audience battle with Ed Sullivan, presented the "Come on Along ... and leave the driving to us," campaign. Edye Gorme and Steve Lawrence sometimes sang the ditty as "Bob" (a part-Indian actor) drove the big bus down the road.[36]

Another program that Greyhound sponsored was Jubilee, U.S.A., a country music show, starring Red Foley. Each Greyhound commercial on this show cost $11,500. Another bargain was on ABC's "Meet McGraw," with advertising at $18,000 a minute. Greyhound was a sometime sponsor of the Huntley-Brinkley Report, and it also put on a number of Jack Benny specials. "Cimarron City," "Cheyenne," and "Sugar Foot" were other popular television series paid for by the Greyhound buses. Generally, for twelve minutes of commercial time, Greyhound paid $184,676; for nine minutes, $169,535.[37] The price was worth it, as profits soared in the first several months of 1959, as Operations Impact and Payload paid off. On into the '60s, Greyhound's affiliation with television grew, changing its emphasis now and then to capture special markets, but always retaining the message that the bus—particularly the Hound—was the best travel bargain to be found.

After several years of adverse publicity and of trial and error in things like diversification and advertising, Greyhound seemed, by the mid '60s, to be settling down to a period of excitement and material advancement. This happened, to a large extent, in the years ahead, but not without some jolting developments that reached right to the top echelons of the organization's management.

"Greyhound Stories"—Silly and Otherwise

A girl once asked a driver for his autograph. He said, "O.K., but I don't have a pencil." Pulling up her dress, she said he didn't need a pencil. She wanted him to put his punch mark on her panties. He accommodated.—Greyhound driver.

One time a woman was sitting on the back row of a bus, holding a huge bag of oranges. Suddenly, the bus stopped, and every orange in the lady's bag spilled out into the aisle. Frantically, she got down on all fours in a desperate effort to retrieve her oranges. She became so upset and excited that she explosively flatulated—so loudly, in fact, that it was heard all over the bus.

It was so volatile that it woke up a drunk. He stirred himself at the noise, looked around, and sized up the situation. Then he looked sternly at the woman who had lost her oranges, and said, "That's right lady. If you can't catch the little sons-of-bitches, shoot 'em!"— Universal Greyhound bus drivers' story.

The greyhound dog on a bus is always to be shown running from left to right ____ Normally, the dog is in greyhound blue. However, any color can be used. The dog is never produced in one solid color (it is produced on a red, white and blue shield), because that encourages the details of the dog to fill up, particularly in the legs and tails.— Greyhound Graphics Manual.

"I hated that son-of-a-bitch so much that I would've paid a thousand dollars to be a pall-bearer at his funeral—and I'd 'a borrowed the money."—Retired Greyhound bus driver, talking about his former supervisor.

There was a cartoon that showed a Greyhound bus going into a repair shop, with a frowning Greyhound dog prominently displayed on the side. The second frame showed the bus leaving the repair shop with the dog, now smiling, and a litter of about nine puppies lying around it.—By Bill Ruble, Newport News Virginia Press, September 7, 1946.

"When I was working in Los Angeles in radio, I went down to the Greyhound bus terminal, somewhere in downtown L.A., to meet my ____ wife, who was coming into town after having visited her

family in Phoenix, Arizona. I approached a driver who happened to be standing about, to see if he knew when the bus I was waiting for might be coming in. The first thing he said—which I've always clearly recalled because his choice of words struck me as so funny at the time—was, 'where do you want to see somebody from?'

It took me a few seconds to figure out that the proper answer to that peculiar question was 'Phoenix'."—Steve Allen, to the author, December 30, 1980.

"I used to have a temper that was hotter'n a two dollar pistol."— Retired Greyhound driver.

A woman got off a bus one night at ———————, and slipped into a snowbank. One foot was in the snow and the other was still in the bus doorway. The driver yelled out to her, "Wait a minute, and I'll help you."

She called back, "No, I can look at you and tell you ain't no gentleman."

The driver responded, "I can look at you, and tell the same thing"—Still the same driver.

"This woman got off at ———— one night. The next night, she wanted to return home, but there weren't any seats left on my bus.

"I said, 'Lady, you better get the next bus, for tonight, I'm loaded.'

"She said, 'That's all right; you were loaded last night, but you drove all right."—And yet the same driver.

Chapter Five
This Lady was a Real Bitch

Nobody knew it at the time, but an event on January 28, 1957, in Clay Center, Kansas, ultimately caused several people to lead a dog's life. It happened at Roy Lee's place, when Little Shamrock, sired by Happy Yet, gave birth to a litter of greyhounds. They were all registered with the American Coursing Association, but one—a high-strung, nervous female—was not destined for the race-track. Instead, she was sold (for an undisclosed sum) to a bus-line, and became the "living symbol" of the Greyhound Corporation.

While still a puppy, weighing only ten pounds, in April 1957, she made her television debut on the Steve Allen Show. (Greyhound was the first transportation company to sponsor shows on television.) She was immediately dubbed "Stevo" by some and "Steverino" by others, a naming that ultimately caused a few problems for Greyhound.[1] When Greyhound moved away from the Allen Show in the early '60s, the latter's agent said to Greyhound, in effect, "of course, you can't continue using the name 'Steverino' publicly." The Greyhound people protested that "Stevo" was the only name the dog had ever known. Privately, therefore, the greyhound continued to be called "Stevo" but publicly her name was changed. Verne Kelly, of Greyhound, always named his pets after Shakespearian characters: Hamlet, Ophelia, Marc Antony, etc. He hit upon "Lady Grey" for the bus-line mascot, after Lady Jane Grey, of Elizabethan England. Then someone suggested "Lady Greyhound." Despite Kelley's fear of "over-commercializing" the dog, the name was successful.[2] The Corporation turned the Lady Greyhound program into an advertising extravaganza that made Madison Avenue history for almost a decade.

Lady Greyhound's primary role in the beginning was to be on hand at the opening of terminals. She bit through a ribbon of dog biscuits, to the tune of the "Greyhound March," when the Detroit facility was inaugurated in 1960 (but she fell asleep at the Milwaukee opening). Newspaper, radio and television accounts of her appearance in Detroit—where 1,500 people came to see her in just one day to get her "pawtograph" (footprint on a piece of paper)—turned Lady Greyhound into a veritable national institution. Silly? Yes, indeed, but Greyhound showed that it was no different from any other corporation in that as long as the program brought cash into its register, the sillier the better.

At full maturity the white and gray Lady Greyhound weighed fifty-four pounds, and had been trained to freeze into a pose everytime she saw a photographer. One of her favorite poses was to be reading a newspaper while wearing horn-rimmed glasses, or to be seated behind a typewriter, or to be "listening" to jazz in some swanky night club. She usually wore a tiara for the photographic sessions.

Her dedications of terminals inspired Greyhound to send the Lady on numerous publicity tours throughout the United States. Always hoopla-ed in the media far in advance of her arrival, she was usually accompanied by her "lady in waiting," Sue Warburton of the Grey Advertising Agency in New York.

Lady Greyhound generally traveled by charter-jet (in her own seat, with safety-belts on) because her own bus company had a rule against dogs. Sometimes, however, a charter was impossible, so she went by commercial air-line. This meant she had to be crated, a condition she "detested." The only problem she ever had with commercial travel was at St. Louis, where officials were in a quandary about where to store her between flights. J.D. Harrigan, an official of the St. Louis Rabies Society, wrote about the incident to J.E. Hawthorne, Greyhound's vice-president for marketing:

> Dear Jim,
>   I'm sorry we screwed up your g----d dog. Couldn't you work out some deal whereby you could use a Mexican chihuahua, instead of one close to the size of a horse?
>   ... Apparently the trouble was, we didn't have any facilities for taking care of mutts in this airport, but since this incident we have been able to work out storage facilities in case something comes up in the future. I am sure there will be no problem in St. Louis in the event you have another trip through here.[3]

Though her home base was New York City, Lady Greyhound— trained and cared for by Lorraine D'Essen of Animal Talent Scouts[4]—traveled approximately 25,000 miles a year. She was twice named Queen of National Dog Week, and was forever turning up in some organization as an "honorary cat." She was once the guest of honor at the homecoming ceremonies of Moravian College in Bethlehem, Pennsylvania. On this occasion, she received an "Associate Degree" in Animal Letters, and was inducted into the Delta Omicron Gamma Society, better known as "Dog." The Lady constantly participated in good causes: she was frequently an honorary marcher in the March of Dimes campaigns, and she was the National Pet Division Director for the 1960 Christmas Seal Program. In Oak Park, Illinois, much-to-do was made when Lady Greyhound visited a little boy who was about to have major surgery. After a photographic session with him, the Lady soothed and comforted the lad, and greatly ameliorated his worries. For deeds similar to this hospital visit, LG was awarded "the most coveted of all dogdom honors," the "Bide-A-Wee" medal from the Society for the Prevention of Cruelty to Animals for her "outstanding work in the promotion of kindness to animals." She also became the symbol for "World Animal Day," sponsored by London-based League for the Protection of Animals. In this regard, she received the Margaret Ford medal: a hand-cast bronze replica of her head; a scroll, framed in glass, accompanied the sculpture. She was also the first recipient of the Fellerette Award, given by the Pennsylvania Chapter of the SPCA.

In Philadelphia Lady Greyhound gave an "interview" on Radio Station WRCB and was made honorary disc-jockey. The "interview" was a tape of about four minutes, produced by Grey. Among other things, LG "talked" about Greyhound's defensive driving practices, particularly as they related to the day-time "lights on" program. She said, "After almost a year of experimentation in various sections of the country, Greyhound is convinced that ... lights in the daytime help other motorists determine direction, speed and distance of vehicles, thereby avoiding serious errors of judgment." Also in Philadelphia, she was named a "canine book reviewer" for *Pet Digest*, and proclaimed as an honorary editor of the Dorrance Company, a subsidy publisher.

In June 1963 Lady Greyhound attended the sixteenth annual chicken festival at Delmarva (Salisbury), Maryland. Perhaps her presence helped to draw 40,000 people to the two-day event. In New York City, she was introduced on ABC's radio station by Herb Oscar Anderson, who devoted two mornings in a row to raising money for the multiple sclerosis campaign. He was made an "honorary dog" by Lady Greyhound. Publicity reports gleefully noted that "both the Greyhound bus and Lady Greyhound were generally mentioned by

Anderson on these shows."[5] Always while in New York, Lady Greyhound's "interpreter" was Mrs. D'Essen.

Pittsburgh's Hotel Penn-Sheraton put "Welcome Lady Greyhound," on both sides of its marquee. While in the Smoky City, the "first lady of transportation" had a lengthy "chat" with popular singer Anita Bryant, and "interviewed" Toki Johnson, the society editor for a black newspaper. On all of her interviews—whatever the medium—Lady Greyhound developed her own inimitable style. For example, she was "dogmatic" on the subject of weather, objecting to the belief by some that animal behavior could predict rain and snow. She would have liked to see the phrase "raining cats and dogs" disappear from the language. She especially disliked any reference to "dog days," believing it should be changed to "people days."

She toured the South, and at Louisville, Kentucky, she visited the editorial offices of that city's morning paper, *The Courier-Journal*, while everyone sipped *coffee a la canine*. Shoppers at Grant's Department Store had a good look at her, and got pawtographed photos. At nearby Fort Knox, she posed with General Everett S. Thomas, Jr., in front of a tank, was made an honorary commander, and given a scroll by the U.S. Army.

In Dallas, Texas, she became an honorary editor of the *Express*, and attended a football game at the Cotton Bowl. She modeled a new fashion in Miami, Florida, known as "poodle-prints," to be manufactured by Serbin, Inc. On another visit to St. Louis, she was given a "leash to the city," by the Mayor (and also in Portland, Oregon). She became a deputy sheriff, and an honorary member of the Girl Scouts, and of the St. Louis police department's canine corps.

She went on to Kansas City, where a band greeted her at the airport and played "The Greyhound March" as she was motorcaded into town. She turned popular W.R.E.N. disc jockey, Jean Zimmerman, into an honorary dog. A street in Clay Center, Kansas, was re-named after Lady Greyhound, and Fred Meeks of the Kansas Legislature, in a special salute to Lady Greyhound, stated his intentions of enacting a bill proclaiming the greyhound as the state's "official dog." In Topeka itself, Mayor Edward Camp turned out to greet her with a leash to the city, and Governor John Anderson shook her paw, while his fellow office workers distributed "Meet Lady Greyhound" folders.

In San Francisco she stayed at the Sheraton Palace, where she had her own bed (she never slept on the floor—for she had to get eight hours of sleep a day), in a room shared by Ms. Warburton. California Governor Edmund Brown announced a "Be Kind to Animals Week," and ceremoniously handed over its Proclamation to none other than Lady Greyhound.

There was also a tie-in between the Lady Greyhound program and the Miss Universe Beauty Pageant, and the Lady had her picture taken with each year's Miss America. When Greyhound became the official bus line of the Mrs. America Pageant, LG's schedule was even more frenzied. In another beauty event, Lady Greyhound was a "lady in waiting" for Mrs. Georgia Conrad, who became "Miss National Transportation" at the 38th convention of Associated Traffic Clubs of America. She played a similar role for Dixie Lee Cook, the "Highways to Hope" Queen. Altogether in 1963, a typical year, Lady Greyhound appeared on twenty-nine television shows, a like number of radio performances; and she was "written up" in 306 newspaper articles. That same year, she also gave out 20,000 pawtographs to eager fans.

Why would politicians and public celebrities make such spectacles of themselves by so obviously "going to the dogs"? A better question, though, is "why shouldn't they?" Their purpose was to gain votes and public attention, so they latched on to any program that might help their endeavors. The great popularity of the Lady Greyhound program was an excellent example of how the American public *likes* to be exploited and manipulated by the media, politicians and public relations departments. That public is fickle, to say the least, and apparently it will do anything for a bit of entertainment.

Such was the case in 1964 during the World's Fair at New York City. As one public relations lure at the fair, Greyhound announced the celebration of its "fiftieth anniversary." (Of course, it was not— it was playing fast and loose with historical fact. To observe its fiftieth actual year, Greyhound legitimately had to wait until 1980.) Another Greyhound PR device at the fair was to make the most out of the Lady Greyhound Program.

Lady Greyhound had her own room at the fair, specially constructed so the tourists could get a good look at her. The room was outfitted with plush-bottom chairs, and a telephone. Visitors received a Travel-Pak (a cosmetic travel kit) from Lady Greyhound, via Ms. Warburton, and watched cartoon shows. A few days into the fair, Greyhound officials had to take care in their newspaper and magazine advertisements to let the public know that Lady Greyhound was actually a dog, and not a human being.

During the fair, the Greyhound people received many letters about the Lady Greyhound Program. None was as enticing as the one from Murray M. Spitzer, of New York's Animal Hygiene Research Corporation. His concern had recently perfected a toiletry product, and he wanted Lady Greyhound to demonstrate its qualities to a waiting world. The product's name was "Poodle-OO," and it was said to be effective, indeed.[6] The Lady used "Poodle-OO" while the fair was in progress, and many visitors to her room bought it. Some Greyhound officials demonstrated an interest in further collaboration; however, no records exist that show any subsequent Greyhound-Poodle-OO connections.

What with all of Lady Greyhound's public exposure, and the running dog emblem on thousands of buses, perhaps it was inevitable that the company run afoul of the Society for Indecency to Naked Animals (SINA). This organization wanted to clothe publicly shown animals, real or depicted, that were higher than four and longer than six inches. The entire country stood amazed in the fall of 1962 as SINA took its battle (known now to have been pretty much a hoax), to the length and breadth of this land. Greyhound did not have a chance of being overlooked by this crusading organization.

SINA's President, G. Clifford Prout, wrote to Greyhound that,

> the membership of SINA have voted unanimously to protest the use of a nude greyhound dog as your symbol on buses. We have no objection to a clothed dog, but object to the indecency of a naked one. Accordingly, the 38,000 members of SINA will make a special effort to encourage all bus travelers to ride by rail or air until some change is forthcoming. I am sure you can appreciate our stand on this, and we trust that steps will be taken to cover this public display of indecency, such as other spirited concerns have cooperated.[7]

Greyhound, however, ignored this letter. It actually made no effort whatever to please SINA, whose motto was "Decency Today Means Morality Tomorrow." When SINA, located on Fifth Avenue in New York, finally determined Greyhound's awkwardness in the matter, it took stringent steps to correct the problem. It sent Greyhound a summons:

> SINA constitution requires that you answer this summons in person or through a sworn statement before the Executive Board of SINA ten days after issuance of this document setting

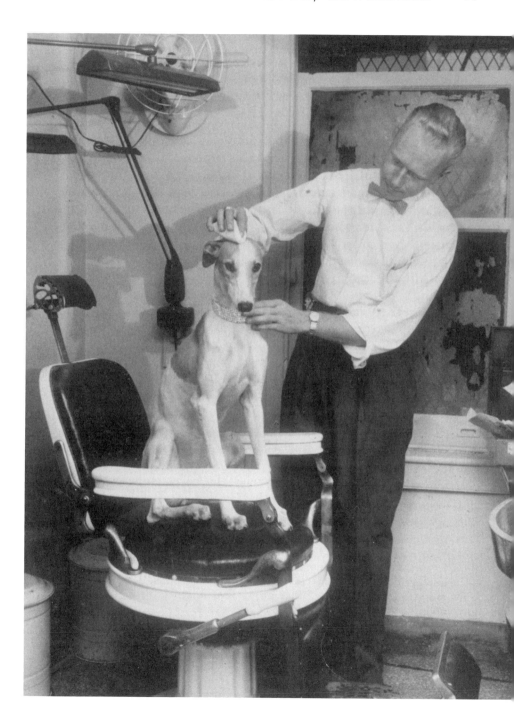

forth a complete explanation of your actions. If the summons is ignored, then in the name of decency you shall be deemed unworthy of ever appearing on the SINA membership rolls, and if you are presently enrolled, you shall be forthwith and permanently expelled from our organization without delay or prejudice.[8]

Alas and alack, though, showing that some people could not get respect, Greyhound cold-shouldered this proposal from SINA, just as it had all the other suggestions for clothing its greyhounds.

Lady Greyhound's wardrobe, however, should have been a real cause of celebration and happiness to SINA. She had a fur outfit for wintertime, and for summer a thin, shiny covering. An umbrella attached to her collar kept her dry during the rainy season. For spring and fall, she sported several different suits that made her undoubtedly the best dressed dog in America—nay, the world.

By the mid-sixties, Lady Greyhound was so well known that it became necessary for the Corporation to lay down several rules by which her appearance would be governed. V.P. Kelly, Greyhound's vice-president for public relations, sent a "confidential" directive to all employees who had anything to do with the Lady Greyhound program.

First, all publicity releases about the dog had to have the phrase, "the living symbol of the Greyhound Corporation." She must always be called Lady Greyhound, and *not* "Stevo" or "Steverino." Kelley went on with his directive:

> She is a lady, a queen, and conducts herself accordingly. [It took quite some time, however, to train her not to urinate in public.] She is always clothed. She is never to be photographed except in a graceful, positive light. She is not a trick dog. She has no routine. She is not an actress. She is not seen in or associated with such places as bars or dog tracks. She hobnobs with important people. She participates in fund drives, visits orphans and children's hospitals, and senior citizens' groups." [And, he might have noted, any other group that might have made a dollar or two for the Greyhound Corporation.]

Kelley's memorandum further dictated that Lady Greyhound would always be accompanied on her trips by a trained publicist, who in no way would ever become involved in controversial matters, on either a national or local level. Lady Greyhound would generally travel by the fastest means available, and that meant air, in which case, she would travel in the baggage section in her own specially constructed crate. If a bus were not being operated publicly, Lady Greyhound could ride on it. Upon arrival at destinations, Lady Greyhound would be met by private car; if such were unavailable, by a taxi. The Lady must get two hours of exercise every day, and work for no more than an hour at a time. Her attention span was thirty minutes. It was important to remember, said Kelley, that Lady Greyhound must be lodged in only the best hotels and motels. He added, parenthetically, that it must be kept in mind that not all such lodging facilities would allow dogs in their rooms.[9] He did not say, however, what Greyhound proposed to do in such a case.

It was important for the Corporation to maintain the image of just one Lady Greyhound (though in fact there were three); therefore, the dogs never made simultaneous appearances.[10] The original Lady Greyhound, the one that was named "Steverino," was retired from service in 1966. Kelley wrote to D'Essen that all LG programs were to be moved from New York to Chicago. He offered to give "Steverino" to her, provided she not use the dog in any commercial activities. D'Essen gratefully accepted, for she had come to love the greyhound.

A year or so before her retirement, Steverino gave birth to a litter of nine puppies. They were all given away to Brownie and Cub Scouts on Linkletter's television show "People are Funny," and Greyhound reaped the benefits of yet another public relations extravaganza.

A while after the births, however, Greyhound showed that if it could not get a lot of publicity mileage, it certainly would not give away, or sell, its puppies. In Winston-Salem, North Carolina, Earl W. Shumate was the director of the "Tiny Greyhound Booster Club." This organization was composed of 125 girls and boys, between the ages of 8 and 13. They consisted of "pee-wee" and midget football teams, majorettes and cheerleaders. Shumate wanted Greyhound to donate a puppy to them, which would be used for carnivals, candy sales and other social events. The puppy, said Shumate, would "always wear a jacket with 'Go Greyhound' sewn on it."[11]

D.A. O'Dell, of Southeastern Greyhound, who received Shumate's request, did not know what to do with it, so he sent it on up to Chicago, where it fell into the capable hands of vice-president Kelley. He replied to O'Dell that "we are not in the dog business, but in the bus business. If we gave to one group, there would undoubtedly be many others also wishing a dog. In your best public relations manner, try to explain the situation to the Tiny Greyhound Booster Club, perhaps on the legal opinion of our avoiding possible liability."[12] Who would be responsible, for example, if this greyhound ever bit someone? The Corporation or the Club? Also, what would happen when the puppy grew into a dog? Would the Club want a replacement? Mr. O'Dell accordingly informed Shumate and his young charges that the donation of a puppy might detract from "our national symbol" and Greyhound had no wish to do that. Just how the puppies being given away on the Art Linkletter show did not detract "from our national symbol," and presenting just one to a small organization did, was never explained. Such inconsistency, however, makes up the wonderful make-believe world of public relations.

An easier turn-down for a puppy came in 1965, when George Wolfe, an agent for Greyhound Van Lines in Portland, Oregon, wanted one to promote his company's activities. Again, Greyhound, through its spokesman, D.K. Behnke, scotched the idea. They would run the possibility, Greyhound said, of two Lady Greyhounds appearing at the same time if Wolfe's request were honored. Behnke explained further that "Greyhound has spent considerable funds to promote *the* Lady Greyhound [$12,689.31 for the first three months of 1966], and it is important that we protect that investment by avoiding the use of bogus Lady Greyhounds."[13]

The Greyhound Corporation certainly had no objections, however, to the creation of "Lady Greyhound Fan Clubs" around the country.[14] On the contrary, it greatly encouraged them, in an action that amounted to yet another chapter in this continuing saga of "the best known dog in history" (with apologies to Lassie and Rin Tin Tin).

By April, 1966, over 6,000 people belonged to the "Lady Greyhound Fan Club." Each member received a symbol from Greyhound, which they proudly displayed on the walls of their rooms and studies. Greyhound encouraged groups rather than individuals to join. The large membership areas were Illinois, Michigan, New York, Pennsylvania, Ohio and Wisconsin. The lowest memberships were in Arkansas, Colorado, Georgia, Mississippi, Nevada, New Hampshire, Oklahoma, Vermont and Wyoming. The most recalcitrant state was unmistakably New Mexico, for it was the only place in the Union without *any* membership in the Lady Greyhound Fan Club.

For the Lady's birthday in 1966 (the ninth one for the original, though she made no more appearances for Greyhound), a contest was put on, for fan-club members only. The idea was for a fan to send in something creative with a Lady Greyhound theme. This could be a poem, a card or even a cake. The winner would receive an all-expenses paid trip, with a parent, to Hollywood, to see the premiere of "The Ugly Dachshund," and to "shake paws" with Brutus, the Great Dane star of the show, and with Lady Greyhound. After the movie, the winner would have an escorted tour through the Disney Studios, and spend a day at Disneyland. The winner of this Lady Greyhound contest of 1966 was thirteen-year old Miss Laura Scheuneman, of Denver, who wrote a short story called "George," and dedicated it to the bus-line mascot.[15] In addition to publicity accruing from "The Ugly Dachshund," Greyhound also benefited from another Disney production, "Winnie the Pooh." In the press books on both movies, a great deal of material was given about Lady Greyhound.

Warner Brothers produced a film, "The Incredible Mr. Limpet" (starring Don Knotts, about a man who could turn into a fish), which ultimately helped Greyhound to a considerable extent. The studio made a ten minute publicity film about the movie, in which a Greyhound bus figured prominently. Film personalities were shown traveling from Ft. Paradise to Weekiwatchee—in Florida—and Lady Greyhound was always the first off at the various destinations. Greyhound officials were obviously pleased, as Warner Brothers gave them two copies of the publicity film, and assured them that the bus and Lady Greyhound sequences would not be cut. It was estimated that the short would play in 5,000 cinemas around the country, reaching approximately 100,000 people.[16]

So successful was the Lady Greyhound program that someone in the organization suggested that a replica of her be placed atop all the buses. The suggestion was treated seriously by the top management until it was realized that a "five foot replica on top of a thirty-eight foot bus would look more like a moose than a dog," and prove to be a safety hazard out on the road. The idea, therefore, was not put into practice.[17]

As the '60s drew to a close, the Lady Greyhound program dwindled in popularity with the public, and in interest with Greyhound management. It was a program that had fairly run its course: the public was no longer as fascinated by the spindly-legged, high-tension dog as it was when she first hit the scene. Also, by the late '60s and early '70s, Greyhound's diversification and acquisition programs put the actual bus-line operations—and along with them the Lady Greyhound program—on a relatively low level in comparison with the Corporation's other holdings and interests.[18] Therefore, at an increasing rate, funds were withheld from the program. Greyhound went from Steve Allen to Fred MacMurray for its advertising, and the slant was changed from showing off the actual dog to proclaiming the virtues of air-suspension rides.

While it lasted, however, the Lady Greyhound program made advertising history. It showed just what could be done when an imaginative public relations staff and a real live, well-trained animal got together. The program was a definite phase of Greyhound history—one that made a distinct mark on the public. Beyond that, it showed what good animal training could do— causing one Greyhound executive admiringly to proclaim, "that bitch is a real lady!"

"Greyhound Stories"— Wheeling and Dealing

"There was a time when a funeral had to be postponed because Greyhound [Package Express] had lost the package containing the human ashes."—James Steelman, Murfreesboro, Tennessee.

"The most unusual article I ever handled was a queen bee, packaged in a section of cane with a cork stopper in each end."— James Steelman

"Driving a bus is very hard work. We earn the salary we get. Drivers are classified according to stress along with airline pilots, control tower operators, railroad dispatchers, policemen, firemen, doctors, secret service agents, all those who for one reason or another must be 100 percent alert while on duty. We must be able to control any situation on the road, or on the bus, and never lose our temper, be immune to being called all the four letter words, and handle the situation in the manner of a United Nations diplomat!"—George Walker, Louisville, Kentucky.

There was this preacher of thirty years who showed up at the Pearly Gates. Gabriel looked at his credentials for a moment, and told him to stand aside.

Then a Greyhound driver of twenty years came up, and Gabriel waved him through.

This puzzled the preacher. "Why did you make me wait, and let that driver go on?"

Gabriel replied, "because that driver has scared the hell out of more people in twenty years than you have in thirty."—Bus drivers' story.

A soldier one time requested that a Greyhound ticket agent cash a traveler's check. When he opened his wallet, he found that he only had one left. He exclaimed "Damn!" only to be accosted for swearing in public. The young man got off by saying that he was only repeating his initials. His name was David A. Millions.—Williston (Fla.) Sun, 1945.

A customer walked up to the window years ago, and asked "What is the bus fare to New York?" The agent ___ answered $19.21,

Ma'am." And the customer then said, "and will the driver pay for all my meals at the lunchstops?"—Ibid.

There was a drunk once in the old days who stood on the treadle which operated the air, and everytime he started out the door, it would close on his neck. He almost suffocated.—Russell A. Byrd, Russ's Bus.

Russell Byrd got a bug in his ear one time while driving a busload of passengers. Here are some suggestions he received on how to deal with the problem: put milk in your ear, put olive oil in your ear, stick a straw into your ear and blow cigarette smoke through it (at least that would anesthetize the creature); or—the only sensible thing—go to a doctor.—Russ's Bus.

"This particular time I went to New York City. We were gone for a week or ten days (on a charter), with the Youth Symphony Orchestra out of Lexington (Kentucky), and I went along with two other drivers. We had the big banners pasted on the sides of the buses, and I was always on the rear end. I was the rear end of everything. But we went through the Lincoln Tunnel, and they went on to the hotel like normal bus drivers would. But I was gawking around, looking at everything in town, trying to see it all in the first two blocks, and I got lost. I kept going around the block there about three times and I finally stopped and asked a policeman ___ how to get to this particular hotel, and he was trying to tell me. He said, "well, wait here a minute, there'll be one of your buses by here—one of your buddies—and you can follow him down there. And, I didn't tell him, but that was me that he had seen pass there three or four times."—Jim Music, Crossville, Tennessee

"Fletcha Amarilla," (Yellow Bus—about an old, used Greyhound in service somewhere in Mexico):

Fletcha Amarilla
Got an arrow in my heart
Though you're loud and though you're dirty
And you'd rather stop than start
I never like the Greyhound
Or the bus I took to school,
But the Flethca Amarilla
I love you like a fool.

If you've got fifty pesos
You can ride 'bout half a day.
The Flecha Amarilla's safe
But it doesn't hurt to pray.
Jesus is on the dash board.
And the blood drips down his side.
He is dying for us
So that we'll get there alive.

Chapter Six
"Akron, Ohio, is the Capital of West Virginia"

Who rides a Greyhound bus, and why? During the past several years, the Greyhound Corporation has spent millions trying to find out. Its investment in "demographics" has largely been disappointing, because as late as 1978, a federal study indicated that "Americans tend to have a negative opinion ... of buses today." Only twenty-six per cent rated them positively, thirty-eight per cent were thoroughly negative, and thirty-four per cent did not know enough about buses to give them any kind of rating.[1]

In 1956 when Greyhound first became seriously interested in demographics, here is how the bus travelers compared with plane and train passengers:

*They were younger and older.

*They were from a lower income group, with a larger proportion of black people.

*They were, on the whole, non-businessmen, most coming from blue-collar occupations.

*Women made up 58.2 per cent of the travelers.[2]

*A majority of the passengers surveyed, 57 per cent, preferred to travel on a bus, while the sizeable remainder, 43 per cent, would have liked better ways of traveling, but used the bus because of its economy and convenience. Also, 51.7 per cent of Greyhound travelers thought the bus the safest form of transportation, while 30.1 per cent picked trains, and 9.3 per cent, planes.

Plane and train travelers generally snubbed the humble bus passenger, considering him as a patron of the absolute lowest form of transportation. Without saying whether or not they had ever been on a bus, here are the general reasons for the train-plane opinions:

*No one would use a bus if they could afford better.[3]

*The buses are dirty and in poor condition, and always overcrowded.

*Some of the people using buses don't even have luggage; they carry their belongings in a paper bag.

*The bus drivers are rude, and don't treat people with respect.

The buses are poorly ventilated, and some passengers are not as clean as they could be.

*The bus is a "low-class hound dog. We wouldn't use this sort of dog for hauling."[4]

Two years later, another study indicated that travel preferences had not changed very much; the impression still abounded that people traveled on buses because they had to, not because they wanted to. Preference was for air, followed by trains and cars. Buses were still in last place. Greyhound and the other bus companies felt they were being unfairly stereotyped, and for the next several years tried—without much success—to turn things around.

In 1959 Grey undertook a massive demographic study for Greyhound. Nothing that had been learned in the past had materially changed; the study did turn up a few new developments:

*People eighteen to twenty-nine showed a sizeable preference for the bus over other modes of travel.

*Short-trip travelers (50 to 99 miles) were twice as numerous as the long trippers (over 100 miles).

*Most trips are made in August, and a preponderance of these are for pleasure.

*The bus traveler is to be found primarily in the southeastern and western parts of the country.[5]

These demographic studies helped Greyhound to embark, in 1963, upon a Special Markets Program. The most important incentive for this program, however, was the dramatic upsurge of the civil rights movement. Greyhound had long been patronized by the black community, and it now wished to demonstrate that the Corporation wanted to serve the Negro, and contribute to his welfare, and show that it was not "just another self-seeking, opportunistic company intent upon exploiting them."

To head the Special Markets Program, Greyhound hired a Brooklyn Dodgers baseball star, Joe Black, the first Negro pitcher ever to win a world series game.[6] After his baseball career ended, Black became a school teacher in New Jersey. One of his "side jobs" was to act as a marketing consultant to Grey, the Greyhound Corporation's advertising representative.

In 1962, Black began full-time work for Greyhound. When he was offered the job of overseeing special markets, Black asked James Kerrigan to assure him that his new position would be as good and pay as well as school-teaching.[7] (Today, Mid-1980s, Black is a vice president of the Greyhound Corporation, and undoubtedly is on a higher pay scale than school teachers.)

Black was well received not only by his own people, but by other ethnic groups as well. He and his staff went into communities[8] with large black populations, and sponsored programs to honor the typically unsung person. An example of this activity was the "Mother of the Year" program in several locations. Black and his team also contacted school-age children, and put on programs of interest for them.[9] Black traveled extensively around the country, attending sports events and luncheons, where Negroes figured prominently. He helped to develop Greyhound advertising that was directed specifically toward the black market. In 1972, Black himself summed up his position at Greyhound:

> Although unnecessary, company pride dictates that I mention that long ago, Greyhound recognized its obligation to people in some of this nation's social problems. And it can be proud of the fact that it is a practitioner of the theory that profit alone is not enough, though profit is still the name of the game.[10]

With Black at the helm, Greyhound set about to win the goodwill of the Negro, and as much of his travel dollar as possible. To help do this, constant studies of black population shifts and changing opinions and attitudes were sponsored by the Corporation.

As is well known, black migration was predominantly south to north. From 1940 to 1972 the black population in the South decreased from 77 to 52 per cent, while in the North it increased from 22 to 40 per cent. Since black people fit the demographic profile of a bus traveler,[11] and since they were now beginning to concentrate in northern urban areas, Greyhound conducted an extensive advertising program aimed specifically at them. It used primarily black-oriented mass media. In *Ebony, Jet, Black Enterprise* and forty-one other black newspapers and magazines, Greyhound got its message across. Much of this Greyhound exposure—not only in printed media but on black oriented television and radio as well—took the form of editorials by Joe Black. His messages, as might be expected, were upbeat, letting the black man know that he had a friend in Greyhound.[12]

Another Greyhound advertiser to have an important impact on black people was singer Pearl Bailey, who sang a ditty, "Say Hello to a Good Buy." (The use of this phrase, as we shall see in chapter seven, got Greyhound into quite a bit of trouble.) Count Basie was also used from time to time. Popular actor Fred MacMurray—though one of the richest men in Hollywood—struck the common chord with his Greyhound commercial (he thoroughly investigated the company before he agreed to advertise for it), and directed black people toward the bus.[13]

Three years into this program of mass black advertising, Greyhound sponsored another study to determine success or failure. The study opened by saying, "In recent years the black population has emerged as a dynamic and viable market, and consumer analysts think this trend will continue. Improvements in the areas of education, employment and income, will strengthen black buying powers. Recognizing the expanding role of the black community, Greyhound has continually increased its advertising specifically directed to black people."[14] The study went on to emphasize that six out of every ten blacks, 78 per cent, lived in metropolitan areas. By now, 1975, 52 per cent of the black population lived in the South, with 40 per cent in the north, and 8 per cent in the West. The cities of greatest black growth were New York, Los Angeles, Baltimore, Miami and Detroit, and, as a result, Greyhound created literally dozens of new routes, because "black people represent a disproportionately high percentage of intercity bus passengers."[15]

None of these cities, however, had a black growth rate like Washington, D.C. The expanding powers of the federal government, and new civil rights laws, brought tens of thousands of blacks into the capital city, so that by the early '70s, they outnumbered the whites. "Main Street in Washington has come to be the Belt-Way," the saying went, as this vast migration continued. Washington's suburban areas were also greatly affected: black population rose quickly in nearby Maryland and Virginia, particularly in the counties of Prince Georges, Montgomery, Fairfax, Arlington and the city of Alexandria. These new Washingtonians, Greyhound noted, were frequent travelers, and planned its routes accordingly.[16] As it turned out, however, the government-employed Negro preferred to fly; thus, Greyhound and the other bus companies did not benefit as much from the exodus to Washington as they had expected. Increased patronage in other cities was higher on a percentage basis than in the District of Columbia.

By 1977, growth projections for the black population showed an increase faster than for whites. The number of blacks in the country in 1975 was 24.5 millions, or 11.5 per cent of the total U.S. population. By 1985, various surveys showed, the black population should be 29.1 millions. Though blacks still preferred large metropolitan centers in the late '70s, their migration to the industrial centers of the North had practically stopped.[17] The majority of blacks were still in the large cities and small towns of the South. This fact obliged Greyhound once again to re-do many of its routes in order to accommodate this re-shifting of populations. (This could also be an important contributing factor to Greyhound's decision in the late '70s and early '80s to restore services to hundreds of little hamlets in the United States—services that had been abandoned largely because of the Interstates.)

Greyhound's relationship with black people in this country is an historical one. The bus line has shown time and again that it was not interested *only* in profit as it dealt with the black community—it embodied the age-old beliefs of numerous economists and reformers that businesses and corporations should extend themselves into the social sphere, and do good works. Not only did the Greyhound buses provide a cheap way of traveling for black people; it was also one of the first agencies to hire them. Many worked at Greyhound terminals—mostly in menial positions, it is true—but at least it was employment. It should be noted, too, that Greyhound hired many black men as drivers long before Affirmative Action became a reality. (Today, Mid-80's, it hires many females, including black women, to drive its buses.) The intercourse between Greyhound and blacks is one of the happier aspects of the company's history—and by projection of the country itself, for in its quest of black patronage, Greyhound has contributed greatly to civil and human rights.

Not only did Greyhound routing affect and respond to black migratory patterns but it had an important impact on white population shifts as well—especially those from Appalachia. Dayton and Cincinnati, Ohio, for example, were inundated with people from Harlan, Boonsborough, Pineville and other eastern Kentucky locales who took the most direct, express route they could find to industrial employment. Cleveland had one white migration from Charleston and Blue Field, in West Virginia, and another from the Pittsburgh oriented area, primarily Morgantown and Fairmont. Black migration to Cleveland tended to come from predominantly Southeastern Greyhound routes that extended in Alabama from Birmingham through Tuscaloosa, Livingston and York on over into various places in Mississippi.

Detroit's black migration was similar to Cleveland's— primarily from the Birmingham area. Memphis and the Delta areas in Mississippi supplied Chicago with black—and also a few white— migrants. New York City had a migration pattern that emphasized North Carolina and Virginia.

It is assuredly true that the Greyhound route system had a great deal to do with where people settled. Then, once the settlements were made, they in turn highly influenced subsequent Greyhound operations. For example, when all these migrants wanted to go home—say, for a weekend—they would leave from a concentrated area in the North and go to dispersed areas in the South. Express buses, therefore, became the chief Greyhound practice north of the Ohio River; south of it, however, it was primarily a "bump and grind" operation. These demographic factors extended beyond the migratory situation. When new routes were created in the North, they were usually express, non-stop from big city to big city— whereas in the South, a more localized operation prevailed.

Generally speaking, it was mostly the white migrants who traveled on the week-ends. The blacks, mostly from Alabama and Mississippi, lived too far away for week-end travel. The white week-enders turned numerous Ohio cities and towns into boom places every Friday night, as they jostled to get aboard an Appalachian-bound Greyhound. Bus people spoke frequently of the "Southland expresses out of Cleveland," as three buses or more were generally necessary to transport passengers to Charleston and other points in West Virginia. Bus personnel also frequently quipped that so many white migrants lived in central Ohio that Akron had become the capital of West Virginia. Finally, by the early to mid '70s, these weekly treks tapered off, and for the most part, ended. The migrant either brought his family up North to live with him, or bought a car and transported himself every week-end.[18]

The Appalachian week-enders made a vigorous contribution to the history of Greyhound, and to the transportation and social history of the United States. Though this market has largely now dried up, bus people remember it with bemusement, fondness and even nostalgia.[19]

To a lesser extent than with the white-black migrants, Greyhound established a reciprocal relationship with the Latino community. It dealt not so much with migratory patterns as it did in taking passengers into and out of the U.S.-Mexican border cities. In 1972, Greyhound built up a "war chest fund" for Spanish speaking peoples—making an exception to company policy of concentrating on major markets—to advertise in towns and cities along the international line. Greyhound estimated in the mid '70s that there were 11.2 million people of Spanish origin in the United States. If one added the "illegals" to that figure, the number shot up to 16-17 millions. And they all wanted to go somewhere! Greyhound strategists noted that "these people (Spanish speaking) have standards, points of view, and motivations which are different and ever-changing. The prejudices against bus travel, so obvious in their elders, may not exist with them."[20]

By 1975, Greyhound was advertising on twenty-three Spanish broadcast TV and radio stations, and in a number of newspapers and magazines, primarily in east Los Angeles, and Miami. It put a specific emphasis on "eliminating the fear of the unknown." It wanted to let Latinos know that "Greyhound welcomes them and will take care of them. Traveling by Greyhound is easy, affordable, comfortable, dependable, reliable and safe. Greyhound is a good way to visit families and friends."[21]

Greyhound capitalized on its "Tia Juana Joy Rides," which attracted the young people of both Mexican and American nationalities. These trips originated in Los Angeles and San Diego, and lasted for a day or two south of the border. Also, Greyhound noted that a large portion of Latinos traveled within the continental limits of the U.S. Many Mexican workers, for example, from Laredo, Texas—for some reason or other—tended to concentrate in Chicago. Others crossed the continent from California to New York to find employment, or to live with families who had traveled before them. Always ready to take them was Greyhound, the "poor man's" carrier.

Perhaps the experiences with migrants and Latinos helped inspire Greyhound to expand its Special Markets opportunities. As one official explained, "We feel our greatest opportunity to build passenger miles lies in reaching the higher fringes of the lower socio-economic groups, and conversely the lower fringes of the higher socio-economic groups. The object behind this premise is that we already have excellent market penetration amongst the lower income and certain ethnic groups. Thus, our primary target should be those people who might consider Greyhound as a reasonable alternative to air, rail, and hopefully, even driving."[22]

One object was the youth market, for more young people than ever were going to college. One "Back to College" Greyhound ad showed a male student passenger looking at the centerfold of *Playboy*. Beside him sat a co-ed, ostensibly reading *Mademoiselle*, but coyly peering over at *Playboy*. In connection with attracting the youth-college crowd, Greyhound started special runs. One was to "Alligator Alley" in Florida. Other special offerings were to race tracks, casinos and baseball games, as well as runs for spring vacations, Thanksgiving and Christmas.

Senior citizens were certainly not overlooked in these massive sales campaigns. The "Tour of the Month" club was begun, in which charter trips were featured. Greyhound believed that the motivations and characteristics of the charter passenger were different from the regular traveler. "On the charter," it said, "the customer is not an individual." Also, the competition was different. It was easier, for example, to lure a group of retirees away from an airline or train for travel to out-of-the-way places than to capture this trade on an individual basis. The charter business, therefore, became quite significant for Greyhound in the '60s and '70s.[23]

Another special market was the military. Dramatic changes occurred in the military consumer market when the draft ended in January, 1973. The overall number of active military personnel decreased, but the percentage of enlisted women and blacks sharply increased. By 1974, approximately 72 per cent of the U.S. military were under the age of 29, and fewer people than before were entering the services without any college or university background. In short, the non-draft military fit Greyhound's traveler profile quite well; the military was, as the *Army Times* reported, "a big, young, mobile, and well-paid consumer market."[24] What more could Greyhound ask for?"

Getting all those people around required Greyhound by 1980 to put 4,400 buses on the road, with total daily runs in excess of 1,250,000 miles. The very act of scheduling all those miles was stupendous, demanding, among other things, expertise in demographics. When the schedules are completed, they are printed in a large book called *Russell's Guide*. Back in the 1880s, a midwesterner, R.W. Russell, conceived the idea of printing all the train schedules in the country in one compact volume. He came up with a four by eight inch volume that listed train schedules and printed a hotel index for the entire country. Needless to say, the little, portable "red-book" became indispensable to salesmen and other people as they traversed the length and breadth of the United States. In 1926 the inter-city bus industry had grown sufficiently to warrant the publication of *Russell's Official National Motor Coach Guide*. From that time, the *Guide* increasingly neglected railroads in favor of buses. Today, it publishes only bus schedules.

Russell's Guide today, headquartered in Cedar Rapids, Iowa, publishes a new edition each month. A comparative study of these guides going back a few years gives a fascinating glimpse of how towns "dried up" or "boomed" as bus schedules responded to their social and economic conditions. *Russell's Guide* is in many ways a microcosm of American society itself.

Of course Greyhound takes up most of the space in *Russell's Guide*; in second place is Trailways. Anyone who believes that there are only two bus corporations in this country—Greyhound and Trailways—will be quickly corrected by a glance at *Russell's Guide*. There are nearly a thousand bus lines in the United States. For them to be listed in *Russell's Guide*, they must prove themselves to be legitimate concerns, and pay a publishing fee.[25]

An increase in traffic volume, despite the energy crisis, is another difficulty facing Greyhound schedulers and their one and a quarter million miles a day. (President Jimmy Carter's statement, "Thanks for Taking the Bus and Saving Energy," was plastered on the back of every Greyhound—largely without effect. Citizens still took to the road so much in their automobiles that many bus-drivers contemplated early retirement.) Two of the most congested areas in the country are highways 31-W between Louisville and Ft. Knox, Kentucky; and U.S. 1 from Ft. Lauderdale to Miami. "It's just awful tough," said one Greyhound official of these two routes. "I mean, the cars come at you from every direction."[26]

The Kentucky and Florida problems are as nought, however, compared to the traffic volume of the "northeast corridor." This route covers approximately 450 miles from Washington, D.C. through New York on into Boston. Though black migration to areas in the northeast corridor diminished in the late '70s, Spanish speaking populations increased, and they generally gave Greyhound their travel business.[27] The number of cars and trucks on these routes has reached phenomenal proportions, and many bus-drivers are "just tired of fussing with the traffic,"[28] and are either retiring or transferring to less hectic locales.

Still another source of anxiety in reference to the number of miles covered each day by Greyhound is accidents. Greyhound's safety record is generally good and, as noted previously, it hired its first Safety Director, Marcus Dow, in 1929. It has constantly conducted studies to determine what risks are being run out on the road. A typical safety study was undertaken in 1951 by Ross A. McFarland of Harvard University's School of Health. This report, "Human Factors in Highway Transport Safety," gave extremely detailed observations of bus-driver habits. For example, on the nine hour run between New York and Boston, the driver kept his eyes to the front 78 per cent of the time; his left hand was 99 per cent on the steering wheel, while his right alternated between the steering wheel (81 per cent) and gear shift (11 per cent).[29] His right foot was on the accelerator 87 per cent and brake 13 per cent during the New York-Boston run.

The maximum time for decelerating for a possible emergency ahead was 7.2 seconds. It took a minimum of 13.2 seconds to pass another vehicle, and a maximum of 29 seconds. The horn was used 50 per cent of the time when passing.[30]

McFarland's study went on, in general, to determine major driver errors, the ones that contributed to critical situations. They were:

*Following too closely ("tailgating" or "bumper-hugging").

*Cornering while approaching to pass; i.e., getting too close to the front vehicle's left rear.

*Inattention, brought on by fatigue or—in some rare instances—intoxication.

*Driving too fast for the range and vision of reaction time.

Human errors (bus, and other, drivers, pedestrians), the report found, caused 90 per cent of all accidents, with mechanical defects taking up the remaining 10 per cent.[31]

It appears from press reports of major accidents that the worst enemies of the bus driver are other bus drivers, and those who are piloting the big eighteen-wheelers. The automobile—though it has figured prominently—is apparently not as much danger to the bus driver as has commonly been thought.

On June 8, 1943, a Safeway Trails bus and a Greyhound collided in Halethorpe, Maryland, killing two persons. Both bus-lines had to be forced into court before making a settlement with the heirs of the victims.[32] The following year, July 23, a Greyhound and a Washington, D.C. city bus hit each other, injuring twenty-eight persons, some seriously.[33]

In the fall of 1951 a Greyhound plunged forty feet off a ramp of the San Francisco bridge in Oakland, California. Seven passengers were killed, and twenty-two injured, as it landed upside down after its fall. Eyewitnesses said that a car hit a chunk of cement and threw it into the path of the bus, which was traveling between forty and forty-five miles per hour. The bus's left front tire blew, causing it to career across the highway, through one hundred feet of a restraining fence, where it spectacularly teetered on the ramp's edge before going on over. Its impact at the bottom was so severe that it shook near-by houses.[34]

In January, 1952, twenty passengers were injured near

Dyersburg, Tennessee, when a Memphis-bound bus struck the rear of another one headed for the same city. Rescue workers had to cut through several inches of steel to free the imprisoned passengers. The cause of the crash was said to be poor visibility and a rain-slick road, which prevented the rear bus from stopping when the front one halted to disembark passengers. The first bus, it was reported, hurtled forty feet into an embankment, and consequently had most of the mishap's casualties.[35]

The worst accident—to that time—occurred in August, 1952, when two Greyhounds collided head-on near Waco, Texas. Twenty-eight people, including the two drivers, perished in that crash. (The previous worst accident was in 1938, when a bus struck a train in Midvale, Utah, killing twenty-four.) The weather was clear and it was near dawn on Highway 81 between San Antonio and Dallas. Within seconds of that impact, fuel tanks on both vehicles exploded, turning the entire scene into a ghastly ball of fire. Miraculously, twenty-five people escaped with their lives, though most were badly burned or injured in other ways. The Dallas-bound bus apparently crossed over into the south lane, and caused the tragedy.[36] The Interstate Commerce Commission investigated the crash for two months. It concluded that twenty-four-year-old driver Milburn Herring, was dozing, causing the accident.[37] Also in August, 1952, a Greyhound ran onto the shoulder of a road during a flash flood in Cape Girardeau, Missouri. It landed in fifteen feet of water. All but one of the passengers either swam to safety or were rescued. One man drowned.[38]

On March 7, 1953, twenty-six of twenty-eight travelers were injured, some critically (one died the next day), when their Greyhound bus smashed into the pillar of an underpass near Los Angeles. The driver, Forrest Luther, who suffered foot and back injuries, was taken into police custody after some passengers complained that he had been handling the bus erratically.[39] He would give no statements, however, because he maintained that it was "company policy" to speak only to ICC investigators after accidents.[40] (Apparently to speak exclusively to the federal agency is still a "company policy"—making it difficult for the public sometimes, through newspapers, easily to learn the causes of bus wrecks.)

In the same year, on June 12, a Greyhound rammed into a parked tractor-trailer on the busy Pennsylvania Turnpike, near Harrisburg. Six women were killed, and thirty other passengers injured. Driver Francis Garaff, held on a charge of involuntary manslaughter, said he saw the truck's flare, but that his bus had run onto the Pike's shoulder and he could not straighten it out in time to avert the crash. His statements were confirmed not only by the ICC but by the Pennsylvania State Turnpike Commission as well, which found evidence that he struggled, to no avail, for 120 feet to get the bus back onto the road.[41]

Another half dozen people were killed on August 6, 1953, when a Greyhound and a car locked into each other on a narrow bridge near Hydro, Oklahoma. Both vehicles plunged into the creek below. Thirty-five injured persons were taken from the wreckage.[42]

York, Pennsylvania, was the scene of a Greyhound-car accident on March 20, 1954. Twenty-two were injured when the bus hit the rear-end of the car, which had inexplicably stopped on a rain-swept road.[43] A few months later, in August, a woman was killed, and twenty-five persons injured in another bus-car collision during a thunderstorm. This was in Charlton, Massachusetts. The bus went off the road after the impact and hit a tree.[44]

The St. Louis symphony orchestra had to cancel an Ohio concert in February, 1955, when fourteen of its thirty-two musicians were hospitalized after their Greyhound skidded on ice and rammed into a bridge abutment near Clifton Forge, Virginia. Police reports indicated that the abutment was most notorious, causing at least one accident a week. No charges were filed against the driver, as several City Fathers promised to do something about the traffic hazard.[45] Near Lexington, Kentucky, a tractor-trailer truck sideswiped a Greyhound just before dawn on August 30. One woman passenger was killed as the bus overturned.[46]

October 15, 1955, was a "double voo-doo" day for Greyhound, as two of its buses were involved in separate incidents. The worse was in Michigan City, Indiana, when a Scenicruiser ripped into a stalled semi-trailer. The truck had not pulled completely off the road, said police—thirty-three inches protruded onto the highway. Six were killed and twenty-one injured in the accident.[47] The other wreck that day occurred near Ft. Knox, Kentucky, when a Greyhound collided with two other vehicles. Though property damage was extensive, the twenty-two passengers were not seriously injured.[48]

A statistically good year for Greyhound in the area of accidents was 1956. None of its passengers died, though one bus was involved in a fatal collision on October 19, near Roanoke, Virginia. A Greyhound and a truck hit each other; two people in the truck died, while there were no injuries on the bus.[49] In December, 1956, twenty passengers were injured, none critically, when their Greyhound careened off a highway near Tangent, Oregon. The driver said a car made a sudden left turn in front of him, forcing him off the road.[50]

There was only one accident each for 1957 and 1958, but they were deadly. Six persons died in Lexington, Virginia, when a Greyhound rammed into the rear of a parked tractor-trailer. The driver, one of the victims, apparently did not see the safety flares set out by the trucker.[51] In December, 1958, seven passengers were killed, and thirteen injured when a Greyhound and a truck collided near Pulaski, Tennessee.[52]

On December 20, 1959, nine were killed and twenty-one injured when a Scenicruiser hit a loaded cattle truck just before dawn on a desert highway near Tucson, Arizona. The trucker and his relief driver, and thirty of their calves were among the victims. The impact was so severe that many of the calves were hurled to the inside of the bus.[53]

On into the '60s bus travel generally remained safe by comparison with cars and trucks, but accidents, of course, were still all too possible. One of the most spectacular was on August 28, 1965, when a truck loaded with heavy timbers ran head-on into a Greyhound. Eleven persons, including the truck driver, died as the timbers fell into the bus. The accident occurred near Vinton, Louisiana, as the truck was passing a car on Highway 90 when it ran into the oncoming bus, which had pulled onto the shoulder.[54]

A 1967 accident brought up questions about the general safety of Greyhound buses. On May 15, a seventy-three year old woman died when her Greyhound crashed near Hackettstown, New Jersey. The bus went off a wet road in a dense fog and slid seventy feet down a wooded hillside. The victim was thrown through a window when the bus flipped on its side.[55] A state police report claimed that the bus's tires were so thin that the canvas showed. Ironically, just three days before this crash, consumer advocate Ralph Nader had said in Grand Rapids, Michigan, that Greyhound was "using grooved, re-treaded tires [which are] extremely dangerous on slippery wet pavements." (It should be kept in mind that Greyhound does not buy tires—rather, it leases them from major rubber companies.) Despite Greyhound's assurances that its tires were safe, several state and federal agencies planned investigations into the accident. The National Highway Safety Administration announced that it would begin extensive testing of re-treaded tires—a testing which ultimately exonerated their use. Apparently, such tires are still in use today—not only by Greyhound and other major bus-lines but by the trucking industry as well.

In 1968, on March 7, nineteen Greyhound passengers perished when their driver pulled around a car to pass and ran head-on into a car going west in the eastbound lane of Interstate 15, near Baker, California. After the impact, the bus careened through the divider fence, overturned and burst into flames. The car that caused the accident was simply traveling on the wrong side of the freeway.[56]

Possibly the most spectacular crash of the '70s was in East Tennessee on May 13, 1972, when a bus and a tractor-trailer collided, killing fourteen persons. The New York bound bus was said by police to have been traveling north in the southbound lane of the two-lane road. Speculation was that the bus had gone out of control after rounding a curve. Both bus and truck driver were killed. It took an hour and a half working with acetelyne torches and crowbars to free the victims.[57]

One question that came up in the '70s in reference to bus accidents dealt with driver fitness. The Transportation Safety Board, investigating a 1973 wreck near Sacramento, California, learned that just before the bus hit a concrete pillar, the driver clutched his chest in pain. Further, it was determined, the driver was quite obese, and required unusual amounts of sleep. The members of this board began to wonder, therefore, if Greyhound's physical requirements were strict enough, and suggested that a medical screening program for bus drivers, similar to that already in use for airline pilots, be established. Some members wanted to appoint a "certified highway medical examiner" to keep a constant surveillance over bus-driver conditions.[58] To be sure, Greyhound, Trailways and all the other bus companies in the United States, vigorously fought these proposals, saying that their own safety programs were adequate. Nothing came of these particular proposals, but the ICC does require periodic physical examinations for drivers, so involvement on the federal level in terms of driver fitness is practiced, at least to some degree.

Perhaps the most spectacular accident of all times in which Greyhound was involved was on May 9, 1980. A freighter, the *Summit Venture*, rammed into the Sunshine Skyway Bridge over Tampa Bay in Florida. Three cars, a pickup truck and a Greyhound bus skidded over the edge of the bridge at about 7:30 that morning, in a rainstorm that had winds up to 80 miles per hour. Altogether, thirty-two people were killed, twenty-five of them from the Greyhound, as they hurtled 140 feet in space and landed upside down in the restless waters beneath. This was the third time in 1980 that the fifteen-miles-long bridge had been rammed. The pilot of the

Summit Venture, John Lerro, had also been piloting the *Jonna Don* in February, when it struck the bridge. An investigation was planned by all the authorities who converged on the scene.[59] (The pilot was later cleared of any culpability.)[60]

With these accidents, Greyhound's legal department was kept busy, dealing with the claims that were filed, both by private individuals and governmental agencies. Generally, the victims, or their heirs, filed for huge amounts, and then settled for a somewhat lower figure. Jerome Bensinger of Cleveland, for example, demanded $2.25 millions from Greyhound for injuries he sustained in a 1963 accident on the New Jersey Turnpike. He was in a hospital for a full year, and had to walk on crutches afterward. He sued not only the Greyhound Corporation but the bus driver as well, claiming that the latter was negligent in driving the bus through a dense fog, with zero visibility. Bensinger collected $400,000 from Greyhound and $250,000 from the driver, and other drivers involved. This sizeable amount was far less than what Bensinger had originally wanted, and it took him four years to get it.[61]

Greyhound is self-insured against accidents, and in addition, carries excess insurance with numerous carriers.[62] The amounts of money handled through these arrangements sometimes reaches astronomical heights. In the Tampa Bay tragedy, for example, the victims' heirs will possibly sue Greyhound, and Greyhound in turn might sue the Pilot's Association. This is a process that can, and probably will, go on for years on end. The matter is further complicated by the fact that the Skyway Bridge is located in three different Florida counties: Pinellas, Hillsborough and Manatee; and that three bodies of law are concerned: Marine, civil and the regulatory liability of the carrier.

Despite all these horrible things that have happened to Greyhound passengers from time to time, a person is still safer on a bus than in a car.[63] What is frequently said of air-line flights is also applicable to bus runs: "You only hear about the ones that don't make it; never about the thousands that do."

In summary, this chapter has ranged from a discussion of *who* rides Greyhound to what has befallen a few passengers who do. Also under consideration is how Greyhound routing has affected, and responded to, the social and economic conditions of thousands of little towns across America. And finally attention is given to the methods used by Greyhound to get as much of the public's traveling dollar as it possibly can. Altogether in these efforts, Greyhound has been most successful.

"Greyhound Stories"—Mostly Drivers

A driver stopped for a traffic light in Covington, Kentucky. It took so long to change that a passenger in the seat behind the driver said, "Driver, here, I'll take care of that damn light for you!" He pulled a .22 calibre pistol and shot it out.—Greyhound driver.

An old farmer got on a Greyhound one time. He put a gallon jug of liquid in the overhead rack. Out of curiosity the driver asked what the liquid was.

"White gas," the man replied.

The driver screamed,' 'Get that damn gas off this bus, you damn fool!"

The old man took the jug and was gone for a few minutes. He then re-boarded, and the trip got underway.

About twenty miles down the road, the driver asked, "What did you do with that gas?"

"Oh, I checked it in at the baggage room," he responded. The driver had to stop and make an emergency phone call.—George Walker, Louisville, Kentucky.

A driver stopped at 4 A.M. at the Columbia, Tennessee rest-stop. He looked around his coach and saw that everyone was sleeping soundly. He decided, therefore, not to disturb them. He went to the rest-room, smoked a cigarette and drank a cup of coffee. He then got back behind the wheel, and went on to Nashville. When he pulled into the station, he turned on all the lights, and announced "Everyone Off! Nashville." He looked around and there was not a single soul on his bus. He had left them all at Columbia. His stranded passengers were angry, to say the least, and they had all ordered taxi-cabs for the thirty mile trip to Nashville. The driver had to pay the taxi fares—Greyhound story.

"One night after leaving Milwaukee at 4:50 P.M., for my trip to Green Bay, a lady went to the rear of the coach entered the washroom, and locked the door. Just about the time she sat down on the toilet seat, one of the right air-bellows blew out. (Drivers referred to a bellow as a "dough-nut.") There was a loud sound like an explosion, along with a large amount of dust, and the right corner of the coach dropped down, about 18 inches lower than the left side. Almost as this happened, the lady was out of the washroom yelling to me that she did not cause all the confusion. I called back and said

123

it must have been her, because nobody else was in the washroom but her at the time."—Ed McHugh, Green Bay, Wisconsin.

"One evening about 8: P.M., a teen-age girl in a white blouse and blue skirt, walked to the rear of the coach, behind the passengers, and began to change her clothes. I'm watching all this through my inside rear-view mirror. When I arrived in ----, this young girl came up to me and told me she wanted off at Washington and 21st Street.

"I asked the girl if she was a fast change artist. She said, 'no,' but she wanted to know why I asked the question. I said, 'you are now wearing hot pants and a tight fitting white sweater, but when you boarded __ you wore a blouse and a skirt. She said I was wrong, so I said, if she had not changed her clothes on the bus, how would I have known that she was wearing a pair of red panties with the word WEDNESDAY written on them.

"She got red in the face and demanded to be let off the bus immediately. I let her off."—Retired Greyhound Driver.

"There is a cartoon showing an old lady asking the driver of a bus, as they crossed into Colorado, "Isn't there some law about taking a woman across a state line?"—Rearview Mirror, *May 1955, cartoon by Wally Falk.*

Another Wally Falk cartoon for Rearview Mirror *(published by Northland Greyhound Company) showed a public relations man standing in front of the sales manager, holding a sign: "August is Dog Days. Go Greyhound." The sales manager is saying, "Virgil, you're overdoing this slogan thing."*

"The man who invented the nickel in the slots and put them on bus toilets is a stinker."—Anonymous (Thank God).

Girl to a late caller: "Did you know that my father drives a Greyhound? Well, he does, and sometimes he takes it apart to find out why it won't go."
Boy: "So what?"
Girl: "So you had better go."—Greyhound story.

Chapter Seven
The Battle for Roads

It was highly predictable, inevitable even, that the two leading bus corporations in the United States would ultimately have a trade war with each other. Trailways had always run a distant second to Greyhound (it had roughly 22 per cent of the inter-city bus business, to Greyhound's 49 per cent), and it finally embarked on a comparative advertising campaign in which, hopefully, it would take away some of the Hound's business. For its part, Greyhound made it clear from the beginning that it planned to keep the "trail" in its rival's name a verb instead of a noun.

The quarrel started in 1968 when both bus-lines[1] turned to nationwide television for their advertising. Greyhound went after the "switchables," people who might be lured into buses and away from their cars. Also, the company felt that some regular air travelers could be enticed once in a while to take the bus. In planning its budget for 1968, Greyhound emphasized that most of its advertising money would go for spots on national television. The only exception to this "national" rule would be "any case where funds were needed to finance a specific, winnable, face-to-face dog-fight with Trailways."[2]

In the early '70s, with Fred MacMurray representing Greyhound, and another popular actor, Claude Aiken, touting Trailways, the TV networks were flooded with bus commercials. Trailways featured "five-star service" and said that it had "America's only bus with a hostess aboard." This claim was quickly invalidated by Greyhound when it started a "VIP Bus-Plus" from New York to Montreal, via Boston. All such buses had "comely hostesses" aboard, and Greyhound gleefully requested that Trailways advise its public relations agency to adjust its advertising copy.[3] It took some time, however, for Trailways to discontinue its "only bus with a hostess" commercials. In August, 1973, Greyhound found it necessary to speak plainly about the hostess question: "We must presume that this was a misunderstanding in the first place ... and would rather settle it by friendly communications than referring it to regulatory or review bodies."[1] This implicit threat of legal action got the job done: thirteen days later, Greyhound learned that Trailways' "hostess" advertising had ended.

Trailways sought to build some public goodwill for itself in the fall of 1975, when it announced its "opportunity fares." Under this program, it reduced its fares fifty per cent for jobless people who wanted to go to downtown areas to look for employment. Greyhound filed a complaint with the ICC over the matter (saying it was a discriminatory fare), and for its troubles was chided by none other than the prestigious *Wall Street Journal*: "Both in an economic and social sense, the idea [opportunity fares] is full of merit." Greyhound, the paper continued, was a victim of "blind legalism that thrives in the regulatory environment." Instead of "picking" at each other, concluded the editorial, jealous rivals "should be encouraged to innovate and compete in the public interest."[5] The *Journal's* editorial helped to intensify Trailway's wounded pride. Its chairman, Fred Currey, wrote that his company was disappointed by Greyhound's "lack of understanding that these times [mid '70s] demand imaginative solutions from business."[6] The "opportunity fares" were discontinued after a time, but not before they became a definite thorn in the side of Greyhound.

"One-upsmanship" flared again as 1975 drew to a close. Greyhound printed an advertising manual, titled "Project Attack." Its purpose was to capitalize on Greyhound's strength and leadership, and "to attack Trailways where it hurts them the most."[7] Plans were announced to create "city-pairs" in urban areas where Trailways had always been strong. "City-pairs" meant the naming of cities that might exchange tourists; and Greyhound intended to overwhelm those pairs with services, special features, sales promotion and advertising—in short, to deliver a hurtful blow to Trailways. Some of the city pairs were New York-Washington (where Trailways had traditionally had more runs than Greyhound); New York-Philadelphia; Philadelphia-Washington; Philadelphia-Baltimore; Dallas-San Antonio; Houston-San Antonio; Memphis-Nashville; Los Angeles-Las Vegas; Boston-Providence; and Hartford-Washington. These runs became quite important to Greyhound and figured prominently in keeping it ahead of all competition.

The Greyhound-Trailways war climaxed in 1976. Each company printed several brochures, with primarily in-house circulation intended. In this "battle of the pamphlets" charges and counter-charges were hurled with reckless abandon, as officials of both companies proved how petty and inane powerful businessmen can sometimes be.

For example, Trailways claimed that its torsion system was superior to Greyhound's air suspension which, it said, treated passengers like cargo on a semi-truck. A torsion system had been designed for Trailways, it said, in 1954, by Kassbohrer-Fahrzeugwerke in West Germany. (Torsion, however, is a product of the Goodrich Company in the United States.) *But*, said Greyhound, the Germans finally realized the errors of their ways and, in 1967, turned to air suspension. All the luxury buses in Europe—Mercedes-Benz, British Leyland, Van Hooter of Belgium and Volvo of Sweden—used air suspension as standard equipment. Trailways' claim of superiority for torsion systems, therefore, was, said Greyhound, ill-advised.

In one of Trailways' public brochures, *Guide to East-Coast Bus Travel*, it spoke directly to the passenger: "You were probably introduced to inter-city bus travel by a ride on a typical bus. The price was right, but something wasn't. It could have been any number of things. *All the things you will never be subjected to on a Trailways.*[8] When you catch a Trailways, you can be sure that is all you catch." (This suggestion that the Greyhound traveler might contact some loathsome venereal disease in a terminal or on a bus, brought a quick response from the company's legal department. Trailways "cooled it" after this incident, as it found its comparative advertising statements increasingly rejected by television networks, and by large metropolitan newspapers.)

The brochure took a swipe at Greyhound drivers by asserting that the Trailways helmsman was a "gentleman and a scholar," and that he had spent at least eight weeks in intensive training at a Trailways drivers' school, at a cost to the company of $2,500. If a traveler were to "spend a day on a bus *not* driven by a Trailways driver," the pamphlet concluded, you can guess the school he has been to: the school of hard knocks."

On into the bicentennial year, the arguments, petty and otherwise, continued. Trailways said its seats were better than Greyhound's and that they were covered in pure, soft fabric. Greyhound countered that all-fabric covers were a safety hazard, because they burned too easily. (Greyhound said it used "festival quality" fabric.) Trailways' seats reclined 145 degrees, while Greyhound's lagged with a mere 122. This additional recline, said Greyhound, was not necessarily better: it could be a real hazard to the passenger behind that seat. Trailways said—on television yet—

that all their buses had footrests. Greyhound called this statement patently untrue: *most* Trailways buses had footrests, but certainly not *all*. Greyhound claimed that comfort derived from footrests was debatable. In some instances, they could very well hinder a passenger from stretching his legs, making him more tired than he should be. Trailways said its drivers were the better paid. Greyhound asserted that Trailways paid its drivers fifteen to nineteen cents a mile. Trailways averred that through superior maintenance programs, its buses lasted longer than Greyhound's. In rebuttal, Greyhound claimed that a Trailways bus had an average life expectancy of 66,000 miles. (The figures cited here by the Greyhound brochure are, of course, wrong. Buses generally rack up about 100,000 miles *a year*, with the first major overhaul coming between 300,000 and 400,000 miles. Many times when a bus is too old for regular passenger runs, it will be put into charter service.)

Trailways got right to the brink again of a court battle with Greyhound when, in 1976, it came out with another "in-house" publication. This poster showed a large photograph of Fred MacMurry advertising a Greyhound bus, dressed in a clown's suit. The company lawyers felt that the poster was "definitely actionable." While it may have been initially produced for private consumption, the fact that Greyhound people had picked up so many copies of it moved it "into the realm of public exposure." The Greyhounders did not ultimately seek a redress of their grievances in the courts, but they urged Fred MacMurray to do so.[9] He did not, however, possibly because of the unwanted publicity that it would have given to him and to Greyhound, and also possibly because he was so busy with his multi-faceted, far-flung "MacMurray Enterprises," headquartered in Los Angeles.[10] Trailways did not have a "second printing" of the offending poster, and ultimately they all became souvenir items.

Trailways' offensives in 1975 and 1976 allowed Greyhound to become extremely self-righteous. "Our attitude is one of long suffering and circumspection," said one Greyhound official. Greyhound decided in its public advertising not to mention Trailways by name, for that would give it unwarranted publicity. "We are the industry leader," the Greyhounders said, "and we speak from that position."[11] Privately, however, Greyhound planned to counteract and "one-up" whatever Trailways planned to do. "We will not attempt to give the impression that we thought [of market strategy] first. Rather, that we are going about our more important business, and any fares offered to match Trailways are ... a reflection of our ... continuing policy of always being competitive...."[12] Greyhound promised a "more urgent program of harassing Trailways...."[13]

Trailways, however, beat Greyhound to it in terms of harassment. Greyhound proposed, in 1976, to cut its fares similar to what Trailways had already done. This meant reducing fares for the unemployed (very much like Trailways' "opportunity fares"), and beyond that, giving free rides to children under twelve. Trailways complained to the ICC about Greyhound's fare-cutting proposal, saying it was "predatory and noncompensatory." When asked about its own reduced fares, a Trailways spokesman said, "We learned in advance that Greyhound would announce these fares, so being in a competitive stance, we made the announcement first."[14] In Phoenix, Arizona, (to which Greyhound headquarters had been moved), James Kerrigan, chief executive officer for Greyhound, was "shocked and astounded" by Trailways' protestations before the ICC,and he was "at a loss" to explain his rival's action.[15] The ICC rejected Trailways' plea that Greyhound not be allowed to reduce its fares. The ICC pointed out that it must preserve, as much as possible, a competitive situation among businesses in the United States—and that included bus lines.

Toward the end of the trade-war with Trailways, Greyhound concluded that it had not been seriously affected by its rival's inroads. Where Trailways grew the most, so did Greyhound. So it was largely a matter of attracting *bus travelers* per se; and not simply having those travelers make a choice between Greyhound and Trailways. Parenthetically, it was pointed out, big supermarkets are usually more successful when they are near each other than when set out apart. The customer is more after the product than the brand; and this dictum works for travel just as it does for consumer goods. The best thing Greyhound could do, it felt, instead of paying too much attention to Trailways advertising, was to emphasize traveler profiles (lower to middle income groups; younger and older; under twenty-five and over forty-five; and traveling for pleasure), and advertise accordingly. This strategy helped to keep Greyhound the industry leader.[16]

There is nothing like a common foe to cause two belligerents to cease waging war on each other. For Greyhound and Trailways alike, the enemy in the late '70s and early '80s was Amtrak. It is true that in the early history of the inter-city bus industry, trains and buses complemented each other. Amtrak, however, the bus corporations felt, was a direct threat to their very existence, because broad governmental subsidies would make it possible for Amtrak seriously to under-cut bus fares, and operate at a huge loss at the same time.[17]

Even as Congress debated and passed the National Railroad Passenger Bill, Greyhound was gearing up to blunt Amtrak's impact on mass transportation in the United States. At the head of the charge was James Kerrigan who, he said, at first tried to cooperate with Amtrak. "If we worked together," he argued, "we would get people out of the car (84 per cent of all trips in the United States were taken by private auto), and we'd all benefit. Well, Roger Lewis' [the first Amtrak President] answer was to run big full page ads saying, 'it [Amtrak] now costs less than the bus,' and that's what started the argument."[18] (It must be reemphasized that Kerrigan has never opposed Amtrak as such; he is very much in favor of federal funding for it for capital improvements. He is definitely opposed, however, to federal funding of Amtrak fares.)

In June, 1973, Kerrigan remarked that Amtrak subsidies were "unique in that they are intended to preserve a declining mode of transportation which, except in a few areas, is non-essential," and he pointed out that Amtrak attracted barely "enough passengers to fill even one bus."[19] Amtrak retaliated with the assertion that it had to build its own tracks, or pay rent to other railroad companies for use of their facilities—either way an extremely costly proposition. Bus companies, the railroaders maintained, did not pay the total cost of highway construction and use—they shared them with users of automobiles and trucks. This meant, they said, that the actual cost and tax burden on the buses was not nearly so severe as on the train systems; thus, they justified the heavy federal subsidies.[20] Instead of bickering with Amtrak, Lewis believed that both trains and buses ought to go after the traffic in large metropolitan areas, where the preponderance of travel was by automobile.

In meeting the train challenge, Greyhound sponsored an on-board survey of a Los Angeles-San Diego Amtrak run in December, 1976. There were more men than women on the federally sponsored train, and the passengers were relatively high in income, compared to the ordinary bus traveler. The percentage on the train who traveled for pleasure and personal reasons was about the same as for buses, as was the number of business travelers. There was, however, a low incidence of ethnic riders on the train, as compared with buses. The best, actually, that the survey could do was conclude that "many people ride Amtrak just for the novelty of riding a train,"[21] an inconclusive judgment, to say the least.

It was true, indeed, that Greyhound chief, James Kerrigan, and Amtrak first president, Roger Lewis, had serious differences with each other—primarily over the matter of federal subsidies for fares. With the second Amtrak president, Paul Reistrup, however, the doughty Kerrigan was in a veritable state of war. For example, for 1977, Amtrak routinely and calmly forecast huge losses, which had to be made up for by the American taxpayer. This caused Kerrigan to comment that "Amtrak re-enacts the great American train robbery every day of its operations." When Amtrak announced plans to let children under twelve ride free on trains originating in various cities,.[22] it was just simply too much for Kerrigan and the other bus operators.

In April, 1977, Reistrup visited Kerrigan in Phoenix. Several hours after Reistrup left, Kerrigan discovered a letter on his coffee-table, in which Reistrup complained at length about Kerrigan's campaign against Amtrak. This caused Kerrigan to write a stormy letter to Reistrup, in which he explained his and other bus people's positions vis-a-vis Amtrak. Because of its importance to recent social and transportation history, Kerrigan's letter deserves some detailed attention.

Amtrak, Kerrigan began, had initially asked the government for $40 million in "seed" money. That sum had now swollen to $2 billion, and government auditors believed the Amtrak budget by 1982 would exceed $4 billions.[23] Amtrak had kept passenger rail service alive since 1971, Kerrigan claimed, "only by systematically gouging the American taxpayer."

Apparently Reistrup had reported that 1976 was a year of "historic proportions" for Amtrak, and that he was "pleased" with its operation. The statement angered Kerrigan:

> Let me understand you, Mr. Reistrup. You have no qualms about applying the word "pleased" to describe record losses of $469 millions. Ridership has risen only 1.8 percent, despite the new equipment, and amenities like subsidized meals. This has resulted in a deficit skyrocketing by 218 percent. Every new passenger you added in 1976 cost the taxpayer seventy-three dollars a head. In short, you have told the American people that things were great for Amtrak in 1976, and they're getting rosier and rosier, when in fact Amtrak is deteriorating, and by your own admission is going to get worse. The only things of "historic proportions" in 1976 for Amtrak were your losses and your hyperbole ... and the incredible naivete of the people who let you get away with those statements .... Your incredible pronouncements that Amtrak is alive and well, and living in

affluent profitability, is proof positive that if the lie is staggering enough, and its propaganda epic enough, the sheer enormity of the deception will carry it along.[24]

The American taxpayer, said the bus-line executive, paid an average of 60 per cent, or $28.20 per Amtrak rider. On the Vancouver-Seattle run, for every dollar of Amtrak revenue, it spent $11.71. From San Francisco to Bakersfield, each Amtrak dollar caused an expenditure of $10.14, or seventy-three cents per passenger to the taxpayer. On the Chicago-Miami route, the cost per passenger to the taxpayer was $122.00 Kerrigan scoffed to Reistrup:

> If you enjoy irony, dwell on this: you could have bought a 'night-air coach' ticket, $99.00 for everyone of your passengers on that route [Chicago-Miami], and flown them to Florida for a taxpayers' savings of $23.00 a ticket.[25]

Reistrup had apparently accused Kerrigan of opposing Amtrak only because it was a competing transportation system to his own. Kerrigan responded that Greyhound did not compete with Amtrak:

> I can't. Because I have to set bus fares at a level to cover the cost of the service. Unlike you, I cannot arbitrarily set prices at a loss and then bundle [them] up ... and ... hand them to the American taxpayer to ante up the shortfalls.[26]

In an interview, Reistrup was quoted by Kerrigan as saying: "I've been trained as a warrior. I know how to fight." Kerrigan urged him to fight for the American taxpayer, who was weary of "spending his hard earned money in support of strangers on a train." If the bus companies and Amtrak worked together, Kerrigan told Reistrup, "you and I and an army of alienated taxpayers can put Amtrak on a firm fiscal footing."[27]

Conditions with Amtrak, however, did not improve—at least immediately. ("Improvement" in Amtrak's financial history has almost always meant the discontinuance of certain routes.) It developed a program by which a child under twelve could ride free *if* he were accompanied by an adult, and *if* he brought with him three boxtops from a Kellogg cereal package.[28] Also, passengers were told that if they paid a full fare (minus the government subsidy) from various big cities in the east to Montreal, Amtrak would bring them back for only $5.00. To be sure, these tactics further infuriated the bus industry—especially Greyhound, with Kerrigan in charge. In

May, 1977, Kerrigan really laid down the gauntlet, and sought television and radio outlets to air his displeasures with Amtrak. He was "willing to travel anywhere in the country" to discuss the matter. He made himself available, also, for person-to-person interviews, panel-type question and answer sessions, and was keenly interested in a "face to face" debate with Reistrup.[29] Most of these ambitions were not fulfilled, because Kerrigan left Greyhound shortly after these challenges, and became pre-occupied with purchasing and re-organizing the Trailways system.

Toward the end of 1977, Greyhound was in a deteriorating condition, brought on in some measure by Amtrak. Other factors contributing to this unfavorable state were the dual effects of inflation and recession, low airline fares and Trailways competition. A Greyhound executive wrote to the regional vice-presidents in September, 1977: "Today our company is at a crossroads. If costs continue to spiral upward as during the past three years, the company will be unable to continue in business as in the past." He went on to say that bus fares were at an all-time high, and that the public "is unwilling to pay" higher prices. He closed his plaintive remarks by asserting that "Amtrak continues to take our passengers."[30] In 1978 and '79, however, things began to improve for Greyhound, as Amtrak shrank, as economic conditions improved, and as the energy crisis drove people away from their autos and into buses.[31]

Beyond its confrontations with Trailways and Amtrak, in its battle for roads, Greyhound advertising became extremely active throughout the 1970s. One part of this thrust was to come up with clever little jingles that would cause people to remember Greyhound the next time they wanted to travel. One was, "How to make Money with a 747? Only Greyhound does it." This phrase was turned down by Greyhound leaders because it was needlessly antagonistic toward the air-lines. Another suggestion was: "A refreshing exception—A Carrier that Makes Money. We charge less than others, but we earn more: No Subsidies." This slap at Amtrak was also rejected by the leadership, on the grounds that it was too self-serving. One phrase, however, that was acceptable was: "Making America Available to all Americans."

Naturally Greyhound wanted to know how its jingles, phrases, etc., compared in public awareness with the catch-words of other organizations. How, for example, did "It's such a comfort to take the bus and leave the driving to us" stack up against "for people who can't brush their teeth after every meal," (Gleem Toothpaste); and

"A brighter future through Electronics," (Sylvania)? Without any prompting, the public recalled Greyhound's phrase 9 per cent; Gleem, 9 per cent; and Sylvania, 1.1 per cent. Most of the public, however, with or without prompting, did not know any of these phrases: 67 per cent were unfamiliar with Greyhound's; 72 per cent with Gleem's; and 98 per cent with Sylvania. What these statistics proved, primarily, is Greyhound's penchant for surveying; perhaps they only meant that people who ride Greyhound brush their teeth with Gleem, and buy their television sets from a source other than Sylvania.

Another clever Greyhound phrase, used mostly in the '60s was "Go Greyhound and Leave the Driving to Us."[32] Greyhound used "We've Got More Going for You," and then discovered that Allegheny Airlines used the same phrase. Its use by both companies was merely coincidental; neither could claim it exclusively.

Not so, however, with "Say Hello to a Good Buy," sung for the bus-line by Pearl Bailey. Greyhound got into numerous difficulties with this phrase. It had been used as far back as July, 1957, by the El Producto Cigar Company. It advertised two of its cigars for twenty-five cents, and adjured its prospective customers to "Say Hello to a Good Buy."[33]

In the Winter of 1975, a children's buying service in New York, operated by Ilene Silver, used "Say Hello to Good Buys." Her clothing service and the transportation classification of Greyhound made the two enterprises diverse enough from each other to prevent serious problems. Different categories of trade, however, made no difference to Victor Ugolyn of Westport, Connecticut. He represented his state's Kentucky Fried Chicken outlets. He wrote to the editor of Chicago's *Advertising Age*: "We have been airing on television 'Say Hello to a Good Buy'; featured with instore counter cards, and window banners. What Greyhound copy writer lives in Westport?"[34] Another company, Midland Pipe and Supply Company of Cicero, Illinois, had also used the phrase for several years.

One company—Identity, Incorporated—began using the phrase about the same time (1976) as Greyhound, and the two ultimately had confrontations with each other over the matter. Identity was a market subsidiary of Miller Advertising, operating out of Ft. Wayne, Indiana, with offices in Indianapolis. The company appeared to have granted "naked licenses" to numerous of its subsidiaries (primarily automobile dealers) in Florida and the mid-west. This practice, Greyhound believed, was inconsistent with rights usually granted through the trademark laws. Ultimately the two companies solved their differences with an out-of-court settlement. The incident with Identity, Inc., encouraged Greyhound to drop the phrase altogether. It was too much of a hassle to compete with all the other businesses who also wanted to use it.

When the Scenicruiser came out in the '50s, Greyhound advertised it by saying, "we've got more going for you." The York Transportation Company of New York had long used the phrase, "We Go For You." At best there would be confusion between the two marks, and possible intrusions that could lead to litigation. Greyhound took the advice of a legal firm, therefore, and discontinued its use of the phrase.

The most recent difficulty with Greyhound phrasing was "I'll Take You There." A singer named Pop Staples composed the jingle, and apparenty Greyhound paid him $10,000 for it. A contract was signed to that effect by Staples and Greyhound vice-president Joe Black. But then, the East Memphis Music Corporation (and its successor, Cream Records of California), sued Greyhound for copyright infringement. It was in the courts in the early '80s without any judgments being given.

The trouble Greyhound (and presumably other companies as well) faced with phrases was that generally they could not be copyrighted. The copyright office in Washington was quite reluctant to "open the doors" to a flood of advertising jingles. This led the bus company to change its format from "musical slogans" to "Greyhound songs," and alleviated at least some of the copyright problems.[35] This did not, however, ease the difficulties with other companies that wanted to use the same phrases. The phrase problem continues to this day (1980s).

Greyhound also set about registering the names of several of its buses and services. These included "Americruiser," "Leave the Driving to Us," "Bus Fuss," "Logo," "Challenger," "Discover America," "Electrocruiser," "Panorama," "Get in Touch with America," "Next Bus Out," "Slumber Stop," "Super Seven" and "Super Cruiser."

With one of their registered trademarks, "Ameripass," Greyhound got into some difficulty, particularly in California. In the summer of 1976, it advertised a fifteen day Ameripass at "one half the regular price." According to California Attorney General, Evelle J. Younger, Greyhound also reduced the allowable travel time by one half, without making this point absolutely clear to the state's consumers. (Apparently the Ameripass in question was valid for a stated, specific period of fifteen days, during which the customer could arrange seven and a half days' travel—quite like the "budget fares" advertised by air lines.) It was no savings, said the Attorney General; in fact, it was downright deception. He wanted Greyhound to be fined $2,500 for each "Ameripass" offense, and to pay $10,000 for court costs. As it turned out, the Court required Greyhound to print written explanations of its Ameripass advertising in numerous state newspapers, to pay a civil penalty of $40,000, and $5,000 in court costs.[36]

Another advertising problem occurred when Greyhound wanted to use jazz artist Count Basie. Its intention was to tell the public that the Count lived only two months a year at his home in the Bahamas. The rest of the year, he "lived" in a Greyhound bus, while touring the country with his musical group. When the ad was comtemplated, it was stated by Greyhound that it would run only in *Fortune, Barron's* and *Forbes*. Ultimately, however, Count Basie's likeness in a Greyhound showed up not only in these magazines but in numerous others as well. This brought a quick, heated protest from the musician's agency, and the ad was discontinued.[37] The incident indicated, perhaps, that Greyhound was no different from most other businesses; it would do whatever it thought it could get away with in order to put its advertising message before the American public.

Still another matter with which Greyhound advertisers had to deal was when an over-zealous agent in Iowa began to give green stamps with ticket purchases. This practice was not only against bus-line rules but also offensive to ICC regulations. Iowa Greyhounders, therefore, had to forego the enticement of the trading stamps.[38]

To be sure, the greatest advertising medium of all is television, and Greyhound used it "to the hilt" in trying to show the viewer that a trip on a bus was not only economical; it was a "romantic adventure" as well.[39] The person at Greyhound who became increasingly involved with TV advertising was Dorothy Lorant (in, 1981, the Corporation's vice-president for Public Relations and Advertising). It was she, as much as any other person, who developed the advertising rules by which Greyhound currently operates.[40]

The destination panels on all advertised buses was "America." The bus always had to be shown with either a full or three-quarter side view (particularly in magazines). On television, it had to be driven fast enough to be realistic, but slow enough for safety. Inside, everything should be depicted as cheery and comfortable, and the "comfort station" should be visible and clearly marked as "restroom," (though on real-life buses, it reads "lavatory," or, in more recent times, "washroom").[11]

The drivers on television buses may be actors, but they must be evenly exposed in terms of their minority statuses. Thus an appropriate number of women drivers, and also black drivers of both sexes, have to be shown.[12] Though drivers are actors, apparently the passengers are not. The college girl going back to school in much of Greyhound's TV advertising, and in other media as well, was required by the Fair Trade Commission to be an actual person.

The TV ads were made as local as possible. Round trip fares were not to be mentioned, unless the one-way fare was also noted. When the trip took less than an hour and a half, its duration was to be stated in minutes; otherwise in hours. As a corollary to its TV advertising, Greyhound began to accept credit cards— Mastercharge and Bankamericard—in 1976, in response to passenger mile decline, to the poor economy, and to rates of unemployment. Through credit cards, it hoped to recapture some of the business that might otherwise have been lost.

In its sponsorship of television programs, Greyhound evolved some rather definite prescreening guidelines. It wanted to be informed by the TV networks if one of its forthcoming sponsored programs depicted bus travel in a bad light. This could include an accident, a grubby looking bus or terminal, and discourteous personnel. Any dialogue or music lyrics derogatory to bus travel were likewise proscribed, as were any and all ideas that public travel might be dangerous. Greyhound did not wish to sponsor any programs or movies about trains or airplanes (though it did not object to brief sequences of "normal" travel on these two carriers.) Completely forbidden were any favorable showings of Trailways (presumably *unfavorable* depictions were acceptable).[13] The idea of yanking Greyhound commercials from programs to which it objected, was "officially" turned down by the TV networks. Privately, however, they were "pretty cooperative" when Greyhound made the request.[14] (Importantly, pulled commercials did not result in any financial penalties against the networks or cooperating stations. The commercials were simply run at another time.)

If any sponsored news program covered a bus accident, Greyhound's commercials were to be pre-empted for forty-eight hours. This pre-emption policy showed an increasing concern by Greyhound to judge the subject matter of the programs it sponsored: it did not wish to affiliate with anything that was "far-out," controversial, vulgar, anti-social or anti-American. It pointed out that "TV programming and print editorial content is solely the responsibility of the broadcasters and editors." While this was as it should be, by the same token, Greyhound adopted the reasonable stance that "we have the right and duty to choose where we place our ads and commercials in the best interest of the company."[45]

In mid-1977, public concern about TV violence reached an all-time high, as many psychologists and sociologists began to claim a correlation between television programs and real-life situations. Accordingly, Greyhound developed a stringent policy of not advertising with "excessively violent" or socially obnoxious programs.[46] It wanted the networks to rate their programs in much the same manner as the motion picture industry had already done. A rating of "G" would mean "general performance," appropriate for viewing by people of all ages: "GP" would mean "parental guidance"; "R" meant "restricted," while "X" would be an indication that the program so designated was not suitable for young people. The networks rejected the rating system, on the grounds that home television sets are not tantamount to the local movie house. They did, however, adopt a policy of saying, before certain programs were aired, that "parental discretion is advised."

In accordance with its advertising policy, Greyhound was relieved from giving commercials on an ABC Monday Night Movie, "Lola-Madonna XXX." Its scheduled message was transfered to a movie on NBC, "Harry in Your Pocket," starring Trish Van Devere and Walter Pidgeon. Greyhound withdrew its commercial support of the June 21, 1975, episode of "All in the Family," where the subject was rape. Also, it transferred to another program all the commercials it had scheduled of David Frost's interview of former President Richard Nixon.

In August, 1977, Greyhound scotched the idea that it sponsor a new TV show, "Hee Haw Honeys," (a spin-off from the very popular country show, "Hee Haw," starring Roy Clark and Buck Owens). Apparently the producers of the new show wanted to feature a Greyhound bus in several of its skits. Greyhound responded that "anyone on a bus identified as a Greyhound must have a regular driver," (though it was well known that the "drivers" in Greyhound commercials were actors). The incidents on "Hee Haw Honeys," said the bus officials, "while very funny, would not be acceptable as things which could happen aboard a Greyhound because of speed, safety, and other similar aspects."[47] Possibly another reason for the Greyhound rejection of "Hee Haw Honeys" was that for several years it had considered Country and Western music as a "subgroup" in the entertainment business. (Even so, it had sponsored numerous country music shows, particularly the ones starring Red Foley. In 1980, statistics indicated that Country and Western was by far the most popular music in the United States. Possibly a reason for the rejection was that there would be too much emphasis on the "Honeys" part of the personnel, and the dress of the very beautiful women on the "Hee Haw" show was inclined to be low-cut and very "risque.")[48]

In addition to relieving itself from unwanted television segments, Greyhound also prepared a list of popular programs, with an indication of its responses, for advertising purposes, to them. There were three categories: "acceptable," "iffy" and "clearly not acceptable."

The "acceptable" included (presumably because of their "wholesomeness"): "The Hardy Boys," "Nancy Drew," "Sixty Minutes," "Wonderful World of Disney," "Eight is Enough," "The Jeffersons," "Little House on the Prairie," "Who's Who," "The Jacksons," "Grizzly Adams," "The Waltons," "Donny and Marie," "Sonny and Cher," "Fish," "Mary Tyler Moore," "Bob Newhart," "Carol Burnett," "Monday Night Baseball," "Welcome Back, Kotter," "Tony Randall" and "Emergency Code R."

The "iffy" programs, ones that could occasionally have objectionable materials from Greyhound's viewpoint were: "Six Million Dollar Man," "M*A*S*H," "Good Times," "The Movies," "Rhoda," "Phyllis," "Maude," "Sunday Night Movie," "One Day at a Time," "All's Fair," "Charlie's Angels," "Tales of the Unexpected," "All in the Family," "Alice," "Quincy," "Rich Man; Poor Man," "West Side Medical," "Barnaby Jones," "Hunter" and "The Rockford Files."

Clearly unacceptable, because of their violence and sometime sexual explicitness were "Kojak" (which happens to be the favorite program of Britain's Queen Elizabeth); "Police Woman," "Police Story," "Baretta," "Hawaii Five-O," "Streets of San Francisco," "Starsky and Hutch" and "Most Wanted."

All things considered, Greyhound's advertising programs reflected the company's concerns about the state of American society. Perhaps it became a bit prudish from time to time in its efforts to judge what it would and would not sponsor. On the whole, however, it recognized that it had a responsibility not only to itself, but to the community as well, and it acted upon that belief.

In its battle for roads, Greyhound ranged all the way from fights with Trailways and Amtrak to widespread, but selective, sponsorship of television programs. These efforts, plus other factors such as fuel shortages, inflation and traffic jams, put more and more people into buses. And Greyhound appeared to be winning the battle of the roads as the '70s closed; ridership was an all-time high, and it was considerably ahead of all competition: a happy situation, to say the least!

"Greyhound Stories"—A Few Legal Matters

Chief Justice Warren Burger, he thought our case was just,
But statutory tolling was sent to bite the dust.
Remanded to the Circuit, we sit around and rust,
And hope the story's ending before we all go bust.

Judge Goodwin has the case now, our spirits still are high.
We think that gold will follow from his ruling by and by.
We've briefed our final theory, we hope that it will fly.
We want to win the issue and beat the other guy.

The Hound can still appeal it, this story has no end.
When will the Circuit Judges their last decision rend?
And will our Crew and Khourie once more to D.C. wend?
They're waiting for the ending—
"From Klamath Falls to Bend"
—From "The Saga of Mt. Hood Stages" (sung to the tune of "Ghost Riders in the Sky"), composed by someone at Broad,Khourie & Schulz, while awaiting the Greyhound decision.

"I had a good safety record at Greyhound, but that didn't mean I didn't have a fender bender once in a while. I didn't report it. Maybe I adjusted it myself."—Retired Greyhound driver.

"It ain't what you do around Greyhound that'll get you in trouble; it's what you get caught at."—Retired Greyhound driver.

"I found out early in the Greyhound game that if you didn't lie to the supervisors, you could get by with a lot of things."—Retired Greyhound driver.

Chapter Eight
Davids and Goliaths

Corporations that grow to mammoth sizes and have multiple relationships with both the public and private sectors can expect to be caught up in controversies on quite frequent occasions. Many times these differences lead the contenders straight to the courtroom. Greyhound was definitely no exception to this pattern, as it faced litigation over the years with numerous adversaries.[1]

In July, 1956, for example, Greyhound and its old friend, General Motors, were at odds with each other. In September of the previous year, Greyhound bought 1,000 Scenicruisers from GMC at a cost of $53 millions. Greyhound President Genet claimed, without being specific, that 570 of them suffered from mechanical defects. When General Motors showed a marked reluctance to alleviate the problems, Genet threatened court action. (Greyhound was GMC's second best customer; in first place was the federal government.) He reported that Greyhound had spent at least a million dollars correcting the deficiencies, and that apparently the only redress from GMC was through the courts.[2]

Ironically, just two weeks before this Greyhound action against GMC, the federal government, through Attorney General Herbert Brownell, had filed an anti-trust suit against both corporations. The government held that GMC conspired with Greyhound,[3] by which it refused to sell buses to competing companies. Since GMC produced 65 per cent of the new buses in the United States, the refusal to supply Greyhound competitors could indeed be serious.

Perhaps it was the government's actions against both companies that caused Greyhound to drop its mechanical defects suit against General Motors. Genet announced that "a completely amicable understanding has been reached between the Greyhound Corporation ... and GMC ...."[4] He went on to assert that "bugs can develop on the road which the best engineers cannot foresee during the experimental phase."[5] GMC had no comment.

In the summer of 1957, the government and Greyhound

negotiated a "consent decree," by which the bus company was required to spread out its purchases, and to publicize all of its patents relating to bus design and manufacturing.[6] Greyhound issued a "full categorical denial" of the government's monopoly charges, but it decided not to fight the case, a decision encouraged by Greyhound's plans to erect its own bus building facilities.[7] A few months later, the government, GMC's best customer, adjourned indefinitely its anti-trust suit against the giant automotive conglomerate.[8]

The next year, in May, Greyhound stood before the Supreme Court of the United States on a matter that had begun in California. In San Francisco's bay area, Greyhound had wanted to increase fares. The state's Public Utilities Commission (PUC), however, disallowed the request, arguing that Greyhound should offset its Bay area losses by profits made elsewhere in California.

To offset the PUC's decision, Greyhound turned all of its Bay area activities over to a subsidiary, Golden Gate Transit Lines, which had its own rate-fixing terms. By this "merger" Greyhound could get through its subsidiary the rate increases that had been denied it as a corporation. The ICC, ignoring the state agency's earlier rulings, permitted the "merger" to take place.

The PUC of California was, understandably, upset at this example of federal bureaucratic dogmatism in league with corporate arrogance, and accordingly sought relief in the federal courts. Finally the case worked its way to Washington, and by a 5-4 vote, the Supreme Court reversed the ICC approval of the Greyhound transfer. Speaking for the Court, Mr. Justice Clark stated that the operative law for the ICC gave the agency powers to approve "genuine mergers," not to create "mere corporate shells." Greyhound's transfer of its Bay area activities to the Golden Gate Transit Lines was "little more than a paper transaction," said Clark, and must therefore be negated.[9]

Other major court actions involving Greyhound during the '60s and '70s included suits that caused it to comply with directives from the National Labor Relations Board in reference to personnel hired at bus terminals,[10] and with hiring bearded people, such as Abdullah Ibrahim, an orthodox Muslim who lived in Brooklyn.[11] Also, Greyhound won a case before the Supreme Court allowing it to prohibit anyone over 35 from applying for a driver's job. The High Court agreed with the lower tribunals that a legitimate safety reason existed for the age restriction.[12] And, finally, Greyhound had to pay $150,000 in damages to a South Carolina woman who was sexually assaulted in a Raleigh, North Carolina terminal. It was determined by the Court that the man who assailed the woman in the terminal's rest-room was later convicted on another charge, and given a sentence of life imprisonment. Greyhound, the Court believed, had provided inadequate security at its Raleigh terminal, and thus had encouraged the assault.[13]

By far the most protracted (and ultimately costliest) court case Greyhound ever had involved a small bus-line headquartered in Bend, Oregon, named Mt. Hood Stages. It was solely owned by William A. Niskanen, who incorporated it in 1931. In 1943, Niskanen's line became a member of the National Trailways Bus System. As early as 1952 Niskanen feared that conditions had developed which made competition with Greyhound, locally or nationally, almost impossible. He believed that Greyhound's monopolistic pattern started when the ICC received the power to regulate the inter-city bus industry.[14] The federal agency, he believed, had not paid sufficient attention to the *overall* effects of allowing Greyhound to pursue what was apparently an unrestricted program of acquisition.

Between February, 1947 and July, 1956, Greyhound systematically acquired numerous bus-lines in the Northwest that ultimately had the effect of encircling the routes used by Mt. Hood. The Greyhound acquisitions and their pertinent routes were: OC&N Stages, operating between Klamath Falls, Oregon and Reno, Nevada; Inland Stages, between Reno and Los Angeles and San Diego; Washington Motor Coach, Portland and points north; North Coast Transportation Company, Portland and the Canadian border; Overland Greyhound, Los Angeles and points north and east; Oregon Motor Stages, Portland and points west; B.C. Motor Transportation, Seattle and the Canadian border; and Pacific Greyhound, Los Angeles and points north and south. The ICC approved all these additions to the Greyhound system.

Mt. Hood, which operated principally on a north-south route between Klamath Falls and the Dalles, and west-east into Idaho, Nevada and Utah, opposed the four Greyhound acquisitions, for fear of encirclement. Greyhound authorities, however, made numerous promises to allay such fears: to interchange traffic and honor Mt. Hood tickets, to quote direct routes (instead of just Greyhound), and publicize non-Greyhound fares and services. Above all, said Greyhound, it had never been its policy to send passengers over circuitous routes; it had no intention of starting now.

Thus assured, Mt. Hood withdrew its objections, and the mergers went ahead. On the sixth acquisition (Oregon Motor Stages), however, Mt. Hood protested again, and told the ICC that Greyhound had now begun a trade war with the tiny bus-line—primarily because, it believed, Greyhound wanted to buy it out, and Mt. Hood did not want to sell. Greyhound was cast into an image of an old-time western "range boss," who wanted to buy up all the property next to him, and who treated recalcitrant sellers very harshly. And Niskanen was, most assuredly, a "recalcitrant seller." He told a friend that he was willing to "throw everything" he had into his fight with Greyhound. "We did not build up this line without fighting," he exclaimed, and "we are not going to give it up without putting up the best fight possible.[15]

Despite Mt. Hood's protests, the ICC approved the sixth acquisition. Mt. Hood negotiated unsuccessfully for the seventh acquisition (B.C. Motor Transportation), and this caused further ill feelings toward Greyhound.[16] By the early '60s, Greyhound had captured 90 per cent of the bus business in the Pacific Northwest, and Mt. Hood claimed a 70 per cent loss on some of its routes because of Greyhound encirclement. For example, Greyhound routed passengers from Eugene, Oregon to Boise, Idaho through Portland over its own route instead of sending them on the money and time saving direct Mt. Hood route.

Despite Greyhound-Mt. Hood differences, the two bus companies had operated, since May 1, 1940, a joint through route between Klamath Falls and the Dalles (Biggs), Oregon. Mt. Hood thus became a "bridge" for the Greyhound run between San Francisco and Spokane. Mt. Hood leased the Greyhound buses for the Klamath Falls-Dalles segment of the trip, making it unnecessary for passengers to transfer to another vehicle. This convenient arrangement went on for several years, to the benefit of both passengers and bus companies.

But then, from May 15 to July 4, 1964, Mt. Hood was hit by a drivers' strike, and the joint through route was necessarily discontinued. When the labor problems ended, Greyhound was disinclined to resume the previous arrangements, giving a sixty day notice of permanent discontinuance. Greyhound argued that the Interstate Highways had mostly been completed between San Francisco-Portland-Spokane. Thus, it was safer to carry passengers on this all-Greyhound route than to subject them to the perils of the two-lane road used by the previous joint operations. Also, said Greyhound, Mt. Hood had never put a regular run on the Klamath

Falls-Dalles route; it had always worked on that run solely in conjunction with Greyhound, whose managers concluded that there were not many profits on a "bridge" operation—thus, it should be discontinued. Even so, said Greyhound, it continued to send more passengers to Mt. Hood than Mt. Hood sent to Greyhound.

The new Greyhound routes with the strong emphasis on Portland added much travel time to a passenger's San Francisco-Spokane schedule. The route, for one thing, was 110 miles longer than by the Klamath Falls-Dalles "bridge," and Greyhound apparently intended to make sure that passengers would not arrive sooner by riding Mt. Hood buses at any stage of the San Francisco-Spokane run. As the ICC explained, by using the new Greyhound schedules, "a passenger could leave the through bus at Biggs (the Dalles), board a MH (Mt. Hood) schedule, have dinner in Bend, arrive in Klamath Falls, wait there almost 3 hours, take a Greyhound schedule to Redding, and there reboard the same bus he left at Biggs."[17]

The all-Greyhound east-west route, via Portland, was also considerably longer than direct runs by Mt. Hood. One route, for instance,[18] was 113 miles longer, and another—through central Oregon—116 miles. Moreover, the shorter, time-saving (up to four hours), Mt. Hood routes ran through some of the most scenic areas of the Pacific Northwest, while the all-Greyhound route traveled the dull and uninteresting Interstates. The ICC very definitely did take into account all these esthetic qualities offered by Mt. Hood as it strove to settle the differences between the two bus-lines.

Mt. Hood took action on October 7, 1964, when it asked the ICC to review Greyhound's acquisitions in the Northwest to see if the bus-line had lived up to all the promises it made against circuitous routing and unfair competition. Then, on May 27, 1965, Mt. Hood filed a petition with the ICC, which sought to restore the Klamath Falls-Biggs "bridge" of the San Francisco-Spokane run. It also asked that Greyhound be forced to stop its destructive competition against the smaller carrier.[19] Hearings were held in San Francisco on November 8-10, 1965; and January 10-11, 1966. Both sides had ample opportunities to air their grievances before the federal agency.

As expected, Mt. Hood lawyers hammered away at the encirclement-destructive competition questions, while the Greyhound attorneys defended their company's actions. They argued that the swings through Portland actually benefited the majority of travelers in the Pacific Northwest by eliminating long stop-overs, or even overnight stays at several places along the way. True, the Klamath Falls-Biggs passengers might be inconvenienced, but Greyhound believed it should adopt the utilitarian principle of "the greatest good for the greatest number." Greyhound, said its legal representatives, was continuing the policies of interchange, as evidenced by swapping passengers with numerous other bus-lines, all for the safety, comfort and convenience of the passenger. It was just that Mt. Hood's routes were not profitable or convenient to Greyhound—primarily because of the speed of the Interstates—and that is why the giant carrier snubbed the little line. Besides, asserted Greyhound, Mt. Hood was a "disappointed purchaser," losing out to Greyhound on a number of key buys. Even so, Greyhound said, its treatment of Mt. Hood had nothing to do with "malice aforethought."

Beyond the belief that Mt. Hood's wrongfulness in bringing the petition against it, Greyhound challenged the authority of the ICC to deal with the matter. The agency, said Greyhound, had fully approved the certificates of "convenience and necessity," which had made it possible for the bus-line to carry out the operations of which Mt. Hood now complained. Once the ICC issued an operable, valid certificate, with proof that it was not based on fraud, Greyhound claimed the Commission then did not have a right to change or terminate it. Only the carrier—in this case Greyhound—or a court of law could do that.[20] Thus, if Mt. Hood had a problem, it was taking it to the wrong place; it was a court instead of ICC that Mt. Hood should contact. Moreover, the certificates were issued thirteen to eighteen years before, and there had been at the time "no express reservations of power to issue supplemental orders."[21] Therefore, even if the ICC did have jurisdiction over the present matter, all statutes of limitation had expired, leaving Mt. Hood with no case.

The Interstate Commerce Commission disagreed both procedurally and substantively with Greyhound's contentions. On April 5, 1968, it issued these orders to Greyhound:

> *It must restore the San Francisco-Spokane through bus service with Mt. Hood via Klamath Falls and Biggs.
> *It must revise its schedules so that interchange of passengers would not have unreasonably long lay-overs at intermediate points.
> *Greyhound agents were required voluntarily to quote joint through routes and fares. (Several Mt. Hood people telephoned or visited fifty-five Greyhound agencies between December, 1955, and October, 1965, making over 100 inquiries into

schedules and fares. Never did the Greyhound agents volunteer
information about shorter and cheaper Mt. Hood routes. In some
instances, said the Mt. Hood group, its fares were inaccurately
quoted by Greyhound agents.)

This was an ICC ruling with which Greyhound simply did not
want to live. First, in April, 1969, it petitioned the ICC for a
reconsideration. ICC refused, and this caused Greyhound to head
for the federal courts. The case was tied up for several months while
the U.S. District Court in Chicago deliberated on it. Then, on
February 5, 1970, it rendered a decision. If the ICC ruling had
disheartened Greyhound, the court's devastated it. Not only did
Judge Edwin A. Robson uphold the previous ICC judgments
regarding the joint through route, schedules and fares; he also
added the following orders:

*Greyhound must show Mt. Hood schedules in Greyhound
folders equally with other non-Greyhound lines.
*Greyhound must eliminate the three-hour lay-over at
Klamath Falls and Biggs for passengers wanting to travel
between these two points via Mt. Hood.
*Greyhound must negotiate in good faith with Mt. Hood to
establish bus schedules most advantageous to the traveling
public.
*Greyhound must show Mt. Hood's connecting routes on its
maps or on equal basis with other non-Greyhound carriers.
*Greyhound must "cease and desist" from discriminating
against Mt. Hood at depots that Mt. Hood occupied with
Greyhound.
*Greyhound must stop trying to influence commission
agents selling both Greyhound and Mt. Hood tickets to favor the
former, to the disadvantage of the latter.[22]

Strong orders, these; and most companies and individuals
would have rushed to comply with them. Not so Greyhound,
however, whose leaders apparently thought they were clever or
influential enough not to have to obey the law. During the next
several months after the court order, the ICC conducted
"compliance" tests and found that Greyhound's quoting errors in
reference to Mt. Hood ranged from 51 to 58 per cent. Mt. Hood's
surveys reported a 75 per cent non-compliance rate, while
Greyhound's, as might be expected, dropped to 22 per cent.

Two months after the court order, Greyhound re-instituted the
joint through route with Mt. Hood. It was not so compliant, however,
with a number of other directives. For eighteen months, Greyhound

did not show Mt. Hood's connecting routes on an equal basis with other non-Greyhound carriers. And when it finally did, it distorted the geographical location of Bend, Oregon, where Mt. Hood was headquartered, giving the impressions to agents and travelers alike that all-Greyhound travel "would in all cases be faster or shorter than a connecting route...."[23] For twenty months, Greyhound failed to show accurate wall maps of Mt. Hood routes; nor did it depict Mt. Hood's routes on Centerfold maps contained in various tour packages.[24] It took nineteen months after the judicial action for Greyhound management even to make a systematic effort to inform all its lower echelon employees that it was under court orders in respect to Mt. Hood. The giant bus corporation was, as various judges concluded, "playing fast and loose" with Mt. Hood, the ICC and the courts.

In June, 1973, an angry Judge Robson, showing that Greyhound ignored his decrees at its peril, issued a judgment of both criminal and civil contempt. He said that a command to a corporation was the same as a command to that corporation's officers. Greyhound and its leaders, therefore, were guilty of "willful failures" to obey the Court's orders of 1970, and of "eleventh hour" adherence thereto. Greyhound had accused the government, via the ICC, of using a "scattergun approach"—i.e., of enforcing obedience to the minutest detail—while the Court spoke of "gun-point compliance," in which Greyhound conceded only when it was apparent that it had no other course.[25]

There had been at least two cases in the past similar to Greyhound's contempt. One dealt with the Kroger Company. In 1947, it was enjoined by the courts to sell products at a profit dictated by the Office of Price Administration. When it developed that this course was not actually followed, Kroger was hailed into court on a contempt charge. It was shown, however, that Kroger's top management had in fact notified its supervisors and employees of the court order, and had disciplined racalcitrant workers.[26]

The other concerned the Holland Furnace Company. The Holland Furnace Company acted differently from Kroger. It was clear to the Court that Holland's top management wished to evade its various rulings. This evasion was based upon management's "intentional policies" to set aside numerous rulings by the ICC.[27] Therefore, the Court fined the company $100,000 and sentenced its chief executive to six months in jail.[28]

Greyhound's contempt, said the Court, was more similar to Holland Furnace's than to Kroger's.[29] The Court was not really impressed when two of Greyhound's top officials, F.L. Nageotte and Bart Cook, President and Vice-President of Greyhound Lines, West, averred that they extensively used the telephone to monitor compliance with the Court's 1970 orders.[30] Unlike the careful and astute businessmen they were supposed to be, however, they kept no record of their calls. Further, the Court said in reference to Mt. Hood that "Greyhound relied on its own employees to police each other,... kept almost no organized records ... and refrained from any threat or imposition of punishment."[31]

It was increasingly obvious that this was one court order Greyhound did not wish to obey. The Court, of course, had something else altogether in mind. It slapped a civil contempt charge on Nageotte, R.L. Shaffer, the President of Greyhound Corporation, and James Kerrigan, President of Greyhound Lines.

Nageotte, said the Court, "was responsible for the decision not to send copies of the [Court] order to Greyhound agents ... and not to discipline any agents for violations that they committed."[32] No document could be found, said the Court, "to indicate that Shaffer ever concerned himself with compliance in any way. It does not appear that he ever issued a single instruction or took a single step designed to achieve compliance."[33] As for Kerrigan, who was in charge of Greyhound East during most of the Mt. Hood proceedings, "he knew of the order and ... that Greyhound agents in the East sometimes were called upon to quote service to the Pacific Northwest. He also admitted that he ... implicitly concurred in the decision not to send any bulletins regarding quoting to Greyhound agents in the East. And he concurred in the decision not to mention the [Court's orders] in the company's bulletins."[34] The three Greyhound officials were not personally fined or imprisoned by the Court presumably on grounds that they fully obey its directives.

The Corporation itself, though, did not get off with just a warning. In January, 1974, Judge Robson found it in criminal contempt of his Court, and imposed a whopping $600,000 fine on the Greyhound systems ($100,000 against the actual Corporation, and $500,000 against Greyhound Lines, for its contempt from 1970 to 1973). Furthermore, Greyhound had to give semi-annual compliance reports to the Court for five years, and the Department of Justice was granted visitorial and document examination rights in a further effort to monitor Greyhound's activities.[35] (The areas served by Mt. Hood were flagged in red on all Greyhound maps and marketing material; and referred to as "compliance country").

As expected, Greyhound appealed this verdict. Arguments were presented to the U.S. Court of Appeals, Seventh Circuit, in May, 1974, and a decision was rendered the following December. The Appeals Court found that Greyhound had flagrantly disregarded the promises it made during the acquisition hearings back in the '40s and '50s; also Greyhound had sought to "excuse its non-compliance" with ICC and court orders "with twisted and strained interpretations...."[36] The Seventh Circuit, therefore, upheld the Lower Court's decision, an action that forced Greyhound to pay the $600,000 fine assessed against it, and caused it to make no further appeals, perhaps because of the possibility of even higher fines than the one it already faced. (Greyhound had objected to the size of the fine, saying it was unreasonable. The courts held, however, that the fine was levied in accordance with "the necessity of ... terminating the ... defiance...." Another consideration in imposing fines was the ability to pay. Since Greyhound Corporation and Greyhound Lines together earned well into the hundreds of millions for 1970, 1971 and 1972, the years for which they were held in contempt, the Court believed the fine to be reasonable, indeed.)[37]

The Mt. Hood people took a keen interest in these contempt proceedings against Greyhound, and the ultimate assessment of fines. Mt. Hood wanted to collect damages from the contempt decisions, but the courts refused. The reason for the refusal was that concurrent with much of the contempt trial, Mt. Hood was suing Greyhound on an anti-trust action under the auspices of the Sherman Act, and by the time the contempt decision was given, Mt. Hood had been awarded a sizeable amount by the courts.

The anti-trust trial, in which Mt. Hood asked for triple damages against Greyhound, began in July, 1968. It was heard in the U.S. District Court for Oregon, with Judge Alfred T. Goodwin presiding. At the trials on the district level, Greyhound lawyers spoke at length about "exclusive jurisdictions" of the Interstate Commerce Commission, and wanted the jury to omit consideration of "all conduct by defendants involving exercise of control over the acquired bus companies."[38] The Court refused this request, which would have seriously curtailed the jury's power over the case. (Greyhound's request in this regard showed a curious, yet interesting reversal of some of its earlier interpretations. At the ICC hearings in 1968, Greyhound had wanted to negate the Commission's authority over what was subsequently done with the Greyhound acquisitions. Now here, in 1973, and beyond, Greyhound wanted the ICC to have "exclusive jurisdiction" over those acquisitions. It apparently favored ICC scrutiny to a jury's.) The District Court, under Judge Goodwin, ultimately awarded Mt. Hood $13,146,090 (after trebling) for all the previous damages done to it by Greyhound. On top of this figure came attorney's fees of $1,250,000, plus court costs. Needless to say, this judgment ruined the day for several top Greyhound executives, and caused them immediately to file appeals proceedings.

The appeal went to the Ninth U.S. Circuit, and its judgment was given in June, 1977. At these hearings now, Greyhound reverted to its initial argument that if the ICC approved the acquisitions in the first place, it then had no authority over whatever conduct that approval engendered.[39] This was tortured reasoning, said the Court. It was clear that Greyhound had an overwhelming monopoly of bus travel in the Pacific Northwest. While mere possession of monopoly power did not violate the Sherman Act, *abuse of it did*.[40] The Court agreed with the earlier jury opinion that approximately 95 per cent of San Francisco-Spokane travelers would have used Mt. Hood's Klamath Falls-Biggs "bridge" if it had been available to them. Greyhound, therefore, was culpable, and must pay damages to the small bus-line. The Ninth Circuit upheld all the previous verdicts against Greyhound.

This judgment Greyhound decided very quickly to appeal to the highest tribunal in the country, the Supreme Court. It seemed now to lean on two defenses for its ultimate salvation. One had to do with proving that it *deliberately* and *systematically* had not intended to harm Mt. Hood. The other dealt with statutes of limitation, with a view to limiting or abolishing the "tolling" (or suspension) of them by the courts.

The first line of defense seemed to be negated by the work of Eugene Crow, whose San Francisco law firm, Broad, Khourie & Schulz, represented Mt. Hood. According to a 1978 article in the Los Angeles *Times*, Crew searched a Greyhound warehouse, on court orders, until he found an incriminating document. The Greyhound confidential memorandum began, "It is exceedingly important that the contents of this letter do not leak out." The document, said Crew, proved that Greyhound was covertly diverting passengers around Mt. Hood routes.

Crew went on to say that "untold thousands of passengers traveling in the West by bus were deliberately not being told by Greyhound of the fastest routes to travel," and the victims were generally "people who had to ride buses, because they could not afford to travel by plane or car .... An extra hour or two on a ... bus ride may not [be] much to many people, but it means a lot to a mother with a child who has a dirty diaper."[41] The Greyhound documents found by Crew turned out to be incriminating, indeed, as they proved deliberateness by the giant bus-line.

The "tolling" question was the one thing that gave Greyhound some measure of success in the case, but that was only temporary. The jury awarded damages to cover the period 1953 to 1973. The applicable statute of limitations, however, was four years. Since Mt. Hood filed its anti-trust suit on July 5, 1968, Greyhound argued that any injuries before July 5, 1964, should be disallowed. Mt. Hood's attorneys, however, maintained that the statute of limitations should be "tolled" (suspended, or held in abeyance) from 1953 to 1960 because of "Greyhound's fraudulent concealment of its wrongdoings," and from 1960 to 1964 by the ICC's intervention in the dispute between the two bus companies.[42] The courts agreed with Mt. Hood's interpretation of "tolling," and allowed the "fraudulent concealment" and "government intervention" period to be "tacked" or "bridged" to each other.[43] Therefore, the way was clear for Mt. Hood to collect damages going back fifteen years.

After its deliberations of the case, the Supreme Court remanded it to the Ninth Circuit, which in turn sent it back to the District. The High Court wanted to make sure that the tolling periods had been instituted equitably and fairly. The District Court again validated these periods and said they were warranted by Greyhound's actions and government intervention. Greyhound appealed this District decision to the Ninth Circuit. The Appeals Judges, February, 1980, wearily pointed out that "this anti-trust case is before us for the third time," (appeal from District Court, remand from Supreme Court, second appeal from District Court). "Mt. Hood has not slept on its rights," the judges said. On the contrary, it had "pursued its claims diligently," by petitioning the government for relief "within four years after becoming aware of Greyhound's fraudulently concealed conduct."[44] Therefore, the Ninth Circuit Appeals Court once more affirmed the District Court's judgment.

Greyhound immediately petitioned the Ninth Circuit for a re-hearing. This petition was denied in April, 1980. Accordingly, Greyhound appealed the case once more to the Supreme Court, hoping that the tolling question would give it at least partial relief. At the High Tribunal's meeting in the fall of 1980, the Mt. Hood-Greyhound case was not called up for consideration; and this meant that the District and Ninth Circuit verdicts were at last allowed to stand.

By this time, late 1980, the interest on the original sum of approximately $14 millions had grown appreciably. When Greyhound finally settled its bill with Mt. Hood, the amount was roughly $23 millions—an expensive gamble, which the Corporation was now left to explain to its stockholders.[45]

From all the evidence presented to the ICC and the various courts, it seems clear that Greyhound actually did want to run Mt. Hood out of business. Of course the Greyhounders defended themselves in the name of free enterprise; one of their lawyers maintained that for Greyhound to recommend Mt. Hood was like asking United Airlines to suggest that its passengers use American.[46] (Of course, as any regular air-traveler knows, when appropriate schedules prevail, most airlines will do just that.) What Greyhound forgot in this case is something that is too frequently forgotten by many people in authority: the free enterprise system works down as well as up; small businesses have just as much right to exist as big ones. For all its protestations of protecting the public good and seeing that fair competition prevails, the ICC gives every appearance from time to time of ignoring this fundamental premise of the free enterprise system. The federal agency has possibly done more for consolidation-minded big corporations (after all, it quickly approved the acquisitions that Mt. Hood feared so much), than it ever has for small concerns. Why else would it allow a huge bus corporation to gobble and gulp, while giving only promises that it would not allow its appetite to consume anything that did not wish to be eaten up? And, while all the time, the intended victim was shouting bloody murder, without getting one iota of attention? When the ICC did deal firmly with Greyhound on the matter, it was probably more because it felt it had been misled than because it believed any fundamental economic principles had been violated.

The Mt. Hood-Greyhound case shows that there is still an element of individualism in this country, and that with tenacity and good luck, it can be successful. Most people gave in to Greyhound; after all, the economic rewards of selling out to it probably exceeded anything that could have been earned as an independent carrier. But William Niskanen saw beyond economics and mere profits; he saw a life-time dream threatened, and he meant to preserve it.[47] Even if it was something of a one-time shot in which the ICC championed the little man, it is still a tribute to the free enterprise system that Mt. Hood won this case.

The case also shows the almost unlimited patience of the courts in this country. How many private individuals could have helped themselves to the judicial system for so long and to such an extent? Over the life of this case, there were at least twenty-one different and distinct judicial rulings; all of them primarily against Greyhound. The case reminds one of an errant child who is being punished by a parent; and the child responding, "But you have been so loving in the past, I really don't believe you mean it this time!" Surely it was that thought that kept Greyhound petitioning, appealing, re-petitioning and re-appealing until the courts cried "Enough!" and forced Greyhound to acknowledge that it, too, must obey the law.

There are several episodes in Greyhound's history of which it can be justly proud: among them, its patriotic activities in World War II; its strong support of minorities; and its living up, generally, to the standards of "service for the unserved," for which its founder, Eric Wickman, was knighted by the King of Sweden. Mt. Hood, though, is a clear indication and proof that top Greyhound management of the past dozen or so years really is composed of fallible mortals, and that they are not the gods to whom they so frequently liken themselves.

"Greyhound Stories"—Some Admonitions

"I have never seen any contribution ever given by Greyhound Lines to any charity in the United States ___in the thirty-three years I have been employed___"—Greyhound driver.

"We have a saying: There is a right way and then there is the Greyhound way, and the Greyhound way prevails."—Greyhound driver.

"___I believe the divorce rate is higher among bus drivers than any other occupation. We are never at home on a Holiday—we work very odd hours, and the wives after many years just can't take it. It really is an occupational hazard."—Greyhound driver, going through divorce proceedings.

"They got more roads in the State of Florida than anywhere else in the world, and Greyhound ran on everyone of them, whether it was any 'count or not."—Retired Greyhound driver.

"Any you people out there working for Greyhound, you be careful if you tell them where to stick a bus. I got fired when I done that." former Greyhounder.

Chapter Nine
Whose Corporation is This, Anyway?

After nearly fifty years of close affiliation with the Windy City, Greyhound decided in 1971 to leave Chicago. One source said that this decision was actually reached on a snowy afternoon in New York when a group of shivering executives on their way from one meeting to another agreed that it was "too damn cold" to run a business in the East. More rational reasons, however, seemed to have been a growing unhappiness with Chicago's congestion, its tax structures, and its increasing costs of labor.

In reality, an "in-house" study had begun long before the New York experience. This investigation concentrated on numerous relocation sites, which included Dallas, Portland, Atlanta, Miami, Cleveland and San Francisco. The chief considerations were relations with state and local governments, "quality of life" and facile integration of the Corporation's diverse entities, particularly if it already had several companies in the area. All signs pointed to Miami, and this city was recommended by numerous Greyhound insiders.

The top management, however, declined the "in-house" study and turned to Fantus, a Chicago-based consulting firm which advises corporations on where to locate. All of the cities studied by Greyhound's "in-house" staff were included; and Fantus added one more: Phoenix.[1] It was that southwestern city which finally won Greyhound's favor.

Why? The answers are almost as numerous as the people who ask the question. Many present and former Greyhounders assert that several insiders bought houses in Phoenix while the Fantus study was in progress, and that an option was acquired on a twenty-story building at Phoenix's Rosenzweig Center—now known as Greyhound Tower—long before the Corporation's Board of Directors approved the transfer. When that approval did come—at a meeting in Houston, Texas—witnesses asserted that it took only fifteen seconds to wrap it all up. One thing was certain: *somebody* wanted to go to Phoenix.

The Corporation's acquisition policies triggered Greyhound's move to the southwest. In 1970, outbidding General Hosts, Greyhound acquired Armour & Company, for $400 millions, and immediately projected plans to have the two concerns—Greyhound and Armour—under one roof. Also, the moving costs out of Chicago could be absorbed, for tax purposes, in the price it paid for Armour.

When Arizona politicians got wind of a possible Greyhound move to Phoenix, they assiduously courted anybody and everybody who mattered in the Greyhound Corporation. A very favorable lease (twenty years with a ten year "escape clause"), for one thing, was offered by the Phoenix city fathers for the building at Rosenzweig Center. Over at the Capitol Building, Arizona's solons obliged Greyhound, and enacted a law by which the earnings of the Corporation outside the State would not be subject to Arizona taxes.[2]

Keeping all this southwestern hospitality in mind, the Fantus people then proceeded to laud the climate, schools, good labor supplies and services, relatively low crime rates (as, at least, compared to Chicago's), and adequate supplies of "reasonably" priced houses at "nominal" interest rates. All these factors combined, plus the Greyhound-Armour cohesiveness that would thus be achieved, made Phoenix the premier city for the Corporation.[3]

And to this day, these explanations for the move from Chicago to Phoenix are routinely handed out by the Greyhounders. The move, they insist, had nothing whatever to do with the fact that Board Chairman Trautman's permanent residence was located in nearby Scottsdale. (He kept a small office at the Phoenix Terminal bus station.)

Even while Trautman was still active in his law firm in San Francisco, he commuted to Chicago, staying at that city's Whitehall Hotel, while he conducted Greyhound business. After his move to Phoenix, his routine for years was to fly into Chicago nearly every week, say on a Monday, and stay until the following Thursday or Friday. Undoubtedly, the jet-lags became burdomsome, so a Corporation move to Phoenix was, for him, welcome indeed.

It is probably claiming too much to assert unequivocally—as some of his enemies do—that it was Trautman, and *only* Trautman that brought Greyhound to Phoenix. (It is frequently claimed, for example, that several "in-house" reports protesting "dust pollution" in Phoenix, searing temperatures in summer, and misleading statistics on crime rates, were promptly thrown into the wastebasket.) On the other hand, those who believe that Trautman's residence in the area had *nothing* to do with Greyhound's leaving Chicago will probably be excellent prospects the next time the Brooklyn Bridge comes up for sale. As the head of what was in 1971 the 29th largest business conglomerate in the United States, Trautman could easily influence home-state politicians toward favorable leases on buildings and tax incentives—two factors that were then pushed by Fantus for a Phoenix move.

The transfer (using Greyhound Van Lines) began in August, 1971, and extended over the next several months. Approximately 800 Greyhound-Armour personnel were uprooted, while a comparable number had their jobs terminated.[4] More than five million tons of household furnishings and office equipment were taken to Phoenix, at a total cost of between $3 and $4 millions.[5] The goods of each department were taken separately: they would leave Chicago on a Friday, and be in place in the Phoenix office ready for use on the following Tuesday morning.[6]

A year after the corporate arrival in Phoenix, Trautman declared that Greyhound had not really moved out of the mainstream of American business, but in many ways had diverted that mainstream to the southwest.[7] Phoenix was about $1,500,000 cheaper than Chicago in matters like locally hired employees, reduced taxes, rents, and communication costs.[8] "I think our people are happy here," Trautman asserted. "Their morale is excellent and there has been less absenteeism due to sickness or bad weather."[9]

(In more recent times, however, Trautman has given a few inklings of misgivings about Phoenix. He has grumbled, for example, about the rising rate of crime in that city, and also about what he regards as a lack of zeal by the Phoenix police in protecting the Greyhound terminal, which is located in one of the city's less noble sections. His remarks have helped to generate rumors of yet another Greyhound move, with San Diego and Washington, D.C., being the two top cities under consideration. Observers point out that San Diego would only compound the time problems already suffered by the Armour people who come to work when the slaughterhouses open in Chicago. A huge, new civic center is being planned for Washington, very close to that city's Greyhound terminal. Also, the Greyhound people could not have failed to note Fantus Vice-President Robert Ady's speech of October, 1980, in which he asserted that the South's historically lower operating costs in comparison with the North's had ended. He believes an increasing number of corporate decisions in the '80s will be made by the politicians in Washington, D.C., "a million miles from reality."[10] It may well be, therefore, that Greyhound at least geographically will try in the next few years to get closer to the seat of power in the United States. If this should happen, there will again be a vast migration of Greyhounders; and also wholesale dismissals of support staff to avoid paying their moving expenses.)

The move to Phoenix consolidated a drive for centralization of authority within the Corporation that had been in the making for some time. Long ago were the days when one could be employed by "Southeastern Greyhound," "Pacific Greyhound" or "Northland Greyhound."[11] There were now "Greyhound East" (for several months headed by James Kerrigan) and "Greyhound West" (with long-timer Frank Nageotte in charge). Greyhound today is divided into seven regions throughout the United States, with a vice-president in charge of each. (Chicago, for example, is in Region Three and San Francisco is in Region Seven.) Each region is made up of numerous divisions.

In the Greyhound Tower in Phoenix is an elaborate communications system known as "Operations Control." Resembling a telephone switchboard, Operations Control tries to get buses to whatever place has the greatest anticipation of use for them. In New York City, for example, on each Sunday after Thanksgiving, more buses than the Region possesses are needed. Also, at certain, largely predictable times of the year, people will want to go South, particularly to Key West, Florida. Operations Control monitors regional and divisional statistics, and sends buses all over the country, where they are needed. Even so, there is an unavoidably high amount of "dead-heading" (coming back empty) out of Florida and other points South.

The Greyhound desk-jockeys in Phoenix present the drivers with schedules that the latter claim are unrealistic under the federal government's law restricting highway speed to 55 miles per hour.[12] As one driver stated, "55 is O.K. if you are on a straight express. *But* if you have to stop at two or three places, you have to go above the 55 MPH to keep the schedules that Phoenix has set." (The individual driver still has to pay speeding fines, and in addition, face disciplinary strictures from divisional and regional headquarters, to say nothing of Phoenix. In some areas bus drivers form a "pool" from which individuals take the fines needed to pay their speeding tickets.) Company policy forbids drivers from bringing aboard C.B. or other type radios.[13] Perhaps that is why Greyhound drivers today closely monitor the big eighteen wheelers on the road, or any vehicle that makes it clear that a C.B. is part of the equipment. They speed up and slow down in accordance with the "homing" vehicle. Also, the Greyhounders have become adept at noting that they are more likely to be caught for speeding by radar from troopers in the opposing lane of traffic than those on their own side of the road.

In addition to disdaining the C.B.s, another element in modern travel (except for the driver) that is neglected is seat-belts. Many drivers point out (probably correctly) that it is only the front seats that would benefit from such safety devices; from the second row on back, they would run the real risk of entrapment during an emergency.

One relatively recent innovation is Greyhound and other lines (by federal regulation) designating places on the bus for smokers. The bus is rarely out of city limits before the driver informs his/her passengers that smoking is confined to the last three rows of the coach. No pipes or cigars are allowed; only major-brand cigarettes. These directives are always accompanied by the admonition not to smoke pot. If marijuana is detected, say most drivers, the first stop will be the police station.

One woman wrote to a Chicago newspaper complaining that her daughter was ill after a Greyhound ride from Champaign. Some men were smoking on the trip, she said, and not cigarettes, "but that funny kind, reefers." The newspaper answered, "Such goings-on don't make Greyhound happy." An official said, "We do insist, and have signs posted . . . [that] marijuana and reefer smoking is strictly prohibited. We are sure that if a driver had been aware of the smoking problem he would have corrected it."

Anyone who has ever ridden a Greyhound or other bus for any distance knows full well that smoking of all sorts does go on, not only in the last three rows but any other place where the fancy strikes the addict. Many times, the offenders are seen and duly reprimanded by the driver. On an almost equal number of occasions, however, the driver *will not* notice the infraction. The reason is obvious. Bus drivers are in a hyper-alert business, and to calm their nerves, they, too, smoke a lot. Like most of their passengers, they are forbidden to light up while the coach is moving, but at stops between destination points (small stations, commission agencies, public rest places), they can and frequently do—on the outside of the bus—go through two or three cigarettes in a span of ten minutes. Since their own taste buds and sense of smell are so saturated with nicotine, it is unreasonable to expect them to be highly sensitive to burning tobacco.[14] A more reasoned practice, they believe, would be for them to smoke if they choose, with fans to keep the unwanted smells away from any protesting passenger.

Greyhound has a fairly rigorous dress and appearance code. When all the drivers were men, the height requirements were at first a minimum of five feet, eight inches; later, this was changed to five feet, ten. Then, when women were employed, and when automatic transmissions made reaching for gear-shifts no longer necessary, the height was again lowered. Men Greyhound drivers may grow a moustache if they wish, but no beard. Their sideburns may not go below their ear-lobes, and their hair must be cut short enough to reveal most of the ear.

In 1980 a new blue-gray uniform was adopted. The pale blue shirt was sixty-five per cent polyester and thirty-five per cent cotton, with the greyhound running dog emblem sewn into it. Patches for safety awards and seniority could be attached to both shirt sleeves and jacket pockets.[15] (Ten years earlier, however, Greyhound balked at the idea of too many decorations on its drivers' sleeves. Bernard Smith, a driver from Laramie, Wyoming, was presented with a twenty year safety award, and told at the same time to remove an emblem of the U.S. flag from his shoulder. Sam Thulin, Greyhound's man in Cheyenne, had asked his bosses—still then in Chicago—whether drivers were permitted to sport the flag, which had been distributed by local units of the Veterans of Foreign Wars. The answer from On High was "No!" The American flag was not an approved symbol for a Greyhound uniform.)

Several drivers filed a grievance with the local union representatives, which said, in part: "Recently this flag has been associated with hippies, yippies, and other radicals, but for many years ... with freedom and justice for the American people...." The drivers said they wished to show their patriotism by wearing the flag. Greyhound, however, on threats of dismissal, forced the erring drivers to abandon the emblems.'[16]

Another thing Greyhound did after it moved to Phoenix was to end its historic relationship with Grey-North, its Chicago-based advertising agency. The company's first ad agency had been Beaumont and Hohman (now defunct), also of Chicago. It was dismissed by Greyhound Chairman Genet in the mid 1950s. He believed that Beaumont and Hohman was not large enough to handle all the diversified actions Greyhund envisioned in the years ahead.

To replace Beaumont and Hohman in 1956, Greyhound

announced that it would entertain proposals from various advertising agencies. The Grey Agency of New York and ad-man *extraordinaire*, David Ogilvie, planned a joint presentation to the Greyhound marketing department (actually at that time a committee of divisional traffic managers) at a meeting in San Francisco. Ogilvie was to "upgrade the image of bus travel," while Grey, represented at the presentation by Arthur Fatt, was to "put arses on the seats."[17]

Ogilvie had a picture of a prim and proper Englishman wearing a bowler about to board a bus. The caption read, "Just look who's riding Greyhound Now!" Fatt's presentation, however, was a cute little jingle: "It's such a comfort to take the bus and leave the driving to us."[18] Ogilvie recognized a good job when he saw one. He exclaimed that Fatt's presentation was "the best I have ever seen," and he counseled Greyhound to "give your *whole* account to Grey."[19] The bus company took Ogilvie's advice and appointed Grey, of New York, as its advertising representative. In the '60s that branch of Grey's in Chicago merged with the North Agency, and was henceforth known as Grey-North. All the Greyhound accounts were transferred to it, with the able Walter Grosvenor in charge.

Twenty years later, however, Greyhound lost its enchantment with Grey-North. The mid-70s were not good years at all for Greyhound. After the Arab oil boycott of 1973-74, traveling again reverted to the automobile, and the general economic slump (which, in fact, had been building since 1966) set in again. The rapid escalation of diesel costs, continued competition with Amtrak (discussed in chapter seven) and deeply discounted air fares brought on by governmental deregulation, all coupled with a "soft economy," contributed to Greyhound's woes.

Under the circumstances, it was fairly easy to come up with a scapegoat, and Grey-North was it. Board Chairman Trautman charged Greyhound President and Chief Executive Officer Kerrigan with improving the company's fortunes. The latter argued that a change in marketing strategy would stem the tide—that an innovative advertising campaign would get the private auto user to take a seat on the bus. (Not that Grey-North had not been innovative. For years Grosvenor recommended harder hitting, more modernistic approaches for Greyhound advertising, only to have his suggestions largely ignored by the bus line's conservative marketing department.) Another conceivable consideration was that Dorothy Lorant, who became the Corporation's vice-president for Public Relations and Advertising in 1976, "inherited" Grey-

North as the corporate advertising agency. Any new agency that came "on board" would be indebted to her. It is highly probable, therefore, that Corporation policies played a major role in dumping Grey-North.[20]

During the Greyhound-Trailways trade war (discussed in chapter seven), Larry Stern was the latter's account supervisor within the Dallas-based advertising firm of Glenn, Bozell and Jacobs (GBJ). Though Stern was the "enemy" at the time, Kerrigan admired his hard-hitting, double-fisted presentations for Trailways (which, as previously mentioned, sometimes caused Greyhound to threaten court action). Just as the trade war ended, Trailways Chairman, Kevin Murphy—for reasons comprehended only by intricacies of the corporate mind—dropped GBJ. This opened the door for Kerrigan to invite GBJ to make competitive presentations to Greyhound, along with the firm of McCann-Erickson, operating out of New York. Grey-North was invited to present bids and presentations in order to retain its Greyhound account. Though GBJ won the contract by offering the lowest bid (at Grey-North, the account had an annual value of $9 millions)[21] and by their "creative strategy" and "depth of experience in bus advertising," it seems clear that Greyhound Marketing, on the advice of Trautman and Kerrigan, predetermined the outcome long before the presentations were made.[22] Though the Corporation does use other advertising firms for occasional and specific jobs, GBJ is still Greyhound's principal agency.

The change of ad agencies in January, 1978, really did not ameliorate very many of Greyhound's problems. The truth was that the company had been deteriorating since 1962 (the last year Greyhound was primarily a bus line). Diversification, quite simply, caused corporate officials to neglect their bus operations. As a result, by the mid-70s, conditions were melancholy, indeed. In addition to the poor economics of the time, Greyhound's public image was one of dirty, dangerous terminals, equipped with high-priced restaurants and filthy toilets; buses on which the air conditioning seldom worked; and a total indifference to customer complaints.[23] Employee morale was so low that GBJ's first assignment was to create a multi-media campaign, directed not at the public but at Greyhound personnel. Many of the missives and messages to drivers, terminal managers and mid-management support staff turned out to be not much more than massively over-budgeted paeans to Greyhound's top officials. Greyhound's internal problems actually postponed GBJ's job of touting the Corporation to the public.

In early 1978 Trautman finally paid some attention to the problems. (He had long had the reputation of not listening to anything he did not want to hear.) He hired fifteen ex-military officers to travel around the country, checking on terminals, driver courtesy, etc. He hired off-duty policemen for added security at terminals.[24] Then he took to the road himself. Once, after a trip from New York to Washington, he complimented the driver, but ordered the bus out of service because "it was smoking."[25] On other trips, he liked to hand out greyhound-engraved golf balls, and surprise drivers and passengers by telling them who he was. Every time he went into a city, by whatever means of transportation, he always visited the Greyhound terminal. In addition to himself, six to eight people, he said, are constantly touring terminals around the country. (One such crusading individual, with a reputation for zeal, according to widespread reports, actually bought a dentist's mirror and used it to inspect the inner rims of toilet bowls in Greyhound rest-rooms.) Suggestions for improvement are made on the first visit; if the improvements have not been carried out by the second visit, the terminal manager is immediately fired.[26]

On his travels, Chairman Trautman "got an ear-full" from drivers, terminal workers, passengers and maintenance personnel, and said it all added up "to a pretty bad picture."[27] He was apparently converted to the opinion, often expressed but rarely noticed, that "hardly anyone at the top [of Greyhound] knew what the hell was going on out on the line."[28] He began, therefore, to decentralize authority, to make it easier for a terminal manager to make a decision without having to get permission from the Division or Region; and to facilitate the latter's activities by freeing them of the necessity to check with Phoenix at every crook and turn.

The problems Chairman Trautman found were so serious that "major changes had to be made fast."[29] Why, they were of such nature, he thought, that he would have to postpone his retirement for a few years. And thereby hangs a tale.

James Kerrigan first worked for Greyhound as a baggage handler and clerk in the Boston terminal. After a stint in the Marine Corps, he was offered a terminal manager's job. In due time, he worked his way to the top—at Central Greyhound, then Greyhound East, and finally to the number two position in the entire Corporation. (Greyhound Corporation President, Raymond Shaffer, retired in 1977. The Board of Directors failed to give that vacated position to Kerrigan. He remained as Chairman of

Greyhound Lines and Vice-Chairman of the Corporation.)

He was 48 years old in 1978, and he fully intended to succeed Trautman, who was 65. (Kerrigan had been referred to by many in the trade as Trautman's "heir apparent.") When Trautman announced his intentions of staying until his seventieth birthday (August, 1982), Kerrigan had a definite reaction. Apparently, the Board of Directors had both Kerrigan and Trautman factions; Trautman simply had more than Kerrigan, so he won on the matter of extending his chairmanship above the age of 65.[30]

August 21,1978, is still referred to in recent Greyhound history as "bloody Monday." On that date, after more than thirty years, Kerrigan left Greyhound Lines.[31] "Why did I leave the Greyhound Corporation?" asks Kerrigan. "Simply because Jerry [Trautman] wanted to stay," he answers.[32] Apparently Kerrigan and Trautman drew up and signed an agreement by which the former would make his departure. He was to receive $250,000 in severance pay, and not work for a Greyhound competitor for at least a year.[33] In addition, he was not to make any public announcements about leaving, because Trautman did not want to "impact the press."[34] Also, apparently the two shook hands, and agreed not to talk publicly about their problems. According to Kerrigan, however, Trautman *did* talk, and soon, after the former's departure. He cited articles in *Forbes* of October 2, 1978 and in *Fortune*, December 31, 1978. Both articles had implications of Kerrigan's "being fired" or "forced to resign" by Trautman.

The *Forbes* and *Fortune* articles, said Kerrigan, caused him to change his mind, and speak up on the matter. ". . . I finally got so fed up with it [Trautman's interviews] that . . . [when] . . . a reporter from the Phoenix paper came . . . I tried to set the record straight."[35] The Phoenix paper was the *Arizona Republic*, and the reporter was Dan McGowan. In the article, Kerrigan was quoted as saying about Trautman: "It was just a classic case of a guy, an old guy, who didn't want to retire."[36] Kerrigan subsequently denied that he used the phrase "an old guy" in reference to the Greyhound Chairman.[37] To this day the question "Was James Kerrigan really fired from the Greyhound Corporation?" evokes a storm of invective from all quarters. "No!" emphatically proclaim Kerrigan and his followers. (Trautman did not have the power to fire him, said Kerrigan.)[38] "Yes!"[39] say Trautman and his entourage, citing falling bus-line profits, deterioration and morale problems as the chief reasons. As long as there are political factions within corporations (and that will, no doubt, be forever), no absolute resolution can ever be given to the Kerrigan-Trautman rift.

After the Trautman-Kerrigan agreement was signed, Kerrigan's office, he said, was immediately locked, though his secretary did stay at her desk throughout that day. That night, **Kerrigan came** back and moved all his personal belongings out of Greyhound Tower. A month later, he returned to pick up his check and, he said, Trautman offered to let him stay in his office until the first of the year. (The agreement, however, for keeping his office, Kerrigan said, was one year, which meant that the vacating date would be August 20, 1979.)[40]

Kerrigan was not the only person who experienced a severe "change of status" on that fateful morning. Frank Nageotte presided over the weekly executive meeting (which was always held on a Monday), and read a letter signed by Trautman. In it, the Greyhound officials were informed that Nageotte had been appointed as President. Earl E. Shew and Frederick Dunikoski were named Executive Vice-Presidents. A year later, the latter became President of Greyhound Lines.[41]

Greyhound Lines, Inc., President Harry Lesko, was demoted to working Greyhound's car rental program in Phoenix. (He had enough years of service for retirement, but was three years too young to collect his pension.) He stayed in this position until February, 1979, when he joined Kerrigan in starting a bus-leasing Phoenix branch of Minnesota based Gelco Corporation. Then, when Kerrigan moved to Trailways later that year, Lesko went with him. (Today, he is President of Trailways, and is regarded by men in the field to be the "best transportation man in America.")[42]

William Quig, a veteran of forty years, who had started out as a Greyhound driver, was told that his position of Senior Director of Operations was being discontinued. He was offered the directorship of Greyhound East operations, at a drop in salary of $10,000. He took his pension instead.

Lesko and Quig apparently got this treatment because they were identified with the Kerrigan faction at Greyhound. Unknown to them at the time was Kerrigan's request to Trautman that he (Kerrigan) be allowed to take the two executives with him, in the business ventures he planned, a request that Trautman was said to have refused.

Several other people suffered uprooted careers on that "Bloody Monday" of August, 1978. They included Jerry Thielen, Package Express Vice-President, with twenty-five years of Greyhound experience—not old enough for a pension—who became an "express solicitor" in Phoenix; General Counsel, Robert Bernard; A.R. Rastro, Vice-President and Assistant to the Chairman; and S. Griffin, Director of Management Control. According to informed sources, many of these men were ordered to leave the building, go home and await instructions from Greyhound about their future careers. When some indicated a marked reluctance to vacate the premises, Greyhound officials (at least those still with jobs) allegedly threatened to have them forcibly evicted by armed guards. Apparently there was a lot of shouting and name-calling that morning, and even a bit of shoving here and there. Altogether it did not present a very pretty picture of the "free enterprise" system in action. Greyhound officials, with Trautman at the forefront, always demanded total, unwavering, even blind, loyalty from their subordinates. And they proved that if they did not get it, any number of "Bloody Mondays" could take care of their problems.

Kerrigan spent most of his "non-competitive year with Greyhound" at the Gelco Corporation. Even before he left Greyhound, however, he had contacts with Holiday Inn executives with a view toward buying National Trailways.[43] He and a group of business associates bought the bus conglomerate in August, 1979, for an estimated $100 millions.[44] Kerrigan is proud that it took him only a few days to raise the necessary capital for Trailways' purchase, viewing the feat as proof of his respectable standing in the business world.[45]

The new President, Nageotte (who replaced Lesko), eight months into his new job, basked in the glory of employee praise. A letter to Nageotte from a driver of Division Four in San Francisco was reprinted in *Along the Greyhound Way*, a house organ for employees. The driver said, "What you inherited amounted to a runaway freight train going downhill. But in a short time you have ... [turned] things around ... and when we mention the Phoenix [Greyhound] Tower nowadays we do not feel we have to clasp our hands under our chin and look up into the sky." All was not completely well, however, as the driver pointed out that there were still some supervisors out in the field who closed their letters with "Do it or face severe disciplinary action."[46]

It is quite true that Greyhound's fortunes picked up from early 1979 on, and it was not exclusively managerial expertise that made this so (though none of the top brass in Phoenix minded that image). High rates of inflation cut deeply into the automobile market, putting many a potential car-buyer into a bus. The continued rise of gasoline prices figured prominently in the buses' come-back, as did the steady shrinkage of Amtrak. Trautman told those present at the 1979 annual meeting that bus travel had been up so much during April that Greyhound "didn't have enough buses."[47] This condition was due primarily to concern over the availability of gasoline, especially on weekends. Greyhound subsidiaries, Motor Coach Industry and Transportation Manufacturing Corporation, were busy at the time building 400 buses for Greyhound, and another 700 for other carriers.[48] The price for each of these new coaches hovered around $120,000. Economically, therefore, Greyhound Lines marched forward as the '70s closed and the '80s opened.

(Internal turmoil, however, continued within the Corporation, and there were additional "gut-wrenching re-organizational blood-baths,"[49] that were reminiscent of "Bloody Monday." Robert Swanson became President of the Greyhound Corporation in February, 1980; he resigned that post in October, 1980. Like Kerrigan of an earlier period, Swanson was widely hailed as the most likely person to succeed Trautman on the latter's retirement in 1982. It was reported that Swanson tried to "replace key corporate executives over the objections of Trautman and Greyhound's Board of Directors.")[50]

It seems that from all the shake-ups in Phoenix the Greyhound employee with the safest job tenure is the driver himself. In November, 1980, a new contract was negotiated between Greyhound Lines and some 16,000 workers (8,500 of them drivers), represented by the Amalgamated Transit Union. The first contract offered by the bus company was rejected by the union. On November 1, a forty-eight hour extension of a strike deadline was announced, but this did not keep drivers from setting up picket lines at some bus stations, primarily in Ohio. Just three hours before the strike was to begin, a favorable contract, to last for three years, was written. Among other things, the contract brought compensation to about thirty-four cents a mile, enabling the average bus driver to earn $30,000 a year.[51]

The question of deregulation cropped up again in the early '80s, and the chances of its enactment seemed to be enhanced by the government's earlier action of lifting some of the controls on the air and truck industry. Certainly Greyhound's leaders want deregulation, *if* it can be total. In a joint interview, Trautman and Nageotte said, among other things, that deregulation should include the freedom of setting schedules and fares.[52] Also it should be "accomplished on a nationwide basis by federal legislation," leaving the states out of it.[53] Greyhound, as the industry leader, would not wish to have "freedom of entry or exit" in terms of routes in one state and have that freedom curtailed in another. Complete deregulation, allowing changes in routes, fares, schedules, etc., would force all bus-lines to compete with one another; and in this respect, Greyhound would have few worries.

The possibility of total deregulation, however, has people like Kerrigan at Trailways worried. While he would like to set his fares without ICC approval, total deregulation, he feels, would allow Greyhound to "eat its competition."[54] Under total deregulation, Greyhound would probably have more routes than it has now, but would cut off services to numerous towns and villages that it finds "unprofitable."

Under total deregulation, Trailways, with its present twenty-two percent of the inter-city bus business, would probably hold its own against Greyhound and its 43-49 per cent. The ones to be really hurt by total deregultion would be the other 750 bus-lines in the United States. In spite of this, the New York *Times* favors deregulation, saying it is time for the government to quit propping up "unworthy competitors." The entire bus industry, the paper said, carries only 1.7 per cent of all inter-city travelers today. If the bus lines could abandon unprofitable routes after giving reasonable notice, and alter fares, either up or down within a "zone of reason," a trend would be set away from the automobile and toward the bus.[55] This would obviously have the happy effect of helping to keep the bus industry solvent, and also of easing the energy crisis. One may expect in the months and years ahead that Greyhound will keep a close watch on the government to see what it will do in terms of deregulation.

And, speaking of watching the government, just such a practice produced the latest spectacle at Greyhound Tower. A Greyhound employee, Jim Skelly, who worked in Customer Relations for $18,700 a year, is also an Arizona State legislator. An intense anti-abortion person, Skelly strongly objected to the nomination of Sandra O'Connor to the federal Supreme Court. His public denunciations became so strong that Trautman "asked him to tone down his criticism,"[56] and be a "little more temperate" on the matter.[57] Instead of acceding to these "suggestions," Skelly quit his job at Greyhound.

The Greyhound explanation came from Lorant:

> We at Greyhound feel that Judge O'Connor is one of the most level-headed, intelligent justices, male or female, ever to

serve on the bench and that her appointment to the U.S. Supreme Court would enhance that body.

Jim Skelly is a fine man and a conscientious legislator, and yet he feels quite differently on the matter of Mrs. O'Connor. We have to respect the sincerity of his feelings ... without in any way sharing them, and it became necessary to ask Mr. Skelly to be a little more temperate in his remarks because the public had begun to believe that his opposition to Mrs. O'Connor was ... as a Greyhound representative rather than ... a private citizen.[58]

The press scorched Greyhound for the incident. Columnist Andrew Zipser opened an article in the *Phoenix Gazette*: "Poor Gerald Trautman. Locked in his ivory tower ... he evidently feels all the world is a bus terminal."[59] The author claimed that "most of us know of Skelly not as a Greyhound employee or as a 'private citizen,' but as a very public figure."[60] He wrote further:

If two weeks ago you had selected a hundred people at random and asked them to name Skelly's employer, I'll wager not more than five would have fingered Greyhound. When Skelly's name is mentioned on radio and television, the only possible connection with greyhounds is Skelly's interest in abolishing the present racing commission. In 18 months of news articles about Skelly, in this paper (*The Gazette*) and in *The Arizona Republic* Skelly's 'Greyhound Connection' has been mentioned only once—in a story about his opposition to vehicle emissions testing.[61]

The Arizona Republic joined in the assault on Greyhound: "Most of the community probably was unaware that he [Skelly] even worked for Greyhound."[62] Just how leaning on Skelly on the O'Connor nomination would do Greyhound any good—when powerful U.S. Senators like Jesse Helms had little chance to block the appointment—escaped the paper, and presumably also Greyhound. By its treatment of Skelly, the *Republic* said, "Greyhound has given itself a black eye, and has done no great favor to business in general."[63]

It had long been the position at Greyhound that anyone who seriously challenged the leadership on matters of policy or economics would soon be dealt with. It was a simple extension from those areas to politics, so the Skelly incident should have surprised no one.

Strong-willed leaders of Greyhound—Wickman, Caesar, Ackerman, etc.—have always set policy and meant to have it obeyed. The pattern of sycophancy, however, has become more intense in modern times than it was in the past, and perhaps this is attributable in part to Greyhound being in the top fifty corporations in the United States (gross annual sales in a recent year were around $5 billion). Being highly diversified, there are so many different things to be seen to that chairmen and presidents have no time to quibble with upstart underlings. Consequently, their power sometimes resembles more that of a military commander's than that of a civilian executive.

And all this makes one wonder just where the "free enterprise" system is in this country today. It is arguable that the bulk of American business is dominated by a few dozen executives, and is subject to all their whims and fancies and childish temper tantrums. Since business and government have always worked so closely with one another in America, and since business has helped itself more than once to tax-payers' bounties, it definitely is the public's right to inquire into how these concerns, including Greyhound, are operated.

These remarks are not meant to be totally disparaging. Most of the people who work for Greyhound today are professional, in every positive sense of the word, and they have a great and honorable history behind them. From the stretched-out touring cars of the teens to the Scenicruisers of the '50s and '60s to the MC 8s and 9s of the '80s, the American public has always had a keen fascination in the hounds as they rolled down the road.

That image is not likely to change.

Chapter Ten
Latter-Day Greyhound: Trials and Triumphs

Gerald Trautman's long-awaited retirement came in 1982, and he was replaced by John Teets, formerly in charge of Greyhound Post House food services. He had no experience whatever in running a bus line. If Trautman's reputation within Greyhound had become unpopular in several circles, Teets' soon was the object of derision. According to widespread opinion, he wished to divest the Greyhound Corporation of its buses, and concentrate on all the other (some dozen or so) corporate entities.

Apparently, Teets had a crusty personality that did not put him in good stead with many of his fellow workers and colleagues. He was described by one former Greyhounder as "domineering and threatening,"[1] a man "unyielding toward unions," reminding others always to be frugal, yet constantly "running around" in the corporate jet. Another former Greyhound executive referred to Teets as "shallow" and more "concerned with his legacy" than doing right by the buses.[2]

On a less hostile note, Teets "pushes people, starting with himself."[3] He saw a relationship between physical fitness and mental prowess. He ran up the 314 steps to his 19th floor office every morning and down them at quitting time. At home, he often jogged where, he said, he got some of his best ideas. After a jaunt, he often telephoned the department officer to whom his idea was pertinent. Frequently the executive would exclaim, "Oh you've been out running again!"[4] He and his wife, Nancy, were the parents of four daughters, and they frequently called him "The Marshmallow," certainly a title that his employees and competitors would never use.[5]

Once becoming Greyhound CEO, Teets set about eliminating and restructuring what he called "flab." Any of his companies with high labor costs and mediocre profits rather quickly got the axe (Greyhound, for example, sold Armour in 1983). "What remains," Teets argued, are the "grunt-type businesses, steady money-makers ...."[6]

Federal deregulation of the bus industry on 20 September 1982 meant that Greyhound would now have to compete with all the other bus lines in the country, particularly in charter business. Greyhound lowered its fares,[7] profits began to fall just after deregulation (certainly by comparison with the "halcyon" period of 1980-81 when the energy crunch put millions of Americans onto a Greyhound seat), and Teets dictated that any of his companies that did not turn at least a 15 to 20 percent profit would be in danger of discontinuance. To offset such a calamity, Teets first asked and then demanded a 15 percent pay cut from the 16,000 Greyhound employees.[8] (And he must have expected a strike from this proposition, for he and Greyhound developed a "contingency plan" called "Operation Sunrise," to operate the firm during a shutdown.)[9]

Greyhound workers met this proposal with a fierce, 48-day strike that began in late October, 1983, and ended in early December. Picket lines formed around major Greyhound terminals, and one striker was killed in Zanesville, Ohio,[10] when he fell in front of a bus being used to train a replacement driver. One former Greyhounder said the strike of '83 was "WRONG" on both sides. On one hand it "pained" him to see his "fellow employees" react so violently when their jobs were threatened. On the other, Teets' hiring "scabs" as replacement drivers "destroyed any possibility" of creating a positive atmosphere between labor and management.[11]

For his part, Teets tried to convince the drivers that it was either a cut in pay or their jobs altogether. With deregulation, airlines were selling "dirt cheap" tickets, and Greyhound could not compete (at one point, it cost $29 by air to go from Los Angeles to Phoenix; the same trip on Greyhound was $45). Teets rationalized that the drivers had to face some hard realities in these early days of deregulation. The buses were the last of the transportation industry to be deregulated. Airlines (deregulated in 1978) and trains (early '70s) had somewhat of a jump on buses in matters of competition,[12] enabling them seriously to undercut Greyhound fares. Furthermore, in three years following the 1982 deregulation, some 2,500 new bus companies had come into existence, almost always undercutting Greyhound in wages and fares.[13] The Greyhound buses were making only 8 to 9 percent of Teets' required profit margin of 15 to 20. Something, he argued, had to give.

The drivers did not believe a word he said. His preoccupation with other Greyhound holdings meant, in Amalgamated Transit Union's (ATU) opinion, that he had seriously mismanaged the bus line. Making matters worse, no one in the executive suites in Phoenix had been asked to take any kind of cut in either salary or benefits. Why not? asked union officials. And, of course, executive salaries and bonuses were generally at least ten times more than those of the average Greyhound worker. If Teets and his fellow executives had taken cuts, this surely would have shown some goodwill toward the buses. They did not, and the problems continued. In December 1983 the employees "who had become convinced that further job action would be ineffective,"[14] stopped the strike and took the 15-percent pay cut (from 40 cents a driver mile to 37)[15] that Teets had decreed. Many drivers began to wear the "hound" insignia upside down on their caps to demonstrate that the "dog is dead."[16]

According to numerous reports, Teets put on a lavish "victory party," after the strike and spent large sums of Greyhound money (some estimates go as high as $105,000)[17] to do it. This bacchanalian feast only deepened the steamy feelings ATU had for Teets and the Greyhound Corporation.

Over the next several months, the Greyhound buses definitely had to adjust to the new rigors of deregulation. Antitrust laws, for example, that had previously been largely overlooked (definitely, however, with the exception of Mt. Hood, discussed in chapter eight), were now enforced.[18] Fare levels were left to individual operators, while the federal and state governments confined their roles to safety standards.[19]

In addition to cutting "flab," Greyhound also spent much time creating a new franchising program—the first the bus line had ever offered. CEO Teets said that "without the franchise program, Greyhound Lines will be dead within three to five years."[20]

In April, 1985, led by Greyhound Lines President, Frederick Dunikoski, the bus company put up about 10 percent of its system—about 70 routes— for franchise.[21] These new franchises were not restricted in the equipment they used. Vans, limousines, and mini-buses, could now join the 40 footers in transporting passengers, either for the long or short haul.[22] All of these vehicles would carry the Greyhound logo, be required to meet stringent safety and quality standards, and take advantage of Greyhound driver training programs.

A franchisee would pay a 10-percent royalty to Greyhound. Some operators felt this was too much because that
amount was all they usually earned after meeting costs.
Greyhound reminded them that each bus of an independent
line had an average load of 16 passengers, while the Hound
had 21. "The extra passengers will more than pay back the
fee."[23] Moreover, the franchises would have exclusive rights to
territories, without any Greyhound competition, with the
exception of charter rights.[24] And, of course, they could use
Greyhound terminals.

Dunikoski labeled the franchising program as "the most
revolutionary change in the bus line's 71-year history."[25] He
believed unionized Greyhounders would benefit from the
franchises because in about two years he expected franchise
expansions to feed additional traffic into the Greyhound network.[26] Such growth would enable Greyhound to serve "cities
and towns now without bus service."[27] In other words, with
franchising, Greyhound could get back to its rural and small
community routes that it had tended to forego during the past
several years. "Wherever people want to go," Dunikoski said,
"Greyhound and its franchises would take them there.[28]

Alas, the franchising program did not pan out. Continued
forays into the Greyhound market by cut-rate airlines such as
Peoples caused Teets and his management at Greyhound
Tower in Phoenix to think of additional ways to cut costs. The
franchises might have worked if they had been given full
attention by management (again, however, the other holdings
of Greyhound seemed to have attracted more attention than
the buses), if Americans had not gone back to their cars for
transportation needs, and if "federally subsidized" Amtrak
had been forced to operate on its own devices.

Suggesting that certain "high cost" terminals be closed
was one of the first money-saving arrangements. To be closed
no later than 1 July 1986 were terminals in Albany, Bingham-
ton, and Syracuse, New York; Harrisburg and Scranton in
Pennsylvania; and Norfolk and Richmond in Virginia.[29] Other
closings were to occur in Ohio, Michigan, Georgia, South Carolina, Indiana, Florida, Louisiana, New Mexico, Kansas, Wisconsin, Missouri, California, Washington, and Arizona.[30] Some
terminals, "while not presently scheduled for closing, will
have their manpower count significantly downsized."[31] Plans
concerning additional closings were "in the development
stage."[32] Replacing many of these terminals were "contract"
commission agencies such as motels and convenience stores.

For many Americans, the days of Greyhound terminal had come to an end. Greyhound Lines president Dunikoski believed these strictures would make the company stronger and viable "for many years to come."[33]

More troubling than closing terminals was Chairman Teets' demand in 1986 that Greyhound employees (drivers, mechanics and maintenance, etc.) give up another 14 percent of their wages, plus decreases in benefits. ATU rejected the proposal outright. Just three years before, Greyhound workers had yielded 15 percent of their pay; it was just too much less than three years later for the executive suite to demand another cut. Everyone in the business looked for a massive walk-out by Greyhound employees. Teets beat them to the draw. He sold the bus line, citing unfavorable competition from the airlines, union difficulties, and the buses not yet making his required balance of profits.

A Dallas investment group headed by Frederick G. Currey (formerly of Trailways, when that bus company was owned by Holiday Inns) started trying to buy Greyhound bus line in 1986. It was not until 2 a.m.[34] on 23 December 1986, however, that the deal was struck, with the formalities completed on 19 March 1987. The cost was $360 million in cash and other considerations ($170 million in cash, $120 million to Greyhound in accounts receivable, $60 million in preferred stock, and $9 million to Paine Webber).[35] At this time, the Greyhound fleet consisted of 2,800 buses, carrying some 30 million passengers a year.[36] Many in the financial world thought the price Currey and his group paid was too high; speculation had been in the realm of some $150 million.

Reactions to the sale of the Greyhound bus line were quick in coming. For the drivers and other Greyhound employees, the mood was, "Thank God, Teets is gone!"[37] and they spoke openly of the "welcome friendliness" of the new owners. In addition to the reputation of fierce anti-unionism, Teets was also known as a man who was good at buying and selling companies, but not at building up ones that suffered from competitive disadvantages.

What, many wondered, would be the relationship between the new Greyhound management and the ATU? A Greyhound spokesman, George Graveley, said that "informal chats" had taken place between management and labor, with "good exchanges of opinion."[38] One should not automatically assume, Graveley argued, that there would be company-union confrontations in the future. Currey pointed out that while the Greyhound deal did not carry with it any obligations toward ATU, he had "no axe to grind" with it. He was "very respectful" toward the Greyhound drivers, and he hoped that continuing talks with union officers would "lead to beneficial things for both parties."[39] Domenic Sirignano of the ATU "assumed nothing" in reference to the new owners, because he wanted "to see where they're coming from." He did say that Currey was "committed to the bus line in a way Teets never was."[40]

Almost everyone who expressed an opinion about the matter noted that with the Greyhound buses moving to Dallas, they would not now have to compete with a dozen other corporate entities in Phoenix. Ever since Gerald Trautman, the Greyhound Corporation had steadily reduced its attention to the buses. They had become the "poor relatives" of the larger corporate concerns. It was better to compete with other bus lines in the country than with companies within one's own operating systems. (At that time, Greyhound owned Dial soap, Traveler's Express, Purex bleach, and many other consumer and service products. As stated previously, the last year Greyhound had been primarily a bus line was 1962.) The only major competitor now facing Greyhound Lines was Trailways, and that situation would not last long.

As for driver pay scales, Currey noted that when he and his group bought Greyhound, they had two options. They could hire new drivers at 22 to 25 cents a mile, or they could re-hire the old workforce for 30 cents a mile. They decided to hire the old drivers (although they had already recruited over 2,000 new drivers), because their experience "would be worth the premium above market wages."[41] With various incentives and conditions, the price could go higher. Most of the old workforce drivers kept the road with these new circumstances, although it meant taking a further cut, from the 1983 level of 37 cents a mile. Perhaps an increased feeling of job security and friendly management helped them to make their decisions.

The new Greyhound management optimistically set about to revamp the bus industry. Not the least of the changes they envisaged was to restore the old Eric Wickman (founder of Greyhound) standard of "service to the unserved." In cooperative ventures with local governments, Graveley reported that the bus company might send 'Greyhound vans' to small communities to pick up passengers and take them to major boarding areas for the buses.[42] Currey elaborated on these points. "Para-transit" vehicles manned by Greyhound-trained drivers, he believed, could transport passengers not only to the buses, but also from rural areas to city-centers, to airports, and to major hospitals for visiting and outpatient purposes. "We have a high sense of urgency," Currey explained, "for services in as many rural areas as possible, but not with a forty-foot bus."[43] Charter services aimed at senior citizens and blue collar workers were in the works, as Greyhound began to give every appearance that its new leaders understood the history behind this great company. These ambitious plans were to be created within the corporate office of Greyhound Bus Lines (GLI) itself; thus, the scheme differed from the franchising efforts of a few years earlier. Unfortunately, most of these plans did not materialize.

Two months after buying GLI, Currey's investment group unexpectedly found that Greyhound historic rival, Trailways, was in danger of extinction. (It had suffered a decline of $61 million from 1985 to 1986.)[44] In fact, they had predicted that ultimately they would acquire Trailways; but not this quickly. They had not provided any financial arrangements for such a transaction when they bought Greyhound bus line. GLI vice-president, Craig Lentzsch, remarked: "When you are in the bus business and both the number one and number two companies are declining, you have to be thinking occasionally about the efficacy of linking the two systems together."[45] Acquisition of Trailways (which did not include Trailways companies like Adirondack, Martz, Capitol, Carolina, and Panhandle) led to a restructuring of the bus line's debt. Through a bank, GLI issued $80 million in bonds to investors (in $1,000 increments) and they were snapped up in one day,[46] although they were unsecured. (The next year, 1988, Greyhound issued another $150 million in bonds.)[47] Management, of course, was pleased at this response; it was another indication of the financial world's growing confidence in the bus line's ability to secure its future.

On 10 November 1987 Trailways formally announced its Chapter 11 bankruptcy. It took another seven months, until 7 June, 1988, for the Interstate Commerce Commission (ICC) to approve the Greyhound-Trailways merger. The federal agency believed the merger would "enhance and stabilize nationwide bus service."[48] The merger brought the Greyhound fleet to 3,754 buses (soon to rise to 3,949),[49] both owned and leased.[50] There were, of course, ongoing expenses connected with the Trailways merger: among other things, terminals had to be sold or renovated, food services revamped, and duplicate routes changed.

Once more, there was an air of optimism among Grey-hounders. The "break-even" point in passenger loads per bus fell to 19.3 from a previous 21.1.[51] Ridership increased some 20 percent in three years after the initial Greyhound purchase.[52] Currey exuberantly exclaimed that Greyhound had returned—in 1987—to the rural scene. With operational costs funded in part by the federal government's Urban Mass Transportation Administration (UMTA), some 69 systems in 16 states were serving 750 rural communities.[53] Another 5 states were slated to be added to this system in late 1989. These "hub-and-spoke" activities were performed by 15 to 25-seat vans, "operated by local transportation systems to the nearest Greyhound facility."[54] Moreover, the new Greyhound invested heavily in sophisticated training programs for its drivers, a resurrection of charter service and package express, computerizing its ticket purchasing system; and then, of course, there was the constant expenditure of building and improving terminals.[55]

Currey noted that "for several years there was growing concern as the company declined. With the turnaround, however, we have begun to hire people again, and jobs are far more secure than they have been in a decade or more.[56] Was Currey's optimism here reflective of hard, cold facts of reality? When he and his group bought the company, they made it clear that they had no particular obligation to the drivers' union. The coldness between the two—GLI and ATU—that had marked the Teets' era, began to return. Contract negotiations were not nearly as sanguine as both parties had previously predicted. These growing differences ultimately produced the most horrific strike in Greyhound history. It lasted for three painful years.

Even many years after the strike, the question remains: what caused it? This is not easy to answer, because both sides had different explanations. Did Currey promise the drivers that he would "make up" for the losses they took, first when he and his group bought Greyhound, and then when Greyhound merged with Trailways? Did the ATU promise "forebearance" in the matter of wages and benefits until Greyhound could get back on its feet?

Chairman Currey believed that drivers were making 8.3 percent more in 1990 than in 1987.[57] He wanted to "lock in" various incentives; safety, for example, which tied pay increases to individual driver performances. The company did not have enough cash reserves to grant only "hard money" increments. Even so, management claimed that its offers in 1990 amounted to a 6.9-percent increase for the first year of the contract, ultimately going up to 13.5 percent.[58] Why then, Currey was asked, did the union still go on strike? Currey did not know, arguing that to "anyone who understands the economic reality of our company, this strike is senseless. It never should have occurred."[59]

The drivers, Currey believed, had seen the buses fill up since the merger and concluded that the company was "rolling in cash." The return of the passengers, however, was predicated on a 10-percent reduction in fares,[60] and very heavy costs in advertising to attract riders in the first place. Moreover, Currey found Greyhound/Trailways garages and terminals to be in dreadful shape, and realized that overhauls were required. This meant that the company had to spend $183 million above and beyond the initial costs of the Greyhound/Trailways assets.[61] (ATU spokesman, Nick Nichols, however, said "our impression is their profits are very ... understated. In our view they've been cooking the numbers all along.")[62]

Despite these statistics, at the first negotiating session, Currey claimed, the ATU wanted a 50-percent pay increase for the first year of a contract, "plus additional pension, health and welfare"[63] benefits. The sad truth from management's point of view was that the company did not have the resources to meet the demands of Greyhound drivers.

For the drivers, the initial negotiations of 1990 were flashpoints of anger, and they were highly incensed at management's claims of inability to meet their requests. They had taken a 15-percent pay cut in 1983; they had been asked for another 14-percent of their salaries in 1986, and some more cuts when Currey bought their company and then additional problems arose in the merger with Trailways. For example, there was a question of seniority: who was to be given preference in this matter? The long-time Greyhounders? The long-time Trailways drivers? Many Greyhound drivers felt they had been deprived of their seniority status when the merger occurred. In fact, even in the early 21st century, 11 years after the strike, more than one Greyhound driver attributes the troubles of 1990 to the merger with Trailways.

If the executive suite had $183 million to spend on advertising, terminals, and garages, the drivers wanted to know why some of that amount could not be spent on them. More-over, in all these matters of asking drivers to make monetary sacrifices "for the good of the company," not one suggestion had ever been made for corresponding reductions in manage-ment salaries.[64] Drivers' sentiments were summed up by ATU President, James La Sala, who said that the strike did not hurt Chairman Currey, "who's pocketing his $500,000-plus annual salary from the sweat of our labor."[65]

The strike began on 2 March 1990, after 92 percent of 19 ATU locals representing 9,300 employees voted against the contract offered by Currey and his Greyhound colleagues. They simply did not believe the melancholy statistics Currey gave them. "Profits are up and ridership is up," they asserted, "and the reward for Greyhound workers has been a slap in the face."[66] Greyhound was reneging on its promise to reward driver sacrifices over the past several years.[67] One of the prob-lems here was fuzzy language. What did "reward" mean? Hard money was what it meant to the drivers. (Currey, however, maintained that most of the incentives he offered—2-1/2 cents a mile for safety, for example—were in the form of hard money.)[68] Lack of a hard money offer became the critical issue in the contract negotiations.[69] "Soft money," in the form of indi-vidual incentives and benefits was what "reward" apparently meant to management. There was a tremendous gap between these two points of view that simply could not be reconciled.

Of course, the traveling public suffered greatly from this strike. Most riders were caught off guard when the strike announcement was made at 12:01 a.m. on 2 March 1990. Thousands were in terminals, waiting for transfers for their onward journeys when they were told that the buses were going nowhere. (To the extent possible, AMTRAK picked up a number of these stranded Greyhound riders, accepting their bus tickets for travel.) The riders vented their anger at both the company and the union for not publicizing the possibili-ties of a strike several weeks in advance. Neither company nor union would take any responsibility for leaving their riders in the lurch. Regrettably, the hardest hit were those who could afford to travel only by bus,[70] and they experienced some uncomfortable nights and days until they could reach their final destination. All in all, these were not some of the happiest moments in transportation history—on either side.

The most contentious aspects of this strike started when Greyhound began hiring "replacement" drivers, or "scabs" as the ATU followers labeled them. (The example of President

Ronald Reagan dismissing the Air Traffic Controllers was often used here as a legal precedent.) By mid-March, Greyhound had hired 1,107 new drivers to run the 33-percent of departures still left to it.[71] As the strike continued, word spread that Greyhound had amassed several million dollars in "strike funds," to make the strikers "irrelevant" by hiring "permanent" replacements.[72] The ATU charged that these new drivers were ill-prepared to jockey the big 10-ton buses over the Interstates and by-roads of the country. Many were truckers, but said ATU, there is a big difference between a Greyhound and a semi. Only a modicum of training had been applied to these new drivers, sometimes a week or less. Numerous politicians became involved here. Iowa Speaker of the House, Tom Averson, was quoted by *In Transit* as saying: "I am concerned for the safety of Greyhound passengers who are being transported by replacement drivers whose qualifications fall far short of the regular union employees."[73] And Ohio Senator Howard Metzenbaum had "serious questions about the training and previous driving records" of these replacements.[74]

Currey called these allegations "absolutely ridiculous."[75] Most of the new drivers, he claimed, had more than a year's experience with other buses or tractor-trailers. They were receiving at Greyhound the same safety and behind-the-wheel training that all the 2,000 drivers had who were hired between 1987 and 1989.[76] Such large numbers of driver applications showed, Greyhound management believed, that the company was a popular place to spend a career. The company hired the new drivers at the 6.9-percent a year increase it said it had offered the old drivers.

Apparently, the replacement offer was popular, because truckers and other bus-line operators flocked to Greyhound personnel offices. One replacement had been driving a truck "off and on" for 25 years, and the most he ever made was $12.79 an hour. He had been a union member in the past, but felt no loyalty to it now. Unions, he said, "never do anything for you. They just take your money."[77] His actions personified much of what was going on at that time with labor unions in the United States—not just ATU, but others as well, such as the United AutoWorkers. All of them were in a precipitous state of decline; they certainly were not as "sacrosanct" as during the immediate post-World War II years. The matter of "permanent replacements," however, in the 1990 Greyhound strike continued to be a main sticking point, right down to the ultimate settlements which would be made after three miserable years of striking.

There was violence, with each side blaming the other. Picket lines went up at every terminal in the country (many signs said "Drop Dead, Fred") and ATU officials in Washington, D.C., urged their own members and workers in other unions not to cross them. In Dallas, Chairman Currey told *Bus Ride* that four striking drivers had been arrested and charged with shootings. Three governors had taken "extraordinary" action to protect Greyhounds traveling through their states, and courts had issued 20 different injunctions (Pittsburgh, Cleveland, Chicago, Philadelphia, Jacksonville, and Sacramento, among others) against ATU to stop the violence. Currey and his colleagues in Dallas filed federal suit against ATU in federal court under the Racketeer and Corrupt Organization Act.[78]

The ATU denied all these charges, saying instead that its striking drivers were the victims. The worst incident was in Redding, California, just two days after the strike began, when a long-time Greyhounder, Robert R. Waterhouse, was crushed to death against a retaining wall by a bus with a replacement driver behind the wheel.[79] Many picketers tried to stop the bus after Waterhouse was hit, but the driver, Theodore Graham of Portland, Oregon—apparently in the interest of his own safety—sped out of town and flagged down a police officer. Police brought him back to Redding, but Graham was not arrested. Greyhound called it a "tragic" accident; ATU labeled it as, at best, a demonstration of how dangerous it was for riders to take a bus piloted by a replacement driver.

A sniper attack in Jacksonville, Florida, that injured eight passengers[80] when shots caused fiberglass to shatter throughout the bus, brought a quick rebuke from Chairman Currey. He traveled to the Florida city for a personal investigation of the shootings, offering a $25,000 reward for information about the outrage.[81] "We will not raise fares," he said at a press conference, "to meet the exorbitant demands of the drivers ... We will not bend because of intimidation and violence."[82] The board of the local union in Jacksonville expressed thoughts that strikers did not commit this crime. One of the board members said, not convincingly, that throughout the ordeal, his strikers had "been like choirboys."[83]

The case of a Connecticut man, Roger Cawthra, ultimately pushed the Greyhound strike into an international forum. Cawthra, a striking Greyhound bus driver, was accused of shooting into the baggage compartment of a bus driven by replacement Carl Harris, with 19 passengers aboard. According to his followers, Cawthra could not get the court to call witnesses in his favor, the damaged baggage door was not presented to the court because it had been destroyed, Cawthra and Harris had had a confrontation three days before the alleged incident, and it was clear that the presiding judge was fiercely anti-union.[84] Cawthra sought help from his union, ATU, but could not get it. He quoted the ATU leadership as saying that it would be "counterproductive" to defend Cawthra "because it might drain their treasury and destroy the organization."[85]

Cawthra was fined and convicted to a prison sentence, later over-turned on appeal. He traveled to Berlin in November, 1991, to speak at an international workers conference. He strongly supported worldwide solidarity of the working man. Using his Greyhound experiences, he told his audience that "We will build on and defend the best traditions of the labor movement and ... stop the misery that big business and the union bureaucrats are creating today."[86] Out of this conference came the International Labor Defense Committee to "unify" support for "class war prisoners."[87] Of course, this bent toward Socialism got nowhere in the United States, and Cawthra and his "movement" soon faded into obscurity.

And in the meantime, this miserable strike ground on. The ATU charged that Greyhound prolonged the strike just to destroy the Union. Greyhound argued that ATU deliberately kept the strike going to force Greyhound into bankruptcy. With perhaps the exception of the sit-downs of the 1930's, no strike in American labor history elicited such acrimonious feelings on both sides of the picket lines. Violence continued, with gun-shots, rock throwing, baseball bat attacks, bomb and telephone threats, and "tail-gating" buses out of town, passing them, getting inches in front of them and sharply putting on the brakes, apparently hoping for some kind of incident or other.

A reporter for *The Los Angeles Times*, Dean Murphy, took a Greyhound from New York City to Los Angeles, and wrote a fascinating article about it. On this 9-day trip, he experienced "chaos, misery, a hint of danger, ... humor, and melancholy moments that come when strangers are brought together in common hardship."[88] He saw numerous strikers wearing ski masks, very skittish "replacement" drivers, one of whom, not very comfortingly, told his clients out of Philadelphia heading for Richmond: "This is my first trip ... If I make mistakes, pray for me."[89] And, of course, there were plenty of exhausted, angry riders ("if we were rich ... we would all be flying")[90] who had no other place to go but the Greyhounds. Ironically, Murphy discovered that the strike had led to improved safety at stations, especially the run-down, seedy ones. Increased law enforcement officials patrolled the area, looking for trouble spots[91] and keeping the peace.

Reporter Murphy's bus pulled out of Dallas amid cries of "Scab! Scab!" A striker grabbed the bus's windshield wiper and snapped it back. Then he twisted the side-view mirror out of position. From Topeka to Denver, most of the passengers stood, crammed very tightly into the aisle, because there were not enough "replacement" drivers to man the buses.[92] Finally, arriving in Los Angeles, the bus driver took back streets into the station, thus avoiding strikers. As Murphy walked out onto 6th Street in Los Angeles, he was beset by panhandlers. "I wasn't in the mood,"[93] he dolefully remarked.

After three months of this absolute nonsense, it was clear that both sides were hurting, but neither would give in. A Greyhound official refused to negotiate with ATU until seven days had passed without any violence.[94] Of course, ATU hooted at this pronouncement, saying that it was "outrageous," and a "desperate attempt ... to avoid GLI's legal and moral responsibilities to negotiate in good faith."[95] At the beginning of the negotiations, Currey said, a federal mediator was "physically thrown out of the room" where he tried to reason with the Greyhound Council (made up of one representative from all the ATU locals).[96] The government man reported to Currey that the union was "absolutely hopeless," interested only in "having a fight."[97] Such attitudes could very well have kept the two parties separated. One stalemate, then, usually followed hotly on the heels of another, and it seemed for quite some time that the sides would kill off each other, both of whom apparently forgot the inconveniences and hardships of the traveling public.

That Greyhound was hurting was seen in its June 1990 filing for protection under Chapter 11 of the federal bankrupcy law, to seek protection from its creditors until it could reorganize. (It had lost some $50 million during the first 3 months of the strike.)[98] The company's Chief Operations Officer (COO), Frank Schmieder (known in some circles as the "doctor of sick companies"),[99] wanted protection from creditors, some of whom were threatening to seize the bus line's equipment if it did not start re-paying its $800 million of debt.[100] Such seizures would almost certainly lead to the company's dissolution.

The buses kept running during the bankruptcy, and the strike wore on, with its sponsors trying to keep its momentum going and bring Greyhound to the bargaining table. Civil Rights activist, the Reverend Jesse Jackson, offered his assistance in accomplishing a negotiated settlement to the strike. He was concerned not only about African Americans who routinely rode the Greyhounds, but with all other Americans of generally modest means.[101]

But time was against the ATU, and perhaps again, this was another reason why Greyhound seemed reluctant to negotiate. Just one year after the strike started, in March, 1991, many picketers had abandoned their posts, demonstrating at bus stations only on a periodic basis. There was no way momentum could be sustained under these circumstances. Moreover, whereas some 600 drivers had crossed the picket lines at the outset of the strike, before it ended, almost 2,000 had.[102] The desertion of many picket lines was accompanied by numerous former Greyhound drivers getting into other trades and occupations. One driver went back to college to study law enforcement, and another found work driving an airport shuttle bus.[103] When these two examples are multiplied thousands of times, it is not hard to see that the union was suffering a steady loss of membership. (By the turn of the century only 9-percent of the private sector was unionized.[104] As a further demonstration of this downward slide by unions, surveys have indicated that in the 1970's some 15-percent of young people joined unions. In 2001 that number had been reduced to 5-percent.[105] The unions by and large were victims of their own successes. Many of the things they had fought for over the years became federal mandates: minimum wages, safety in the workplace, workman's compensation, and sick and maternity leaves.)

To accentuate these developments, many labor organizations stopped publicizing their sentiments with the strikers. At the AFL-CIO's 1991 annual meeting the Greyhound strike was "rarely mentioned."[106] In the past it had always been the thought that "an injury to one is an injury to all," but now with Greyhound, a labor official remarked, "we tend to have forgotten it."[107] Not only did labor leaders start to ignore the strike, they actually criticized ATU officials for not trying on-the-job demonstrations in the first place, before calling for a contract or strike vote.[108] It was, of course, sheer speculation about whether or not this tactic would have prevented the strike.

And another development boded ill for the union. The Greyhound bankruptcy ended in October, 1991, just 16 months after it began. During that time, the bus line grew considerably. Its debt was re-financed, and it accelerated Greyhound de Mexico (founded in the '60s) to cash in on the growing Latino market (over 70-percent of the Greyhound market in Southern California was made up of elderly Hispanics, traveling to Tijuana for medical appointments),[109] installed a computer system for reservations and schedules (replacing the old Russell's Guide, though reinstating it at a later time for schedules),[110] and began earning profits in 1992.[111] It emerged from the bankruptcy as the only nationwide provider of intercity buses, with 2,600 destinations in the lower 48 states.[112] In addition, it had cooperative agreements with several independent bus lines (which did not always work to their advantage), and it upgraded auxiliary services such as package express, charter, and restaurants at certain terminals.[113]

It was perhaps this strengthened position that caused Greyhound to return to the bargaining table. Federal mediators, under the direction of U.S. Labor Secretary Robert Reich, brought the two sides together for a few marathon sessions and several routine ones. At long last, on 7 May 1993, this strike—which never should have occurred in the first place—came to a somewhat anti-climactic end, when the two sides under prodding from the National Labor Relations Board (NLRB) ratified a six-year collective bargaining agreement.

The compact called for $22 million in back pay,[114] recall of striking drivers and reinstatement of some strikers who had been accused of misconduct and violence. Driver wages would increase from the present (1993) $13.83 an hour to $16.55 by March, 1998,[115] with pension plans that included 401(k), vacations, sick and bereavement, and health plans. In effect, conditions were roughly the same as they would have been if the proposals of 1990 had been instituted.

One of the sticking points in the strike, and at the bargaining tables, was the matter of permanent replacement drivers. When the strike began in 1990 and Greyhund hired new drivers, many in the organization claimed that the strike was over, or at best irrelevant. The old Greyhounders, they believed, had voluntarily given up their jobs and had been replaced by new ones. This idea was not as cut-and-dried as some in management believed. The NLRB ruled that workers who go on strike purely for economic purposes (wage increases, primarily) *can* be replaced. For those on strike, however, for reasons that included unfair labor practices "must be given their jobs back if they ask to return to work.[116] NLRB General Counsel, Jerry Hunter, claimed that the strike generated 175 unfair labor cases for his staff during its tenure.[117] Thus, Greyhound began to restore the old drivers, merging them into a retention of the new drivers, a process that lasted until 1995.[118] (And, of course, by that time, many old Greyhounders had found other occupations.)

The successful outcome of the bargaining was in part due to a new CEO at Greyhound, Frank Schmieder, who was able to "connect" with ATU leadership in a way that Currey had not. (Many still referred to Currey as the "Frank Lorenzo" of the Greyhound Lines, a charge he vehemently denied.)[119] ATU president La Sala and Schmieder comported with one another from the beginning. Apparently both believed that a continuation of the strike would mean a further diminution of the union and a strain on Greyhound, preventing any further innovations in the fields of transportation.

La Sala believed the end of the strike symbolized a new foundation for both ATU (he had at least saved the union) and Greyhound. It was time to put the past behind, and get on with the work at hand. There was a "renewed understanding" that a company cannot be successful "if its workers are dispirited and underpaid."[120] By the same token, however, he yielded to the thought that "workers ... cannot ask a company to give so much in negotiations that it will go out of business and destroy the very livelihood the workers seek to protect."[121] With Schmieder's flexibility and La Sala's cooperation, a new day was in store for Greyhound. Many observers remarked, "It's about time!"

Who won the strike of 1990-1993? In a word: nobody. When the strike started in 1990, ATU represented 19 local unions. By 1993, this number had been reduced to 4. The transit union spoke for over 7,000 Greyhound members in 1990; only 4,000 by 1993.[122] This was progress? Hardly!

Was Greyhound Lines better off than the union? In 1994, barely a year after the strike ended, management announced that it expected to lose up to $28 million in the second quarter.[123]

Also, apparently there was some confusion at Greyhound about its role in surface transportation in the United States. It was universally billed as the country's only transcontinental carrier; yet it fussed and fumed about its regional image, and definitely participated in the increasing fragmentation of the bus industry. Schmieder wanted to create five regional companies to concentrate on "high-demand, short-haul urban markets."[124] This strategy within each of the regionals eliminated many rural routes, quite contrary to those "para-transit" units Currey had envisaged in 1987. The trend once again became "big city to big city." "Regionalization" said one bus analyst, was "rash and unnecessary,"[125] and meant that additional Greyhound jobs would be sacrificed. The regions would "lose drivers, mechanics and customer service associates, ticket clerks and baggage handlers wherever service proves unprofitable."[126] If workers were not let go entirely they were furloughed, all in efforts to allay further expected quarterly losses.

Of course, one could say that there was no connection between these melancholy events and the 1990-1993 strike. A recession was in progress in 1992, and this, coupled with the strike, adversely affected Greyhound fortunes. Schmieder reported that the busline's number of passengers "has been five to 10-percent below 1990, due to lower consumer confidence" [did this come, one wonders, in large part, from the strike?] "and the recession. We are adjusting for this downturn by continuing cost cutting measures ...."[127] Although Greyhound had come out of its bankruptcy showing some profits, ICC Commissioner Gail McDonald, remarked that the "company's financial position remained 'tenuous.'"[128]

These "on again, off again" patterns of solvency and loss must have been caused in large part by the lack of steadiness within Greyhound itself. Being regional one day and transcontinental the next certainly did not create any uniformity of purpose among Greyhound leaders. The "feeders," or secondary lines which had served thousands of small towns were discontinued when the strike started, and never returned.[129]

While these conditions prevailed, the strike became almost a cultural war between GLI and ATU, reflecting some of the social divisions within American society itself. There were the "haves" and the "have nots," the "rich" and the "poor," and "conservatives" and "liberals." The volume was turned up high throughout the country on vitriolic diatribes, with little or no opportunity for moderation. A phenomenon known as "multiculturalism" arose, where insults, real or imagined, frequently wound up in the nation's courts. In large part, the continuing strike should be viewed in the context of these nation-wide social discourses. Economic gains, along with various benefit programs, seem to have been forgotten as both Greyhound and the union prolonged the strike unnecessarily in the pursuit of the thought: "I'm going to win this struggle, no matter what I have to do." In the end they both lost, along with a considerable portion of the traveling public.

Ironically, one of Schmieder's "casualties" was himself. The CEOs at the bus company apparently came to resemble football coaches who didn't win enough games. Not enough profit: out with you! He was replaced by Thomas G. Plaskett who, apparently, never did want to be a "permanent" CEO (not that there was such a position). He was a member of the Greyhound Board of Directors, and became the Interim President and Chief Executive Officer.

In November 1994, Craig Lentzsch became the new CEO at Greyhound. (Among other positions, he had been a Greyhound vice president in the past.) A native of Charlottesville, Virginia, he was a mathematics major at Georgia Tech and received an MBA in finance from the Wharton School at the University of Pennsylvania. Under his leadership, the Greyhounds seem to have flourished in the past six years, and the future is promising.

First, he had better relations with ATU than all the Greyhound CEOs of the previous 15 years combined. He gives full credit for this happy arrangement to Schmieder of Greyhound and La Sala of ATU. "They laid the foundation"[130] upon which Lentzsch could operate. La Sala saw the need to "normalize relations with GLI,"[131] and convinced Schmieder that cooperation could take labor and management into mutual benefits that permanent contentiousness could not. The good relations between GLI and ATU over the past six years have been enough, in all likelihood, to have kept Karl Marx awake at nights. (Diehard labor activists usually call such arrangements "tuxedo unionism," meaning that the unions have come closer to being in corporate "pockets" than they would like.)

Secondly, Lentzsch retained and built up some of Schmieder's previously formulated ideas. One of them was the increasing Mexican connection, represented by a company called AZABACHE. (The word stands for a black horse in Mexican mythology, and it symbolizes speed, style, and beauty.)[132] "It was an effort to operate a more Latin-friendly specialty service."[133] This line, headquartered in Texas, was to make non-stop express runs to Mexico from California cities as far north as Fresno and Salinas.[134] For various reasons, Greyhound severed its ties with AZABACHE, looking instead for other avenues to relate with Mexican bus companies.

Lentzsch brought a philosophy to Greyhound of labor cooperation: "We are not going to grow this company on the backs of the hourly work force. The way to grow this business is by improving the product."[135] He also set in motion a plan to retain the permanent replacement drivers from the strike and also over time to bring back the old drivers, with full restoration of seniority, as the company needed them. This process was completed in 1995. At the union's national meeting in Las Vegas in 1995, at his own initiative, Lentzsch promised ATU members that in the future he would never hire replacement drivers.[136] Of course, under the circumstances of friendship building up between the two entities, perhaps the need, imagined or otherwise, will never come up, at least in the foreseeable future. (Today, in 2001, drivers to a person have nothing but praise for Lentzsch. One driver, out of Greyhound work for over 4 years, lauds Schmieder and Lentzsch for ending the strike and making it possible for him again to be a Greyhounder. The strike could have been avoided, he said, if labor and management had worked toward goodwill for each other rather than being possessed with hateful rancor.)

Without union pressure (for a change) and immediate economic considerations, Lentzsch could concentrate on some of GLI's biggest problems. One was being on time. Lentzsch said that in the past 12 months, "We weren't making it easy for customers to buy our product."[137] Through improved computer systems, Greyhound, both at national headquarters in Dallas, and at various regional points throughout the country, data could be processed not only on bus arrivals and departures (if too much variance here, extra buses could be utilized), but also on the number of passengers on board each bus, and on the tons of baggage scattered around the system.[138] Not the least of all this progress was the creation, in 1995, of a Greyhound web site, www.greyhound.com. All these procedures were accomplished, said Greyhound Executive Vice President, Jack Haugsland, "as a result of creative thinking, not increased spending."[139] This was, indeed, a welcome message at Greyhound.

This "back-to-basics" strategy focused on "customer-orientation,"[140] with flexible scheduling, meeting peak travel demands, and low prices. (The typical traveler, Greyhound found through surveys, had an annual income at or below $35,000.)[141] Did these innovations pay off? In 1998, the company generated revenues of $846 million with substantial net earnings.[142] Obviously, something was going on at Greyhound management that had been lacking for many years. The strategy was to induce first-time and repeat travel,[143] and it succeeded marvelously.

And the positive relations with ATU under these circumstances of growth not only continued but flourished. Negotiations began in early 1998 on a contract scheduled to expire in 1999, and the acrimony of the past was noticeably absent. (Chicago-based Local 1700 voted electronically. Out of 2,276 telephone calls to the central office, 64-percent voted for the contract; 36-percent against.[144] This was typical of the over-all union vote.) Lentzsch did something here that, if it had been done fully in 1983 and 1990, might have prevented those troubling strikes. He opened the Greyhound accounting books for full inspection. He told ATU that "anything they wanted to know about the finances of the company, we would make available."[145] (In all fairness, it must be pointed out that Fred Currey had offered balance sheets and auditors to the ATU in 1990. Still, there was an aura of disbelief when he said the company could not accommodate the wage increments ATU wanted.)

Since Greyhound was a public company and had taken Chapter 11 during the strike of 1990-1993, it was required to open its books.[146] Beyond this gesture of goodwill, however, Lentzsch and the union agreed to meet periodically and exchange ideas and work on the process of labor-management.[147] There is, of course, no law in the universe that says mutual cooperation is less efficacious than constant combat. "Such fence-mending," said the *Wall Street Journal*, "has become symbolic of Mr. Lentzsch's efforts to reverse the big bus company's fortunes during the past three years."[148]

The new contract, approved by both sides long before the current one ran out, was hailed throughout the industry as a milestone of mutual respect and cooperation. One long-time ATU member and critic of Greyhound, Jim Cushing-murray, remarked that he had never voted in favor of a Greyhound contract until now. He remarked: "'So far, if he's given his word, he's always made good on it,' he says of Mr. Lentzsch. 'I think he's a decent man.'"[149] Robert Molofsky, ATU General Counsel, echoed Cushing-murray's thoughts, saying it was the "enlightened leadership"[150] of Craig Lentzsch that turned things around. Leadership at the top (both GLI and ATU) combined for open books and joint meetings which could only produce respect and trust between the two parties. These statements by two leading union men are astonishing, given the past disillusionment and disdain between GLI and ATU.

Under the new contract, running through early 2003, drivers (who make an average of $32,000 a year)[151] will receive some 2.5 percent "over each of the next five years,"[152] causing hourly wages to go from $15.99 to $18.27.[153] This was a real coup for Lentzsch and La Sala. Not only did they please drivers and other personnel within the framework of Greyhound—including everyone from mechanics to ticket clerks—they convinced more than one creditor that Greyhound was a "vehicle of growth,"[154] an extremely important consideration for future accomplishments. With its 18,000 daily departures for 2,400 different destinations,[155] Greyhound was once again "riding high." The recent labor negotiations were "solid proof," said Lentzsch, that the atmosphere at Greyhound had "changed substantially, meaning that we can deal with problems flexibly in the future." The bottom line was "It means that the trust is there."[156] In 1998, Greyhound announced a new carrier, the 55-seat DL-3, with the largest capacity of any bus in the company's history,[157] helping the customer base to grow at a rate "that exceeds the U.S. population" growth.[158] It was as though everything negative of the past had been overcome.

Much of this "customer base" was composed of passengers who made relatively modest household incomes. (Twenty percent of Greyhound riders, however, earn $50,000 or more a year and apparently "value money more than time.")[159] Much of the fleet caters to African Americans, Asians, and Hispanics. In reference to the third group, "Hispanic corridors" have been opened. One route goes from Matamoras, Mexico, to Brownsville, Texas, through Houston, and on to Miami, Florida. There is an express route from Juarez through El Paso to Albuquerque and Denver and to Phoenix and Los Angeles. Another line goes from Tijuana to Yakima, Washington.[160] These are just a few of the innovative route patterns that Greyhound has followed in the past few years. A part of Greyhound route planning apparently includes the decision to locate terminals in numerous small towns (those of 40,000 or less) as near to interstate exits and entrances as possible. (A case in point is Bowling Green, Kentucky, where the station has been moved to the north end of town, some five or six miles away from city center. The thought must have been that passengers can call a cab as easily from the edge of town to get home or elsewhere as they can in the middle, and save the bus several minutes in getting back onto the freeway.) This procedure obviously has not led to many passenger complaints, as Greyhound continued to be well thought of in the eyes of its riding patrons.

Its route expansions accounted in large part for Greyhound being the first bus company in the United States to join the Airlines Reporting Corporation (ARC), which allowed travel agents to sell Ameripass.[161] Greyhound joined three railroads, two theme park operators, and 140 airlines in its ARC participation. In other route innovations Greyhound hooked into the growing market of theme parks, with its "flightlink" program, taking passengers from small towns to major airports. (This had been a Greyhound ambition during the Currey years.)

A symbol of popularity of Greyhound with the general public and the historical-mindedness of the "new" Greyhound, was the opening of the Greyhound Bus Origin Center, on the exact spot in Hibbing, Minnesota, where Carl Wickman had started the whole thing. The mastermind behind this glorious tribute to Greyhound was Gene Nicolelli, a long-time collector of Greyhound memorabilia. The center opened on 10 July 1999 in a 10,000-square-foot building; among the honorees at the ceremonies was Jack Haugsland, Greyhound vice president, whose company contributed $90,000 to the project.[162] Fleets of old buses, some going back as far as the touring cars, are displayed at the museum, as well as a replica of a ticket agency, and guided tours which include "driving" a Greyhound.

Furthering this momentum of goodwill, Greyhound joined Federal Express to take 90 children and senior citizens from Memphis (headquarters for FedEx) to Ontario, Canada, to tour the highlights, in western New York and eastern Michigan, of the "Underground Railroad," the system that had helped so many African Americans in the 19th century to escape the miseries of slavery in the American south.[163] (For a time, there seemed to be plans for Greyhound to join FedEx in package shipping, or if not with FedEx, then perhaps to cooperate with United Parcel Service.[164] Greyhound did create an arrangement with MultiPack, primarily in California.)

Amidst these flurries of activities, Greyhound relocated
its Melbourne, Florida, terminal to the airport, the 89th
"intermodal terminal" for the bus company.[165] Certainly, it
took advantage of increased gaming enterprises throughout
the country when it introduced schedules from northern California to Caesar's Casino in Lake Tahoe.[166] Greyhound even
offered hourly service from Philadelphia to the Atlantic City
gambling areas, including, among others, Taj Mahal, Hilton,
Trump Plaza, Tropicana, and the Sands.[167] It sought a new
terminal in Atlanta, claiming that it had been "pushed out" of
its old place in 1995, because of the city's hosting of the
summer Olympics in 1996.[168] The new facility was to be built
in "the gulch," between Forsyth and Spring Streets (but, as of
2001, that facility has not yet been built). It also opened a
"Flightlink" in Milwaukee, giving passengers a "low-cost
alternative to the automobile when flying in and out of that
Wisconsin city.[169] These were just a few of the nation-wide
efforts by Greyhound to go where the riders are. These ambitions entailed large, on-going studies of demographics which
included finding the most logical routes for bus travelers.
Where are the passengers, and where do they want to go?
Greyhound proposed to be their carrier.

Offsetting these positive developments was the blasting
Greyhound received at the hands of the National Transportation Safety Board in regard to a 1998 accident in Pennsylvania that killed seven passengers and injured several others.
The bus had rammed into the back of a parked tractor-trailer.
(Historically, most Greyhound accidents have involved 18-
wheelers.) The Safety Board concluded that the driver had
used antihistamines. Greyhound challenged this finding,
saying that the cause was most likely a heart or angina
attack.[170] (In 2001 the NTSB has reopened its investigation
into this 1998 accident, reconsidering the Greyhound claim
that it was, indeed, a health problem that caused it. "This is
great news," said a Greyhound spokesperson, "and is unusual
for the NTSB to reopen closed cases.")[171]

The Safety Board, nevertheless, faulted Greyhound "for
not using traffic violations in assessing drivers' safety, allowing 'widespread speeding,' and for not adequately tracking ...
complaints about drivers."[172] Among other things, the Board
suggested installing electronic devices in buses "to monitor
speeding, sudden stops and other activity."[173] Over the years
Greyhound and other bus lines have provided as safe a
ground transportation as it is possible to get. As stated ear-

lier, the buses are like airplanes: the public only hears about the few that didn't make it, not the millions that arrive safely.

Greyhound experienced some difficulties trying to comply with the American Disabilities Act. Fourteen disabled passengers claimed that they had been "denied boarding assistance, or injured, or verbally harassed."[174] Greyhound settled the matter by paying $17,500 in damages to the 14 complainants and stated that it would guarantee lift-equipped buses if passengers gave a 48-hour notice of this necessity.[175] (Greyhound was not alone in scrambling to obey the ADA law. United, American, Continental, Delta, and Southwest Airlines responded to charges, as did Days Inn and MGM Grand Hotel in Las Vegas. Most of these cases were settled by monetary payments.)

An event of 1999 unsettled many Greyhounders when the bus company was sold to Laidlaw, Inc., operating out of Ontario, Canada. Laidlaw ran many buslines in Canada, sold school buses to educational systems, and ran ambulance services. Some drivers and maintenance personnel feared that this sale would bring them back into unfavorable and unwanted competition with other entities within the Laidlaw Corporation. It had not been all that long ago when Gerald Trautman seemingly had forgotten the buses in favor of other business interests. At least, however, Laidlaw was primarily a bus line, and this situation ameliorated the worries of Greyhound employees. Furthermore, many wondered how the new owners, Laidlaw, would comport with the drivers' union, ATU, and affect management-labor relations. This was a needless concern, since Laidlaw has nothing to do with ATU; the labor contract is between GLI and ATU.

Why would Greyhound sell itself to Laidlaw? Despite its vigorous activities of the late '90s, Greyhound still needed sources of financing. If it was going to continue its boom period, Greyhound had constantly to expand into new operations and improve old ones. (A case in point was the Beaumont, Texas, terminal. The state Transportation Department granted $282,150 to improve services at this location. Other terminal upgrades just in Texas alone included Abilene, Austin, Big Spring, Brownsville, and Corpus Christi.)[176] These were huge expenses, and Greyhound needed to assure its lines of credit for the future. And that is where Laidlaw comes into the picture.

The Canadian corporation paid $650 million[177] in cash and other considerations for the Greyhound Bus Lines. Greyhound was a "plum" for Laidlaw as well for, among other things, it meant that Greyhound could expand its operations in Canada. The purchase seemed to be a good deal for both parties. Merger hearings were held throughout 1998 and on 1 February 1999, the final deal was struck.

Not more than 18 months later, however, trouble struck. Laidlaw began to lose millions of dollars, in part because of investments in "poorly performing" American health-care institutions,[178] scandals at its South Carolina waste firm, and increases in the cost of fuel. These losses, of course, meant that Laidlaw's credit would be restricted and its debt ratings severely lowered. Its indebtedness in the United States alone was $3.4 billion.[179]

What did all of this mean for Greyhound? First, it caused Laidlaw to suspend any and all financial backing to the bus line.[180] Speculation soon spread on whether or not Laidlaw would bankrupt. Greyhound CEO Lentzsch expressed the thought that "a bankruptcy filing by Laidlaw would be good news for Greyhound,[181] because under its protection, Laidlaw could once again borrow, and keep a cash flow coming in to its constituents, including Greyhound. The busline continued to operate normally, but was temporarily prevented from pursuing its numerous plans for expansion,[182] using its own cash reserves to keep running. Laidlaw did, however, continue to support some of the internal growth at Greyhound, such as enlarging its fleet of charter buses, improving package delivery, and replacing aging buses with new or refurbished ones.[183]

By August, 2000, however, Lentzsch wanted to seek financing outside of the Laidlaw circle, since Greyhound had an interest payment coming up in October. Laidlaw accommodated Greyhound by authorizing it to "seek third-party financing from outside sources."[184] Lentzsch opened negotiations with some institutions with whom Greyhound had worked in the past. In October, 2000, the bus company received a $125 million credit facility from the Foothill Capital Corporation, a part of Wells-Fargo.[185] Not the least of Greyhound strength here was the almost unprecedented growth of the company since Lentzsch took over in 1994 as CEO. These new loans would keep the buses on the roads.

Both Greyhound and Laidlaw, however, received some criticisms from the federal Surface Transportation Board, which found Laidlaw's condition—and by extension, Greyhound—"troubling."[186] During the acquisition hearings, the

Board was told that "Laidlaw's financial strength would help reduce Greyhound debt while providing investment for growth."[187] Nothing of the sort occurred, and some members of the Board intimated that they might have been misled. (By September, 2000, Laidlaw reported that it "should be able to satisfy working capital."[188]) Laidlaw continues to own Greyhound, although the latter had secured its own financing, and was apparently flourishing as a result.

As the new millennium began, the Greyhound buses seemed to be secure, not just for the short haul, but for the long one as well. By comparison to bygone days, its leadership is enlightened and knowledgeable. As a result, its employees—as represented by ATU—are contented, and pleased to be Greyhounders. (As noted, their next contract negotiations do not come up until 2003.) Still the most visible and best Greyhound employees are the drivers themselves; in fact, they constitute an American institution. It may be true that management and stockholders actually own the company, but in a way, the public "owns" it too, for it has become an integral part of their lives as well.

In 2001, Greyhound had 12,500 employees in the United States, with a fleet of 2,300 buses. It has 2,600 destinations—most on a daily basis—and 350 major terminals, 109 of them owned directly by the company (these numbers do not include the agencies). And with its own financing, the road ahead seems open. Greyhound has a great and honorable history behind it, and in the minds of millions of people around the world, they are still and will continue to be, "The Hounds of the Road."

Appendix A

Trains vs. Buses

By the mid-Twenties, the bus industry had grown so much that it had created one seemingly implacable foe: the railroads. Ever since World War I railroads had been losing large amounts of passenger revenue, and this loss was widely attributed to bus operations. Railroads had been nationalized during the war, and their transport of materiel had caused a severe decline of passenger travel. When the traveling public found the railroads mostly closed to them, they naturally turned to the buses. Perhaps the war broke the public's habit of depending on trains, and pointed them toward buses as the best way to travel. When the war ended, and trains were de-nationalized, the public did not go back to them in the numbers anticipated by the railroad companies.

Then, too, buses could go more places than trains. In the opulent Twenties, vacations became much more commonplace than before. Buses could take people to scenic areas and resort hotels that were by-passed by many railroad routes. The American public may have had a long "love affair" with the railroad, but once it was clear it could not give them what they wanted, they jilted it for a younger system.

To be sure, the railroads fought back. They organized propaganda campaigns against the "irresponsible," "unregulated" buses which were ruining highways built by the public's tax dollars. Some railroads established their own bus subsidiaries, and engaged in price-cutting to kill off several vulnerable bus lines.

One railroader, however, differed from his colleagues about the impact of buses on trains. He was Ralph Budd, President of the Great Northern Railroad. He had a study carried out to find exactly why railroads were losing profits. He checked the decline of ticket sales from 1920 to 1924 at eleven Minnesota stations "where bus competition had appeared, and found an average decrease of 63.7 per cent. Then he checked the decline at fifteen stations where *no* bus competition had appeared, and found a decrease of 64.6 per cent. That was enough to convince him that it was not the bus that was to be blamed. It was the automobile. (See *Fortune*, "Jitney Into Giant," Vol. 10, No. 2; August, 1934, p. 110). The obvious thing was for railroads and buses to complement each other, rather than compete. Budd started the cooperation between trains and buses that lasted, for the most part, down to the Amtrak era.

Appendix B

Anatomy of a Take-Over

The Greyhounders, under Wickman and Caesar, took over many bus systems in the United States in the Twenties and Thirties. These included systems in Texas, Louisiana, Kentucky and Florida. One could discuss mergers and consolidations, *ad infinitum*, and without knowing the behind the scenes deals and activities, miss the human drama of it all. Unfortunately Greyhound and its affiliates did not retain many of the working papers in these various transactions (or if they did, they are keeping them well hidden). Such is not the case, however, with the formation and subsequent relationship with Greyhound of the Midwest Transit Company, based in Indiana. All of the records pertaining to that acquisition are stored at the American Heritage Center at the University of Wyoming.

The Company was formed on September 12, 1925, with capital stock of $25,000 furnished by Wickman's Duluth group. Incorporated in Delaware, the company's president was H.A. Spearin, and the secretary-treasurer, William E. Tracey. Both these men, "parties of the first part," went to the Midwest—primarily to Ohio and Indiana—to acquire new bus lines and all the equipment necessary to run them. Eric Wickman, one of the "party of the second part," remained in Minneapolis, and served as Midwest Transit's vice-president. His job was to keep a steady flow of money to Spearin and Tracey. Their job was to spend it.

Scarcely two months later, Wickman obviously had second thoughts about Spearin as he had the latter investigated by the firm of R.G. Dunn. "In some quarters," the agency reported, "[Spearin] has been reported more or less arbitrary in his dealings, but he is generally recognized as of good ability as a bus line executive, and is energetic." It seems that Spearin and Tracey had been entrusted with $80,000 of Duluth money to cover franchises in Ohio and Indiana, and make down payments on equipment. Wickman, having had no reports from the two by mid-December, and learning that only $12,000 of the eighty could firmly be accounted for, sent an emissary, L.W. Dow, to Ohio, charged with the task of finding the whereabouts of the remaining $68,000, and also of furthering the business of bus consolidations. Dow had wanted to keep his investigation into the missing money a secret, but Tracey was too sharp for him. "Tracey [when he found out the truth] . . . was cool enough. . . to have come from Duluth, or farther North." Tracey was considerably upset that Dow was "down here spying" on him and Spearin.

In terms of Spearin, personally, Dow believed he could make more enemies in fifteen minutes than the average man in a month: "Without some good level-headed man with him, he will never get anywhere, and what little success he may have will be accidental, or plain bull-headed luck, and he is not the man to be in full charge of any such business, especially where character and diplomacy are so essential." After several days of intense study, Dow accounted for $75,000, and it was at this point that Spearin finally caught on to Dow's true mission. He fired off a hot letter, December, 1925, to E.L. Firmine, of the Duluth group:

"I have always had a lot of respect for you and have done you a lot of good in more than one way in the past few years. But when it came a time that you could help me, there seems to be a question as to my honesty and way of doing things . . . . Your sneaky way of going about things I do not like, using and sending Dow down here unbeknown to anyone. Looks like a small piece of business, and if there is any question in your mind about your money, I will make a way to get it back to you, and damn quick."

All apparently was forgiven, therefore, through the process of explanation, accountability and stern letters to Duluth. Spearin was, obviously, like Wickman, a man not to be trifled with.

The respite was only momentary, however, as problems again flared between Spearin and Wickman just before Christmas, 1925. On the 22nd, Wickman received an unwelcome telegram from the Fageol-Frey Company in Kent, Ohio, saying that Spearin was past due $2,600 on four coaches—coaches whose down payments were supposed to have been financed by Wickman's original $80,000. Fageol noted that it would have to re-possess the coaches unless Wickman guaranteed orderly payments. Wickman agreed to do so, but at the same time sent an ill-tempered message to Spearin, advising him to get his house in order. In early January, 1926, Spearin wrote to Wickman that all was well: ". . . Went over to the Kent factory and paid $4,000 on notes and made [our] Jew friends happy again." He talked of how "hard-nosed" Fageol-Frey was on financial matters, and then he hit up Wickman for a loan of $5,000. With the new money, he felt, "I will make the grade all right." Wickman refused to honor his request, and he stepped up his efforts to find the $5,000 still missing from the original sum subscribed by the Duluth group. Wickman did, however, comply with Spearin's demand on January 19, for $1,000 to get a "certificate of necessity" to start a run between Washington and Hillsboro, in Ohio.

The troubles with Fageol-Frey eased somewhat a few months later. L.H. Scultze of Fageol wrote to Wickman in the Spring of 1926 saying that at the moment, all of Spearin's notes were paid. He said to Wickman, "I sincerely trust that you will give us your moral support in keeping these accounts in this position, as this is the first time they have been paid since the coaches were delivered." Wickman, always quick to give his moral support, did so, and reckoned the Spearin difficulties at an end.

Two months to the date, however, the problem re-emerged. Wickman got word from Fageol-Frey that Spearin had again defaulted. This was too much for Wickman. He sent a sizzling missive to Spearin:

"I cannot understand why these people have to wire me every month these notes come due. I should think that you have been in business long enough to know that these notes have to be paid, or you will lose the amount of money you have paid so far on the equipment, and will plan a couple of weeks ahead to meet this payment. You must think I am in a position to raise five or ten thousand dollars anytime it is needed. Your business must be poor, or something is radically wrong, as you now have been operating for two or three months and have not been able to meet one note without paying it from here." Wickman's letter set Spearin straight, for their relationship was relatively calm from then on.

Not so, however, for the ties between Spearin and Tracey. The next year, 1927, started out on a sour note between the two, and got progressively worse. It all had to do with Spearin's presidency of the Southland Lines (not to be confused with Southland-Red Ball of Texas) which ran from Indianapolis through Cincinnati to Louisville, Wickman's desire to manipulate it for acquisition purposes in Georgia, and finally to absorb it completely. By this time, 1927, Wickman and Spearin were on fairly good terms—at least they were not calling each other names. Steadily, it became Tracey who was left out in the cold.

It started this way: Andy Wickman, Eric's brother, wanted to start a bus run between Atlanta and Macon, in Georgia. In return for his shares of stock in Southland, Andy got two buses from Spearin. The question arose whether the new operation would be under Southland's aegis, or whether Eric was going to put some Duluth money behind it. At one time, Spearin gave the impression that he wanted to control the Georgia activities; at another that he only wanted to furnish Andy with two buses. Either way, he was bound to run afoul of several stockholders, primarily Tracey. If he secured control of the Georgia Line, this would be an expansion without first securing the stockholders' or even the Board of Directors' authorization. If he merely wanted to sell two buses, this could possibly be the start of a line that in time could seriously compete with Southland.

Eric wrote to his brother, John Wickman, in February, showing his concern over what Tracey might possibly do in reference to the relationship between Southland and the Atlanta-Macon line. He said, "If this thing is going to be done, do it so that you can stand a lawsuit from ... Tracey, and beat him, for you may rest assured that he will start some trouble, because [of the] two buses [sold to Andy Wickman] for his stock in [Southland]." He further suggested that the Georgia line be registered completely in Andy's name—this to relieve Spearin of any legal troubles from Southland's stockholders. Then Eric turned paranoic in his letter to John. He had learned, he said, that Spearin had written several memos to Andy, telling Andy to "do this" and "do that" with his Georgia plans. According to Eric, these memos should not be kept in any of the company's files:

"The man working with you in the office should not know a thing about it. How do you know but that Tracey might be paying him a few dollars on the side for certain information. I can see no reason why you need any help in the office from now on, and why the office cannot be moved to the garage like we suggested." (Without any culpability whatever on his part, the poor clerk lost his job because of Eric's letter.)

Eric then told John that he intended to send Andy $10,000 to help with the Atlanta operation, further dimming the line of authority between Spearin and MTC. He instructed Andy, through John, to organize his company as a Delaware corporation, and then gave a short discourse on lawyers. Perhaps an Atlanta attorney could draw up the incorporation papers, but he advised:

"Before engaging any attorney anywhere, an understanding should be had how much he would charge for his work. You do not find an honest man ... to deal with only one out of ten times. The bigger the practice for an attorney or firm of attorneys, the better the treatment from such firm, but when you get a single attorney that only gets a job once in a great while, the amount he will charge for such work is unlimited."

Eric completed his long, rambling letter to John by admonishing him to:

"Please keep this letter out of your company files, and keep it to yourself and read it often enough so that you will understand what I mean all the way through. And have Mr. Spearin and Andy Wickman also read it over a half dozen times."

The expected trouble from Tracey about the Georgia activities did not materialize. But it became increasingly obvious that Wickman and his Duluth partners intended to take Southland as their own, and to this plan Tracey vigorously objected.

In November, 1927, Spearin traded three small Whites for three new Yellow coaches, and also had two Yellows overhauled. He did not ask the stockholders or, more importantly, the Board of Directors, for permission to make these transactions. He simply did it, and then fired off a telegram to secretary-treasurer Tracey demanding an immediate $16,000. Tracey was not slow in recognizing the implications of such a move. Many times just before a larger company consumed a smaller concern, the president of the smaller company would put it in an untenable financial situation to make affiliation with the large company appear to the majority of stockholders as desirable. Tracey wrote caustically to Spearin:

"I would first like to know who authorized you to purchase three new Yellow buses .... Personally I am getting awfully tired of the methods and tactics pursued in reference to the purchase of new buses. For a long time and, in fact, ever since the operation [Southland] started, you have gone ahead and purchased new equipment on your own initiative, without inquiring before doing so, where the money was coming from to make payments for same." Then came the crux of Tracey's letter: "It looks to me very much as if this was an attempt to create a situation as a leverage to force some of the stockholders of the Southland to turn their stock into the Motor Transit Company, upon a basis dictated by certain individuals interested in the project. This same method has, in my opinion, been used before to create situations for like or similar purposes." Tracey made sure that everyone saw the bold letters on this correspondence showing that he had sent a copy of it to Eric Wickman. He closed by asserting: "Personally I feel that the investors in our bus operation have been buffeted about sufficient to cause them to stand up and demand their rights .... I think the investors have been more than patient, and have been asked to go to extremes, which no man of judgment will stand for. Your wire asking for $16,000 and desiring information as to when you can receive it ... is in my opinion, perfectly ridiculous."

Though Spearin wrote back to Tracey in a commiserative tone, the future of Southland was all too clear. Its stockholders, with the exception of Tracey and a certain Mr. Snyder, strongly favored swapping each share of preferred and common in Southland for three shares of B preferred and three shares of common in MTC.

Thus did Wickman's and Greyhound's empire continue to grow.

Appendix C
Eric Wickman: Some Profiles

In the late Twenties, Wickman went to California to acquire bus lines. Upon his completion of Pacific Greyhound in 1929, the MTC became nationwide for the first time.

While in California, Wickman demonstrated some insights into his character. He became involved, for example, in one of his employee's personal matters—not, it should be pointed out, by choice. Wickman got a letter from Helen Stoudt of Duluth's child welfare board stating that a certain John Larson, a Greyhound employee, had skipped out on child payments to his estranged wife, Marie. Worse information yet for Wickman was Stoudt's assertion that Wickman was one of Larson's bondsmen, guaranteeing orderly and timely support for Larson's children. Eric quickly got an investigation underway. He found that Larson worked for Motor Transit Management Company in Chicago (a subsidiary of MTC), and gave Mrs. Stoudt his address. Nothing happened, however, over the next few months and Stoudt wrote again to Wickman. The Greyhound executive then sent an irate letter to Glen Johnson of TCMC, ordering that Larson settle the matter. At the same time, however, Stoudt informed Wickman that his signature as a bondsman could not be found: "The mother ... told me that a bond was signed ... and that you were one of the bondsmen. I was not in the office at that time [and] I accepted her statement, but since then have been trying to locate the bond, and have not been able to do so. Unless there is a file which we have not yet located, I think Marie must have been mistaken." (Correspondence relating to this episode is at the American Heritage Center, University of Wyoming.) With Wickman breathing a huge sigh of relief, nothing more was heard of his efforts to get Larson to live up to his paternal duties.

Wickman also showed in California just how meticulous he was with money matters. Ralph Manuel bought Wickman's house in Minneapolis when the latter moved west. Arrangements were made for Manuel to pay it off in installments. A few months later, however, Manuel wanted to liquidate the entire debt, and asked Wickman for a discount because of prompt payment. Wickman responded that he had taken a big loss when he sold the house and was not at the moment "pressed for ready money," so he refused to discount any of the remaining contract. Manuel paid it off, anyway.

Wickman's personal income tax for 1930 was $35,959, a sum

that indicated that he was well paid for his Greyhound services. One would not have thought so; however, in a letter Wickman sent to the Pacific Gas and Electric Company, as he and his family prepared to move back east: "If you will please refer to my account, you will note that I sent you a check for $13.55, covering the April bill. It would appear to me that I have a refund coming on the deposit of $5.00 less balance due of 51¢, for a total refund of $4.49."

Tediousness with finances had always marked this penny-pinching Swede, and that is probably what put him in such a good stead with his stockholders for so many years. He lost a bit of his austerity, however, when he returned from the west. He treated himself to a five passenger Fleetwood Cadillac sedan. He paid $4,968 for it. (Sources for the material in this appendix come from the American Heritage Center, University of Wyoming.)

Notes

[1]Hal Boyle, *Duluth Herald*, August 11, 1951.

[2]Named after Robert C. Hupp, who got his start in automotives working for Ransom E. Olds. After service with Olds and, then for a time with Ford, Hupp raised enough money to strike out on his own in 1908. Though he left the enterprise in 1911, the Hupmobile continued to flourish. See John B. Rae, *The American Automobile: A Brief History*. Chicago, 1965, p. 24.

[3]Some sources indicate that it was Anderson who made the big success out of using the Hup for livery service, and that it was only this success that re-interested Wickman in the business.

[4]"Jitney Into Giant," *Fortune*, Vol. 10, No. 2, August, 1934, p. 43.

[5]Scott L. Holtzlander, "The Bus Business," unpublished notes, 1938; n.p. American Heritage Center, University of Wyoming. Hereafter cited as AHC.

[6]G.D. Taylor, Unpublished history of Greyhound, n.d., n.p.; Trenton, New Jersey, Motor Bus Society. Hereafter cited as MBS.

[7]Graves was President of Northwest Greyhound and Sundstrom of Eastern Greyhound.

[8]Albert E. Meier and John Hoschek, *Over the Road*. Trenton: Motor Bus Society, 1975, p. 15.

[9]R. Redden, Sr., *Greyhound, 1926 to 1948*. A Portfolio. Lynn, Mass., 1980, n.p.

[10]This was a decision that Bogan never regretted. He went on to organize the Gray Motor Stages at Janesville, Wisconsin, and also the Interstate Transportation Company in Indiana, known widely as the Blue Goose Lines. He is sometimes credited with the idea of painting his company's buses blue and white. Another Greyhound personality, however, Orville S. Caesar, appears to have been the official who finally attained color uniformity. Bogan worked for a long time at Greyhound headquarters in Chicago, as the company's vice-president. In World War II, he served in the Office of Defense and Transportation in Puerto Rico and Alaska. He helped to plan and build the Alcan Highway.

[11]Redden Portfolio, n.p.

[12]Ibid.

[13]Ibid. The story of this trip to Duluth showed that the early bus driver had to be versatile—capable of adapting to any situation. This is what gave him such a position of high regard in the neighborhood. He was a "take charge" individual, who reacted positively to events. This, too, is what gave him such authority while actually on the road. It was frequently asserted that the only thing a driver could not do enroute was marry people.

Many retired "old-timers" today feel that the present bus driver is more a technician than a driver, with all the Interstates and automatic equipment at his disposal. They are not particularly envious, however, of the traffic jams. For the contemporary truck driver, the retirees have only scorn. "Amateurish, ill-mannered boors, with nothing but merchandise for a cargo," was the way one of them put it.

[14]Of course, many individual bus owners lengthened cars for themselves. As we have seen, "Bus Andy" stretched out the Hup. In 1914, William E. "Buck" Travis, in California, started lengthening his fleet. The Eckland Brothers, however, were the first ones to specialize in the process. In later years, the Ecklands, along with another bus-builder, Carl H. Will, became an important manufacturer for Greyhound.

[15]To be sure, this statement is disputed by several bus historians who say that, among others, Buck Travis' body building shop, started in 1914, preceded the

Fageols. In the mid-20s, the Fageol operations moved to Kent, Ohio.

[16]Meier and Hoschek, p. 19.

[17]Indeed, most of the original partners in the company "fanned out" in the '20s, creating numerous new bus lines all over the country.

[18]This was a most important merger, not the least because it brought Orville S. Caesar into the Wickman Circle. Caesar most assuredly made transportation and Greyhound history in the years ahead.

[19]"Jitney Into Giant," p. 110.

[20]Hannah Campbell *Why Did They Name It ———?* New York: Ace Books, p. 174. There is much evidence elsewhere, however, to show that this version is more fanciful than real.

[21]C.L. Turner to J.M. Wickman, April 17, 1950. AHC.

[22]Ivan Bowen to R.A.L. Bogan, June 10, 1941. AHC.

[23]E.C. Eckstrom to Arthur Bostwick, May 5, 1949. AHC. The blue and white uniformity of which Mr. Eckstrom speaks, however, was not exactly the creation of Eric Wickman. Many companies which merged with the Wickman group resisted re-painting all their buses to conform with the blue and white scheme. Several who did agree immediately to the new colors had to wait—for economic or utilization reasons—weeks or even months to have their buses re-painted. The point is that for some time under MTC, and even Greyhound, there were all kinds of color combinations. The Greyhound leader who ultimately gained color uniformity was Orville S. Caesar. In a letter, May 18, 1934, R.E. Maxwell of Greyhound, told D.W. Hulburd of *Time*, that "even some of the Greyhound subsidiaries carried their original names and painted their buses differently. An important decision, for which Caesar was largely responsible, was to adopt a uniform name and color and to apply them to a national system...." AHC.

[24]"Greyhound and Yelloway Unite," *Greyhound Ltd.,* Vol. 1, No. 7, March 1929, pp, 1-30. Travis went on to become President of Pacific Greyhound, a position he held for many years. He died in February, 1952, at the age of 81, leaving behind an estate valued at $2.5 millions. He willed the University of Nevada approximately $300,000 to help pay for its new Student Union Building. The news of the bequest was enough to warrant an extra edition of the student newspaper. See *The Sagebrush*, Vol. XXIX, No. 16, Feb., 6, 1952.

[25]. Meier and Hoschek, p. 48.

[26]Ibid., p. 16.

CHAPTER TWO

[1]"It's a necessary part of the business," said one Greyhound official about "spotting." "We don't have as many as we used to in the form of people hired out to check for cash fares, etc., We don't have any cash fares—we don't pick up people at 'Jones' Cross Roads; or this mail box, etc. These people now have their own automobile, and we've lost that type of traveler .... We have company spotters [checking on safety, speed, etc.]."

[2]Nathan Asch, "Cross-Country Bus," *The New Republic*, Vol. 78, April 25, 1934, pp. 301-304.

[3]Letter, T.T. Davis to Greyhound Corporation, undated, MBS.

[4]Byrd, *Russ's Bus,* pp. 100-114.

[5]Ibid.

[6]Ibid.

[7]Greyhound Brochure, MBS.

[8]"Jitney Into Giant," p. 114.

[9]Ibid.

[10]Ibid.

[11]Taylor Notes, MBS.

[12]New York *Times*, May 27, 1933.

[13]Ibid., April 30, 1933.

[14]See Edo McCullough, *World's Fair Midways*. New York: Exposition Press, 1966, p. 94.

[15]New York *Times Magazine*, May 28, 1933.

[16]New York *Times*, April 30, 1933.

[17]*Fortune*, "Greyhound Still Growing," Sept., 1944, p. 125.

[18]"Jitney Into Giant," p. 114.

[19]The theme of societal unification in *It Happened One Night* figured prominently in its adaptation as a stage play, entitled *New York-Miami Bus*. The play gave an especially valuable message in unity-seeking America during the years of World War II. The Russians found the play useful, too, as it became Leningrad's most successful performance during the war years.

[20]Meier and Hoschek, p. 63.

[21]*Newsweek*, August 22, 1936, pp. 30-32.

[22]"Jitney Into Giant," p. 117.

[23]In one case, at least, a bus became a "train." In 1932, the "Cotton Belt Passenger Service" was inaugurated between Texarkana and Pine Bluff, Arkansas. By applying driving mechanisms through four-wheel drive axles, a Yellow W coach was converted into a rail car. Equipped with lavatories and other conveniences, the "coach-car" weighed 2,500 pounds more than its counterpart on the highway. Its gas tank had a capacity of 134 gallons, on each of which it averaged five miles. With a capacity of twenty-seven passengers, its forward speed was 64 MPH, and 60 in reverse. Cotton Belt's President, Daniel Upthegrove, said the line started "when local passenger trains ceased to make money . . . and rolled up big deficits." See "Heavy Highway Equipment on Rails," *Motor Transport Section*, Vol. 98, n.d., p. 306.

[24]"Jitney Into Giant," p. 117.

[25]Telegram, Ralph Budd to L.C. Gilman, Nov. 7, 1928, AHC.

[26]"Jitney Into Giant," p. 117.

[27]New York *Times*, August 1, 1935.

[28]Today the problem of regulation has grown to horrendous proportions. Greyhound director of transportation E.W. Simmons said that a schedule change just from Jacksonville, Florida to New Orleans, Louisiana requires at least five different requests for approval, along with tons of paper work for each; with Florida, Alabama, Mississippi, Louisiana and the big one, the ICC—all this for such a short distance. Simmons Interview, June 30, 1980.

[29]See "How Greyhound Grew Up From a Mere Pup," in *Motorman, Conductor, and Motor Coach Operator*, March, 1954.

[30]These accounts of violence in the 1937 Greyhound strike were gleaned from press reports, primarily in the New York *Times*, Nov. 24, 25, 27, 29, and Dec. 1, 2, 1937.

[31]New York *Times*, Dec. 2, 1937.

[32]The "hold-outs" were Vermont, Idaho, Washington, Wyoming, Nebraska and Utah. The reasons ranged all the way from taxing structures to prohibition of "foreign" companies within a state. In Vermont, the Champlain Transportation Company hauled people around, and in the other five non-Greyhound states, Union Pacific Stages exercised that function.

[33]See "Greyhound Still Growing," *Fortune*, Sept. 1944, p. 125.

[34]*MSS*. MBS.

[35]*Newsweek*, August 22, 1936, pp. 30-32.

[36]See M.C. "Mike" Cuzek, "A Million Miler at the Wheel," *Popular Mechanics*, June, 1939, p. 808.

[37]See Lewis R. Freeman, "The Bus: A New Giant in Transportation," *American Magazine*, Sept. 1929, pp. 42-45, 81-82, 84.

[38]*MSS*. MBS. In 1929 the rate of mortality for inter-city buses was 58 per 1,000,000 passengers, compared to 10.4 for railroads. In 1933, however, Greyhound passenger fatalities were only three.

[39]Today the most coveted prize among Greyhound drivers is the Marcus Dow Award. To get it means that a driver has been graduated to the "big time" among professional bus-men.

[40]Byrd, *Russ's Bus*, pp. 170-180.

[41]Meier and Hoschek, p. 9.

[42]*Knickerbocker Press*, May 14, 1932.

[43]New York *Times*, June 27, 1935.

CHAPTER THREE

[1]The units were Pennsylvania Greyhound, Eastern Greyhound, Eastern Greyhound of New England, New England Greyhound Lines, Ohio Greyhound, Capital Greyhound, Northland Greyhound, Illinois Greyhound, Southwestern Greyhound, Pacific Greyhound Lines, Atlantic Greyhound Lines, Richmond Greyhound Lines, Dixie Greyhound Lines, and Teche Greyhound Lines.

[2]There were claims, too, that Wickman no longer enjoyed the best of health. He apparently had diabetes, and by the '40s had developed a heart condition. Unsubstantiated reports state that Wickman had a drinking problem (as, reportedly, did most of the other founders)—that he would have to stay home for several days at a time because of it—and this condition caused many stockholders, including Caesar, to think increasingly about getting rid of him as President by "promoting him upstairs" to the Chairmanship of the Board. That action, however, did not occur until 1946.

[3]Indeed by the '40s, the entire bus industry systematically studied "shifts and trends" in the traveling population of the United States. These "demographics" became an important index in the years ahead to the vicissitudes of bus travel. Chapter six treats bus demographics in some detail.

[4]O.S. Caesar to Greyhound Operating Heads, Oct. 11, 1939. AHC. The recalcitrant units were Southwestern Greyhound, Central Greyhound, Illinois Greyhound, Pacific Greyhound, Pennsylvania Greyhound, Northland Greyhound, Atlantic Greyhound and Teche Greyhound.

[5]Other important suppliers with similar problems were the Spicer Manufacturing Company of Toledo; Ohio and Clark Equipment Company of Berrien, Michigan and Timken Axle of Detroit.

[6]J.C. Neph of Greyhound to A.W. Koehler of the National Association of Motor Bus Operators, Dec. 16, 1943. AHC.

[7]H.J. Wassen of GMC to Mr. Gunsaullus of Greyhound, June 11, 1943. AHC.

[8]Greyhound Memorandum, August 4, 1943. AHC.

[9]Minutes, Greyhound-GMC meeting, August 5, 1943. AHC.

[10]Ibid.

[11]Babcock to Caesar, Feb. 21, 1944. AHC.

[12]Neph to C.L. Stephens, March 20, 1944. AHC.

[13]Caesar to Babcock, March 24, 1944. AHC.

[14]Greyhound Memorandum, April 11, 1944. AHC.

[15]Babcock to Caesar, April 20, 1944. AHC.

[16]Babcock to Caesar, June 26, 1944. AHC.

[17]Babcock to Ceasar, May 1, 1944. AHC.

[18]The speed restriction continued to have repercussions, even after the war. When it was imposed in 1942, drivers for Pacific Greyhound received an eight per cent pay increase. In the fall of 1945, a speed limit of 45 MPH was restored, and Pacific

Greyhound accordingly planned to reduce drivers' pay by four per cent. This certainly did not comport with the twelve per cent raise that the operators wanted. (They were being paid at the rate of 5.13 cents a mile.) A strike occurred in which 2,700 Pacific Greyhound employees became idle. "Not a single one of our buses is rolling anywhere in the West," said company President Frederick W. Ackerman. R.E. Hasselman, representing the drivers' union, said: "Our belief is that Mr. Ackerman and the Pacific Greyhound Lines would make an acceptable offer to the union if not prevented ... by the Greyhound Corporation, which has offices in the East, and is trying to hold the western employees down to the lower eastern wage standard." The strike was settled in late October. The drivers received a 10.5 per cent pay increase over the pre-war mileage rates (of about four cents). Pacific Greyhound's action certainly did not go unnoticed, as drivers elsewhere agitated and struck in 1945 and 1946 for an increased mileage rate. In most instances, they were successful. New York *Times*, Oct. 6, 23, Nov. 1, 1945.

[19]New York *Times*, Oct. 31, Nov. 2, 1940.

[20]Ibid., May 4, 9, 1941.

[21]Ibid. Dec. 4, 6, 23, 29, 31, 1941; Jan. 1, 1942.

[22]Ibid. June 24, 25, July 9, 13, 1944.

[23]"Greyhound Still Growing," *Fortune*, Sept. 1944, p. 121.

[24]Russell Byrd, *Russ's Bus*, pp. 175-180.

[25]This was largely the case with Greyhound operatives elsewhere. Greyhound was one of the first businesses in the war to train women to replace men who had gone off to fight. Thousands of wives, mothers, daughters and sweethearts worked in Greyhound garages and maintenance shops, and drove buses along routes that had once been the exclusive province of men.

[26]The Mare Island bus operation and the "Dime-Catcher Runs" are thoroughly discussed by Robert A. Burroughs, in the April 1973 edition of *Motor Coach Age*.

[27]"Greyhound Still Growing," *Fortune*, Sept. 1944, p. 125.

[28]"Report on Development of Post-War Bus," *The Greyhound Corporation*, June 27, 1944. AHC.

[29]GMC continued to build buses for Greyhound, but not quite to the same extent as before. The last bus Greyhound bought from GMC was in 1967. Simmons interview, June 30, 1980.

[30]Caesar to R.W. Budd, May 25, 1945. AHC.

[31]Perhaps a reason for yet another change in the development of the Scenicruiser was the suicide of Carl Will. A half hour before he shot himself in the head with a .38 caliber revolver, he telephoned his friend, Eric Wickman. "Everything is all messed up, and this is the last call I'll ever make to you," Will said to Wickman, according to press reports. Wickman sped to the Will home, but arrived too late. Also, see Meier and Hoschek, pp. 118, 119.

[32]New York *Herald-Tribune*, Oct. 14, 15, 1946.

[33]L.A. Rossman to Orville Caesar, Jan. 25, 1946. AHC.

[34]This veto was reprinted in a memo from R.W. Budd to Orville Caesar, April 25, 1946. AHC.

[35]Caesar to H.S. Fairbank, Aug. 23, 1946. AHC.

[36]C.J. Randall to Orville Caesar, Dec. 17, 1947. AHC.

[37]L.A. Rossman to Robert Driscoll, Feb. 10, 1947. AHC.

[38]Robert N. Jones to L.A. Rossman, Jan. 23, 1947. AHC.

[39]Caesar to Ackerman, April 11, 1947. ACH. Today, 1981, Clark County (Las Vegas) permits the 102 inch bus. The rest of the state does not.

[40]The first 102 Greyhound bus was the MC 6, the prototype for which was constructed in 1967. One hundred of these 102s were made in all, mostly in 1969 and 1970. Fifteen of them went to Canadian Greyhound Lines (now not in use); and the remainder were to be operated in California and Nevada (which obviously changed

its speed limits for wide vehicles). The 102s were concentrated in these western states because of the ready availability of parts for their V12 engines (since re-powered to V8s) from storehouses in Los Angeles and San Francisco. Simmons Interview, June 30, 1980.

[41]*MSS.* AHC.

[42]It was not until the mid '50s, with Greyhound's flooding of the highways with Scenicruisers that the forty foot bus was generally approved nationwide. By 1953, forty states and the District of Columbia had approved a forty foot bill. The holdouts were California, Colorado, Delaware, Idaho, Missouri, Nebraska, New York and Tennessee. In time they too relented.

[43]*Reader's Digest*, August, 1946, p. 76.

[44]*Mack Bulldog*, n.d., n.p., MBS.

CHAPTER FOUR

[1]Chicago *Daily Tribune*, May 5, 1950.

[2]Clem Jarvis, a retired bus driver from Bowling Green, Kentucky, says of the Chattanooga incident: "Really, I don't think the head officials of the company condoned [the tactics of the special agents]. I don't think they knew it was going on. But the people who were handling this investigation took it upon themselves to do it. [i.e., lock up the drivers]. We [the drivers] didn't condone any stealing, but we resented that type of tactic. That's getting to be Nazi type. We went on a strike, and it got a little bit tough in that particular case. My policy was just to go home and stay out of it."

[3]Chicago *Daily Tribune*, May 5, 1950.

[4]The Chattanooga incident was one of a kind. Afterwards, Greyhound strikes were more "normal," that is, they revolved around the usual things like shorter working hours and higher pay. Pacific Greyhound seemed to be the most "renegade" of all the systems. In March, 1952, a strike of 3,600 drivers and station workers halted services in Utah, California, Oregon, Nevada, Arizona and New Mexico. the operators wanted a forty hour week, and a pay increase from $7.26 per hundred miles to $8.59. After ten weeks of idleness, they accepted a 4.6 per cent rise in wages, a settlement that Greyhound had offered at the beginning of the strike. The Union, however, claimed a "moral" victory.

Overland Greyhound was struck in June, 1953, in the settlement of which, among other things, drivers received eight and one-half cents a mile for their services. Other divisions that experienced labor problems were Pennsylvania Greyhound, Atlantic Greyhound, Southeastern Greyhound, Eastern Greyhound and Central Greyhound. Wages, hours and working conditions were always the principal points of contention. New York *Times*, March 3, May 12, 1952; June 30, Nov. 8, 25, 1953; Dec. 10, 1954; April 2, 1955; August 30, Nov. 2, 1956; Sept. 17, 18, Nov. 6, 7, 1958; Sept. 30, 1959; Nov. 6, 1960.

[5]As late as 1980, however, charges were still being made that bus drivers drove too fast. A disgruntled passenger wrote to the most popular arbiter in the country, Ann Landers, on the subject, "Afraid to leave the driving to some of them" asserted that one driver did 75 MPH in a rainstorm," steering with one hand and eating an apple with the other." Another driver went "75 MPH at night in a storm."

Ann Landers replied that she sent "Afraid's" complaint to the "top of the biggest," Board Chairman Gerald H. Trautman at Greyhound. She concluded that "Afraid" was the same person who previously sent Trautman a four page, single-spaced typewritten letter without signing it. In his letter to Landers, Trautman claimed that the "complainant was asked to identify himself and was invited to a hearing at company expense, but he refused on both counts." (Just how the invitation was given to an anonymous writer, and how his refusals were rendered, was never made clear.)

Landers concluded by saying, "So Trautman makes a far better case than you do, Mr. Afraid. What's more, he signs his name to his letters." And so it goes. See Park City *Daily News* (Bowling Green, Kentucky) December 14, 1980.

[6]J.D. Getny to Florida Greyhound Manager, Feb. 5, 1951. MBS.

[7]Greyhound's image was salvaged somewhat in a good will gesture that it made to South Korea, when it presented President Sygman Rhee with fifteen used buses. Eugene Taylor of the American Korean Foundation wrote to Caesar that the news of the gift was carried on all of that country's radio stations in Korean and Japanese, and circulated widely in the national newspapers, including one in English. Taylor said the buses would go far in cementing good Korean-American relationships. News of the gift also received wide attention in the United States, especially in trade and economic journals.

What happens to old Greyhounds? At one time, many of them were simply destroyed. In the Motor Bus Society files at Trenton is a photograph of several buses, with the caption, "Waiting for the Torch." This meant they were to be burned. There is also a memorandum to the effect that the disposition of unwanted Greyhounds was "confidential." However, of more recent date, it is common knowledge that Greyhound sells its old buses to whomever will buy.

In 1972, for example, Greyhound sold 356 old buses. Their disposition was: 131 to various brokers; 89 to bus-lines; 64 to individuals for recreational vehicles or offices; 22 to schools, colleges and camps; 13 to churches; 8 to sports fans and teams; 13 to singing and other entertainment groups; 9 for mobile offices and businesses; 3 to charitable groups; one was exported.

They cost between $22-23,000 each. Several foreign bus lines buy old Greyhounds, too, especially in Korea and South America. The only stipulation is that the buses be re-painted and all Greyhound identification stripped from them. (In the Mexican state of Chihuahua, an emblem of a running rabbit is imprinted on the aged buses.) According to E.E. Simmons, director of transportation at Greyhound, no buses have been sold since 1979. "We've been building up our fleet as a result of the energy crisis." Simmons Interview, June 30, 1980. In March, 1981, however, Greyhound announced a new sale of old buses.

[8]Caesar died in the mid '60s.

[9]The "half-way point" for the Interstates is generally reckoned to be 1964.

[10]Interview, James Kerrigan, Feb. 23, 1981.

[11]This was ironic, to say the least. Greyhound had always been a strong supporter of the Interstates, believing they would bring increased patronage. Such was not necessarily the case. Moreover, the Interstates contributed to Greyhound's decision to put in service more and more "expresses," often by-passing the little towns and villages that had always been its life-blood. Only in the late '70s and early '80s did Greyhound restore service to many of these "victims of the Interstates." The energy crisis, which really did cause people to leave their cars at home, was a prime reason.

[12]Arthur S. Genet, "Profile of a Greyhound," Speech to the Newcomen Society, March 13, 1958.

[13]Simmons Interview, June 30, 1980.

[14]One Greyhound employee said that at one time the Corporation had almost as much money tied up in cars as it did in buses, and that Genet did not set up an organization capable of handling them. Cars were reportedly found in storage at bus terminals and airports five and six years after Genet left the Corporation. Jarvis Interview, July 30, 1980. If buses had held out the proper lures to get passengers, said James Kerrigan, people would not have gone to their private automobiles, and Genet's plan would conceivably not have been created. In defense of Genet, Kerrigan said, "There wasn't anything that Arthur Genet did that the Board of Directors didn't approve of." Kerrigan Interview, Feb. 23, 1981. The claim that Genet did not "keep

tabs" on the car-rental system is not entirely true. He had a special bus, a Scenicruiser, Number GXI, which took him and his staff to many parts of the country.

[15]New York *Times*, June 7, 1964.

[16]Ibid.

[17]Simmons' Interview, June 30, 1980.

[18]Today Greyhound has a car-rental program, in only a small number of states, but it has all the guides and controls that were lacking in Genet's time.

[19]Kerrigan Interview, Feb. 23, 1980.

[20]Ackerman retired from active management in 1961, and was succeeded by M.C. Frailey who, like Ackerman, had been associated for several years with Pacific Greyhound. Then came H. Vance Greenslit of Southeastern Greyhound, based in Atlanta, followed by Raymond F. Shaffer, long associated with Eastern Greyhound, headquartered in Cleveland.

[21]*MSS.* MBS.

[22]Stephen J. Sansweet, "The Greyhound Set," *Wall Street Journal*, April 3, 1969.

[23]Simmons Interview, June 30, 1980.

[24]Interview, John Adkins, June 30, 1980.

[25]Kerrigan Interview, Feb.23, 1981.

[26]Ibid.

[27]In 1975, Greyhound built an assembly plant in Roswell, New Mexico, and its buses have come from there ever since. The Pembina plant still operates, and it is the principal supplier for Canadian and independent buses. GMC is no longer in the inter-city bus manufacturing business; it concentrates now on building big city transit buses. Simmons and Adkins Interviews, June 30, 1980. The anti-trust problems with GMC are also discussed in chapter eight.

[28]New York *Times*, Feb. 18, 1944.

[29]Simmons and Adkins Interviews, June 30, 1980.

[30]Today the Greyhound Corporation is a holding company that owns a bus line. The buses, actually make up only a small part now of the Corporation's overall activities. Some of the other properties of the Greyhound Corporation are Armour & Company, Post House Restaurants and several computer and money-order agencies.

[31]John A. Kuneau to Verne F. Kelley, March 17, 1960. Grey-North Archives, Chicago (hereafter cited as GN).

[32]A few years later, in the '70s, Greyhound did put hostesses aboard some of its runs, but primarily to strike back at Trailways, with whom it was in an advertising war.

[33]*Wall Street Journal*, April 4, 1966.

[34]*MSS. GN.*

[35]Ibid.

[36]Steve Allen to the author, Dec. 30, 1980.

[37]*MSS.* GN.

CHAPTER FIVE

[1]Lady Greyhound also made several appearances on Jack Benny and Danny Thomas specials, and on the various Art Linkletter shows, particularly "People Are Funny."

[2]Interview, Verne Kelley, July 28, 1981.

[3]J.D. Harrigan to J.E. Hawthorne, March 12, 1963. AHC.

[4]In 1959, Mrs. D'Essen wrote a book, *Kangaroo in the Kitchen* (New York: McKay & Co.) in which she talked briefly about Lady Greyhound. Mrs. D'Essen died in the early '70s.

[5]*MSS.* AHC.

[6]Murray M. Spitzer to V.E. Kelley, 1964. AHC.

[7]G. Clifford Prout to Greyhound, Sept. 24, 1962. AHC.

[8]This "summons" is at the American Heritage Center, University of Wyoming, Laramie.

[9]This "confidential" directive, plus others, is at the American Heritage Center, University of Wyoming.

[10]V.F. Kelley to Sue Warburton, August 19, 1964. AHC.

[11]Earl W. Shumate to D.A. O'Dell, March 9, 1962. AHC.

[12]Kelley to O'Dell, March 9, 1962. AHC.

[13]D.L. Behnke to Ken Dahlstrom, Dec. 1, 1965. AHC.

[14]The Lady Greyhound fan club, and the subsequent contest, were handled by Aaron Cushman Agency of Chicago, with Greyhound's Sid Cato in charge.

[15]"George," by Laura Schueneman:

George is our dog. We didn't name him, our uncle did. Our uncle is an absent-minded old man who is always getting people's names and animals' names mixed up. He generally calls me "Lady" and my twin "Duke." Back to George, he is a very pretty dog with some very wild ideas. He stands almost three feet off the ground on all fours; five feet on his rear legs. He's always on some sort of whim, one chasing cats and keeping them treed all day, another time howling whenever he hears music. The whim we are dealing with tonight is probably the prime one of his existence. He was on a "steal and bury" kick. At first we thought it was just our things he was taking, but soon we began to get complaints from our neighbors. Then one day he—well, I'd best start at the beginning.

I remember the day clearly. I was sweeping off the patio when I saw George go by with something shiny, carrying it to his secret burying place. I called him—he didn't come—but I wasn't too concerned because I remembered Gwennie Parkins had just won a ten cent tin ring at the county fair. She hadn't wanted it at all. Sometime later I heard someone shout. "Chris, Kate, Ann! Anybody! Come quick!" I ran to the door as quick as I could. Mrs. Sherwood may be rich and slightly excitable, but she still didn't come running and yelling like she was now for nothing. "What's up?" I asked.

"Oh, Kate, it's my diamond ring! Your dog took it. Nan saw him!"

"You're sure Nan is sure. She's getting on in years, you know."

"Of course I'm sure," she panted indignantly.

"I'll get Chris and Mom. Be right back." Chris (my twin sister), Mom, Mrs. Sherwood and I racked our brains for a solid hour, trying to think of a way to find George's burying place. Then Chris yelled, "I know. Boy! This is sure to work."

"What!" the rest of us asked excitedly.

"Listen in. We'll go downtown and get a rubber bone. George loves to bury them. Then we'll buy a half dozen or so balls of string. We'll tie the string to the bone, put it where he'll find it, and the string will lead us to his hiding place."

Well, the next day we tried it, and it worked like a charm. George picked up the bone and trotted away with it. After a while the string stopped and we found his place, a clearing in the woods. We dug and dug and dug, but couldn't find it. Then George came along, looked at us, and started digging. In a few minutes he trotted up to me. He had the diamond ring! He dropped it in my lap.

"Oh George, you little devil!" I whooped. And that's the story. I never heard of him taking anything again.

C. Laura Penniman; Used by permission.

[16]MSS. AHC.

[17]Ibid.

[18]By 1967, the Greyhound Corporation had approximately thirty-eight different affiliates, which employed over 35,000 people.

CHAPTER SIX

[1]See *A Survey of American Attitudes Toward Transportation*. Washington: Department of Tramsportation, 1978, p. 25.

[2]This is an interesting statistic, because during the days of the "Snoose Line," and for several years afterward, hardly any of the passengers were women. The change can be attributed in part to the increasing comfort of the bus, to more women than ever going to college and needing transportation to and from their homes (generally speaking, a co-ed was less likely to own a car than her male counterpart). Also the "man of the house" historically used the auto for work, leaving the bus as his wife's only viable transportation alternative.

[3]As noted previously, a large minority of bus travelers agreed with this suggestion.

[4]These statistics came from a study made by Maxon Research, Inc., in Nov. 1956.

[5]Grey Demographic Findings; Jan. 1, 1959.

[6]See Roger Kahn, *The Boys of Summer*. New York: New American Library, 1973, pp. 253-264.

[7]Kerrigan Interview, Feb. 23, 1981.

[8]The initial emphasis was upon Washington, Baltimore, Pittsburgh, Cleveland, St. Louis, San Francisco and Oakland.

[9]Various interviews, Sept. 1980.

[10]Joe Black, *Negro Market Proposal*, 1972.

[11]I.E. younger and older than the general population and in lower income groups.

[12]"Advertising Strategy," Chicago, p. 15.

[13]A few years ago, Steve Allen used this line in his night club monologue: "I'm not sure that all television commercials are as believable as they should be. I mean we have Fred MacMurray ... doing commercials right now for the Greyhound bus people, and when you see the commercial you actually see Fred stepping off a bus. Now, really—when do you think was the last time this multi-millionaire actually traveled anywhere by Greyhound?" Letter, Steve Allen to the author, Dec. 30, 1980. David Letterman used this same story one night when he was hosting the Johnny Carson show. According to reports, the Greyhound people were no more amused by Letterman than they had been by Allen.

[14]Grey-North Master Plan, 1975, Book 2, p. 2.

[15]Ibid.

[16]"SOS, Strategy for our Survival in the Washington, D.C. Area," Chicago, July, 1976.

[17]Employment opportunities for the blacks were as good, or better, in the South as in the North by the late '70s. Civil rights laws had made their impact, so that opportunities in housing, education and equality in the South were generally superior to those in the North. For many of the blacks in the North in the late '70s, it was a matter of "coming home."

[18]A limited amount of such travel continued into the early '80s. Brooks Bus Line, of Paducah, Kentucky, ran a Paducah-Detroit "auto-plant migration" once a week.

[19]Much of the information about the Appalachian week-enders came from an interview with Kenneth White, a Greyhound official, in Phoenix, June 30, 1980.

[20]"Spanish Speaking Advertising Strategy," 1972.

[21]"Spanish Language Plan," 1975.

[22]Memo, 1972, Walter Grosvenor, GN.

[23]"Charter Sales Marketing Plan," Chicago, Dec. 1, 1976.

[24]"Military Consumer Market, A Demographic Profile," Nov. 1974.

[25]Most larger libraries around the country receive at least two different editions of *Russell's Guide* each year.

[26]Simmons Interview, June 30, 1980.

[27]"SOS, Strategy for our Survival in the Washington, D.C. Area; Eastern Corridor Analysis," Chicago, July 1976. Also "Northeast Corridor Market Study, Chicago, Dec. 1976.

[28]Simmons Interview, June 30, 1980.

[29]The report did not account for the remaining eight per cent. It was presumably spent stretching and scratching.

[30] See Ross A. McFarland, "Human Factors in Highway Transport Safety," a special study sponsored by the National Trucking Association, the National Association of Motor Bus Operators, and the National Association of Automotive Mutual Insurance Companies, pp. 1-200. AHC.

[31]Ibid.

[32]New York *Times*, June 9, 1943.

[33]Ibid., July 24, 1944.

[34]Ibid., Oct. 29, 1951.

[35]Ibid., Jan. 3, 1952.

[36]Ibid., August 5, 1952.

[37]Ibid., Oct. 25, 1952.

[38]Ibid., August 13, 1952.

[39]Ibid., March 8, 1952.

[40]Ibid., March 9, 1953.

[41]Ibid., June 13, 1953.

[42]Ibid., August 7, 1953.

[43]Ibid., March 20, 1954.

[44]Ibid., August 8, 1954.

[45]Ibid., Feb. 7, 1955.

[46]Ibid., August 31, 1955.

[47]Ibid., Oct. 16, 1955.

[48]Ibid.

[49]Ibid., Oct. 20, 1956.

[50]Ibid., Dec. 12, 1956.

[51]Ibid., Jan. 5, 1957.

[52]Ibid., Dec. 24, 1958.

[53]Ibid., Dec. 21, 1959.

[54]Ibid., August 29, 1965.

[55]Ibid., May 16, 1967.

[56]Ibid., March 8, 1968.

[57]Ibid., May 14, 1972.

[58]Ibid., Feb. 6, 1975.

[59]Ibid., May 10, 11, 12, 1980.

[60]Many Greyhound bus drivers are extremely bitter over this accident—to a great extent because they believe it could easily have been avoided. If Greyhound management did not so stringently prohibit C.B. radios, the driver could have heard the news that the bridge was out. A driver remarked: "But no. A good driver, twenty-five people and a $100,000 bus had to go into Tampa Bay," in part because of policies set in Phoenix.

[61]New York *Times*, March 4, 1967.

[62]Simmons Interview, June 30, 1980.

[63]Besides accidents, there is a remote chance of hijacking. On February 27, 1980, a gunman entered a Greyhound bus in Cincinnati, and took six hostages. He killed one of them. According to witnesses, the assailant talked "wildly" about the Iranian hostages, and said he had no reason to live. He was finally overpowered, and taken into police custody. See New York *Times*, Feb. 28, 1980.

In June, 1981, a man, saying that he wanted the FBI to arrest him, hijacked a

Greyhound in Texas, and held the driver at gunpoint until the bus got to Erick, Oklahoma. He then ordered the bus stopped, stepped out and surrendered to waiting state troopers. See *Park City Daily News* (Bowling Green, Kentucky), June 21, 1981.

Bus driver stories are plentiful about disturbed people traveling on their coaches. One such threw a heavy coat over a driver's head once as he sped down the Interstate. He stopped the bus without damage or injury, but the incident did help him to make up his mind toward early retirement. A woman passenger near Birmingham, Alabama, once became so deranged and dangerous that not even the police would take her. A lot of mentally unbalanced passengers have tried to jump out of buses, and many of them are quick to inform the driver that "they're after me." One obviously insane person killed an infant in a bus's washroom. Such incidents, however, are not more numerous than on trains and airplanes. The chances a person takes of confronting situations like these on a bus are remote indeed.

CHAPTER SEVEN

[1]Trailways was now owned by Holiday Inns.
[2]"Market Strategy for 1968," p. 3.
[3]C.D.Kirkpatrick to G.G. Roundtree, July 19, 1972.
[4]Walter Grosvenor to Don Griffin, August, 10, 1973.
[5]*Wall Street Journal*, Sept. 25, 1975.
[6]Ibid., Oct. 6, 1975.
[7]"Project Attack," Nov.-Dec., 1975.
[8]Emphasis included.
[9]Memo, Walter Grosvenor to E.C. O'Connor, Jan., 21, 1976.
[10]C.L. Van Sickle (of MacMurray Enterprises) to the author, June 5, 1981.
[11]C.D. Kirkpatrick to James Kerrigan, Jan. 22, 1976.
[12]"1976 Advertising: A Critique," Chicago, Oct. 27, 1976, pp. 1-200.
[13]Ibid.
[14]*Wall Street Journal*, Dec. 31, 1976.
[15]Ibid. Ironically, today—1980's—Kerrigan is the President and Chairman of the Board of Trailways.

[16]It should be noted, however, that in the mid '70s, Greyhound and all the other bus companies faced declining economies. These were due to continuing bad news out of the Middle East, causing fuel prices to skyrocket.

[17]The American public seems to be of several minds about governmentally sponsored railroads. It is very difficult for many people living in an area not served by Amtrak to see the connection between their tax dollar and lower fuel bills. If all these commuters in the giant cities could not go by train, they would probably go by car, thus compounding an already impossible situation—especially in the Northeast Corridor—creating additional gas shortages, and driving its price even higher than it is now, to say nothing of an increased rate of casualties on the highway.

Is Amtrak socialistic? If you live outside its area, yes, of course it is. If you live within its area, well, to be sure, it is not. Like TVA, Amtrak shows that people's political ideologies are frequently formed by the condition of their pocketbooks.

When the "Wind-Fall Oil Profits Tax" was being discussed by Congress in 1979 Senator Russell Long of Louisiana proposed an amendment to give bus companies an additional credit of 10 per cent against their income taxes for increasing their capacity to transport people. (They already had a regular 10 per cent investment tax credit.) Since buses got 113 "passenger miles" per gallon of fuel, compared to a car's 41 (a "passenger mile" is one passenger transported one mile), Long thought his amendment was justified. Needless to say, Greyhound and Trailways agreed with this supposition, for they stood to gain almost $50 millions during the six year life of the credit, from 1980 to 1985. Despite extensive lobbying by the two bus companies, the Long Amendment failed. See *Wall Street Journal*, Nov. 19, 1979. It seems clear, therefore, that the bus industry is not opposed to subsidies *per se*, only if they do not get any of them.

[18]Kerrigan Interview, Feb. 23, 1981.

[19]"Greyhound Bares Its Teeth at Amtrak," *Business Week*, June 9, 1973, pp. 48-50.

[20]Ibid. This is still Amtrak's argument today, as put forth to the author in an interview with an Amtrak official in Feb. 1981.

[21]"Amtrak On-Board Survey," Phoenix, Research Information Center, Inc. Dec. 1976, pp. 1-120.

[22]Washington, D.C., Seattle, Louisville, Houston, Chicago, Portland and Kansas City.

[23]That prediction has not materialized, primarily because of severe cut-backs in Amtrak routes in late 1979. In 1981, the administration of President Ronald Reagan promised fewer subsidies for the ailing railroad system. It was widely reported and believed that Amtrak was viable mostly in the Northeast Corridor, and that the American taxpayer was simply buying the tickets for New Yorker and Bostonian commuters.

[24]James Kerrigan to Paul Reistrup, April 21, 1977.

[25]Ibid. Kerrigan's statistics seemed to be borne out by other writers. Scott Burns' article, "Amtrak Railroading the American Taxpayer," Boston *Herald-American*, April 7, 1977, claimed that each Amtrak passenger from Boston to New York paid $17.50 for his ticket. Each fare was subsidized, however, by the government $24.59. This made the actual fare $42.09, or eighteen cents a mile. By air, the same trip cost $36.00. By private automobile, it cost $11.00. And by Greyhound (which left Boston hourly), and took four and a half hours—as opposed to five for Amtrak—for the trip the cost was $16.85.

Another article, in *Reader's Digest*, "Time to Get Amtrak on Track," by Earl and Miriam Selby, April, 1977, attracted a lot of attention, and undoubtedly encouraged the impetus of the late '70s to curtail the governmentally sponsored railroads.

[26]Kerrigan to Reistrup, April 21, 1977. Another Greyhound executive who attacked Amtrak was Ballard L. Peyton, a regional vice-president, based in Chicago. A letter of his appeared in the September 2, 1980 edition of the Chicago *Tribune*. It said, in part: "It is incredible to me that in an era of heightened interest in government economy and fiscal conservation that our politicians can continue to justify expenditures of millions of tax dollars for the rail passenger service for a small segment of the traveling public. These people could be accommodated on another mode at virtually no cost to the government and with lower fares, less pollution, and greater energy efficiency. . . .

"We in the intercity bus industry would have no quarrel whatsoever with rail service if it were operated on the same basis and under the same rules that we have to observe. But there simply is no reason that rail passengers should receive heavy government subsidy at the expense of the general taxpayer when no basic public is serviced. There is no marketing reason that rail service should not be self-sustaining on a route where it provides an important public service, and there is no reason that rail passengers should not pay at least the cost of providing that service. It is not a valid marketing assumption that passengers will not pay compensatory rates when the service is important to them. They pay what it costs to ride the airlines and to ride the buses, and there is no basic reason to believe that rail passengers will not pay the cost of their trip when they go by rail if it is, in fact, an essential service."

[27]Kerrigan to Reistrup, April 21, 1977. Today, 1981, with Alan Boyd as President of Amtrak, there is apparently a new feeling of cooperation with bus-lines. He and Kerrigan have discussed possible joint ventures by which Trailways (which

Kerrigan now heads) might "feed" into an Amtrak system. If this becomes a reality on a large scale, it will be a historic "throw-back" to the early days of the bus industry. Buses complemented train routes back then at a profit, and there probably is no sound reason why the same program cannot be practiced today. Kerrigan said of the bus-train possibilities: "I think we'll have a larger market, and we'll all participate." Kerrigan Interview, Feb. 23, 1981. Greyhound has several Amtrak connections already; for example, at Harrisburg, Pennsylvania.

[28]Alfred Michaud, Amtrak's Vice-President for Marketing, said in 1977 that the railroad's free children program was inspired by the bus-lines, including Greyhound, doing the same before.

[29]Letter to N. Pinsoff, May 3, 1977.

[30]Memo H.J. Lesko (Greyhound President) to Greyhound regional vice-presidents, Sept. 9, 1977.

[31]This "turnabout" in Greyhound fortunes is discussed in some detail in chapter nine.

[32]The tune was developed by a man named Bob Kirschbaum.

[33]Its ad appeared in the New York *Daily News*, July 9, 1957.

[34]Victor Ugolyn to *Advertising Age*, Jan. 18, 1977.

[35]George T. Christie to J.E. Hawthorne, Dec. 13, 1962, GN.

[36]State of California *vs* Greyhound Lines, Superior Court for the County of Nevada, August 27, 1976.

[37]Willard Alexander to Mary Jane Bryan, July 12, 1976. GN.

[38]E.C. O'Connor to R.O. Lande, April 21, 1977. GN.

[39]Only in its advertising, apparently, did Greyhound want to evoke a "romantic image." In reality, its leaders portray themselves as fearsome business men and women, who have little or no time for the gushy, sentimental stuff. Their business is "running a bus-line," not indulging in historical romanticism. Perhaps that attitude caused Charles Kirkpatrick of Greyhound to counter Charles Webb's idea, in 1975, to write a "romantic history of the buses." Kirkpatrick told Webb (mistakenly) that the buses had "more of a business beginning than a romantic beginning."

Nevertheless, when Al Meier and John Hoschek (both members of the Motor Bus Society), came out in 1975 with their history of the inter-city bus industry, *Over the Road*, there were several individuals affiliated with Greyhound who criticized it on the grounds that it was not "romantic" enough. ". . . The book makes no real attempt to portray the romance and excitement that were so much a part of the growth of the business." (Though, in their preface, Meier and Hoschek distinctly disavowed any intentions of discussing "romantic origins.") The Greyhound people complained, too, that Meier and Hoschek had a "preponderance of information" about the growth of the inter-city industry in the West, as compared to the East. Some people who had figured prominently in bus-line history had been only perfunctorily mentioned, or omitted altogether. *Over the Road*, the Greyhounders said, had an "undercurrent of bias" against Greyhound, which is occasionally depicted as the ogre, devouring everything in its path," and buying a company to eliminate competition, and then dismembering it (which was, in fact, the truth). The book also neglected, the management believed, Greyhound's expansion into other fields, particularly as compared with Trailways. The book's greatest sin, however, was when it suggested that Trailways' torsion system (Torsilastic, put out by B.F. Goodrich), was superior to Greyhound's air suspension. (This question at the time, 1975 and 1976, was an important contention in the Greyhound-Trailways advertising war.) Walter Grosvenor to Charles Kirkpatrick, July 31, 1975. GN. It should be noted that Greyhound bought many copies of *Over the Road*, and printed its own dust jacket for it. The bus company handed out hundreds of complimentary copies of *Over the Road*, so it could not have been too displeased with the book.

[40]A stickler for grammatical purity and some semblance of reality in advertising,

Mrs. Lorant once soundly rejected a promotional piece from an ad agency, called "Greyhound Mountain Travel Guide." Its writing "was miserable," with phrases like "Try the regular, but good, rate," "Anyone lets you be a real free spirit like no other way to travel lets you," and "We want to save you." Because of this, and other shoddy pieces of writing, Mrs. Lorant's department set up various screening and editorial procedures by which she and other officials would approve the final copy of major promotional pieces. Inter-office Memo, Dorothy Lorant to Charles Kirkpatrick, May 23, 1977.

[41]Memo, Walter Grosvenor to Creative Group, August 27, 1974. Letter, Grosvenor to E.H. Holzer, Oct. 28, 1976.

[42]Grosvenor to Account Creative Groups, Oct. 5, 1976.

[43]Greyhound Memo, March 25, 1975.

[44]Letter, L.E. Kronsnoble to D.A. Davis, March 2, 1977.

[45]Greyhound Memo, March 25,1975.

[46]*Wall Street Journal*, May 11, 1977.

[47]Letter, Walter Grosvenor to Henry Siegel, August 11, 1977.

[48]With all the women who ride Greyhound buses, one wonders why the company did not advertise extensively on the daily soap operas. Maybe the answer is that the waiting list was long indeed, after all the detergents and washing powders.

Chapter Eight

[1]Some important court cases involving Greyhound have already been discussed. In chapter four, some civil rights suits were mentioned; in chapter six, a few suits involving accidents were noted, and chapter seven talked about some copyright infringement actions. The present chapter must be selective—focusing on the obviously more significant disagreements. In general, suits arising from lost or damaged luggage or other similar matters are not discussed.

[2]New York *Times*, July 25, 1956.

[3]Three other companies named in the suit were the Hertz Corporation of New York, National City Lines of Chicago, and Public Service Co-Ordinated Transport, of Newark, New Jersey.

[4]New York *Times*, Oct. 12, 1956.

[5]Ibid.

[6]Ibid., June 28, 1957.

[7]These facilities were briefly discussed in chapter four.

[8]New York *Times*, Jan. 16, 1958. The matter rested until the early 1960s, when the government re-opened the case. It is beyond the scope of this chapter to discuss fully the Federal suit against General Motors.

[9]New York *Times*, May 20, 1958.

[10]Ibid., March 24, 1964.

[11]Ibid., Sept. 28, 1970.

[12]Ibid., Jan. 21, 1975.

[13]Ibid., March 18, 1979.

[14]William Niskanen to Donald Schafer, March 20, 1952. Broad, Khourie & Schulz, San Francisco.

[15]Ibid.

[16]Bad blood between the two lines was also stirred in 1962, when Greyhound wanted to sell some Oregon routes it considered unprofitable. Its favored buyer was Ben Franklin Hauck, doing business as Valley Stages. When Mt. Hood also applied to the authorities to purchase these routes, both Greyhound and Hauck withdrew their own applications, presumably to keep Mt. Hood in an inferior position, competitively.

[17]Interstate Commerce Commission, *Mount Hood Stages, Inc.—Petition for*

Modification; No. MC-F-9136, April 5, 1968; p. 461.

[18]Albany-Eugene to Oregon-Idaho state line.

[19]For example, after several acquisitions in the Pacific Northwest, Greyhound began, said Niskanen, "a very vicious and effective advertising program," using such phrases as "Only Greyhound has three routes to California," "Only Greyhound has four routes to the East," "Only Greyhound has 20 schedules to California," etc. In Niskanen's opinion, if Greyhound's "predatory" growth continued, it would be able to advertise "that only Greyhound has service anywhere." Niskanen to Schafer, March 20, 1952.

Niskanen expressed the thought that unless things ultimately changed, Mt. Hood "would be placed in the difficult position of competing with Greyhound only by their sufferance." William A. Niskanen to Donald Schafer, May 17, 1952; Broad, Khourie & Schultz, San Francisco.

[20]ICC. *Mt. Hood Petition for Modification*, p. 473.

[21]Ibid., p. 458.

[22]Greyhound Lines *v* United States of America and Interstate Commerce Commission; 308 F. Supp. 1033 (1970), pp. 1040-41.

[23]United States v. Greyhound Corporation, 363 F. Supp. 525 (1973), p. 529.

[24]Ibid., pp. 529-530.

[25]To show how Greyhound operated nuisances against Mt. Hood, the court cited the instance of Salt Lake City. If a passenger wanted to go to Burley, Idaho, or Cedar City, Utah, via Salt Lake City, he was told—if he asked—that a Mt. Hood carrier could get him to his destination two hours and thirty five minutes faster than a Greyhound.

But, the passenger was further informed, the Mt. Hood terminal was four blocks away, and the time difference between Greyhound's arrival in Salt Lake City and Mt. Hood's departure was only ten minutes. Therefore the passenger could not possibly make the connection, so he had better ride Greyhound. The clincher, though, to this whole problem was that Greyhound refused to allow Mt. Hood's buses into its terminal at Salt Lake City—and it used this refusal as "an alibi for its agents' failure to quote shorter or faster interline service with Mt. Hood." Ibid., p. 551.

[26]Ibid., p. 555.

[27]Ibid.

[28]Ibid.

[29]One wonders, then, why certain Greyhound officials did not go to jail. It was F.W. Ackerman, then President of Pacific Greyhound, who gave Mt. Hood most of its troubles vis-a-vis encirclement and competition. It was Gerald Trautman, then vice-president and general-counsel of Greyhound, who "rendered the crucial advice in 1964 that Greyhound's representations at the merger proceedings should not inhibit it from cancelling the through-bus." Ibid., p. 556. Neither Ackerman nor Trautman, however, was named in any contempt proceedings. In light of what ultimately happened, Trautman turned out to be a very poor prophet.

[30]Ibid., p. 559.

[31]Ibid., p. 556.

[32]Ibid., p. 571.

[33]Ibid., p. 572.

[34]Ibid., p. 571. Kerrigan said of the case, "Bill Niskanen and I were always friends, and stayed friends. He ... was very quick to say publicly anywhere he was that had I been the chief executive officer of the Greyhound Lines during those days of the '60s, the case would never have occurred. It would have been settled." Kerrigan Interview, Feb. 23, 1981. Though Kerrigan may have professed friendliness toward Niskanen, the evidence indicates that most other Greyhound officials held him in utter contempt. Likewise several Greyhounders remarked on Niskanen's "brittle" personality.

[35]United States of America v The Greyhound Corporation, 370 F. Supp. (1974), pp. 883-886.

[36]United States and Interstate Commerce Commission v The Greyhound Corporation, 508 F. 2d. 529 (1974), p. 541.

[37]United States and Interstate Commerce Commission v The Greyhound Corporation, 370 Supp. 881 (1974), p. 885.

[38]Mt. Hood Stages v The Greyhound Corporation, 555 F. 2nd. 687 (1977), p. 695).

[39]Ibid., p. 693.

[40]Ibid., p. 697. Emphasis added.

[41]Philip Hager, "Tiny Bus Line Takes on Giant: Mt. Hood Stages and Greyhound Near a Showdown," in Los Angeles Times, Feb. 11, 1978.

[42]Mt. Hood Stages v The Greyhound Corporation, 555 F. 2d 687 (1977), p. 698.

[43]Ibid.

[44]Mt. Hood Stages v The Greyhound Corporation, 616 F. 2d 394 (1980), p. 400.

[45]In anticipation of having to pay damages, Greyhound set aside a sizeable sum of its savings, and collected interest on it. Therefore, when the damages were finally paid, Greyhound could claim that the payment had no major effect on the earnings of 1980.

[46]Los Angeles Times, Feb.11, 1978.

[47]Niskanen died in the spring of 1981, just a few months after his victory over Greyhound before the Supreme Court. Before his death, he sold Mt. Hood Stages to Baldwin-United Music Corporation of Cincinnati, Ohio.

CHAPTER NINE

[1]According to numerous sources,the Greyhound person who first picked and then continually supported Phoenix was Jesse C. Nicks.

[2]This is not an unusual action by states that are wooing industry. This very practice helped Delaware for many years to achieve pre-eminence in corporation friendliness.

[3]Of course the Armour people suffered because of the time difference between Phoenix and Chicago. Cattle in Chicago start for the slaughterhouses at 4 A.M. each day. This meant that Armour personnel monitoring their company's kills would have to be on the job by 2 A.M. In late 1983, Greyhound was negotiating a sale of Armour to the Conagra Corporation of Omaha, Nebraska.

[4]See John H. Jennrich, "The Lawyer Who Rides and Drives Greyhound," Nation's Business, Feb., 1980, pp. 52-58.

[5]See William Gruber, "Greyhound Alive, Doing Well," Chicago Today, April 19, 1972.

[6]Ibid.

[7]Ibid.

[8]Ibid.

[9]Ibid. Also in his annual report for 1971, Trautman told his 80,000 plus stockholders that "the transfer to Phoenix is proving to be beneficial to Greyhound and Armour and specifically is resulting in lower costs of operation and improved employee morale."

[10]Robert M. Ady, "Changes Impacting Facility Location Decisions in the New Decade," Speech, Southern Industrial Development Council, Kansas City, Missouri, Oct. 21, 1980.

[11]It is true, however, that the retired drivers' groups from these companies continue to use the old classifications, and some, such as Northland, still print their own magazines and letters.

[12]Passed in late 1973, the federal law had at least one ironic and inane effect. The roads in Kentucky, with the exception of the Interstates, had 60 MPH imposed on

them in the daytime, and 50 MPH at night. The federal law for a continuous 55 MPH had the effect of lowering the daytime speed by 5 MPH and increasing the nighttime speed by the same amount.

In all fairness to the schedulers in Phoenix, it must be pointed out that schedules are not arbitrarily set. It is official company policy that "if you leave late, you arrive late." Moreover, it is true that many drivers rarely start loading people early enough to leave the terminal on time. Then, to make up for the lost time, they may speed; even possibly getting a speeding ticket, for which they then blame the Phoenix schedulers.

[13]Many Greyhound drivers swear that Trailways, and other drivers, smuggle C.B.'s aboard their buses, while the supervisors look the other way. Whenever one Greyhound driver meets another on the road, if he sharply thrusts two downward pointed fingers up and down, that means that the place is crawling with State Troopers, and to slow down.

[14]Many drivers have found the Greyhound ban on smoking to be a launching pad for ridding themselves of the habit. Others convert from one form of tobacco to another: It is not unusual to see a driver's jaw puffed out like a baseball pitcher's, full of chewing tobacco. He brings along an empty coffee cup filled with napkins to spit in, and finally dispose of, his "chaw." Needless to add, he goes through his Beech-Nut and Apple-Cured as surreptitiously as he possibly can.

[15]For photos and descriptions of the proposed new uniforms, see *Along the Greyhound Way*, March, 1980, p. 5.(They did not get accepted, as shown.)

[16]See Bob Blum, Laramie *Boomerang*, Dec. 17, 1970. Another embarrassment for Greyhound was when it became the sixteenth corporation in the United States to pay a fine because of the Watergate Scandal. Corporate funds, it was adjudged, to the amount of $16,040 were given by fifty-five Greyhound employees to various political candidates. Greyhound was fined $5,000. See *Wall Street Journal*, Oct. 3, 1974. Trautman himself is a Democrat. He organized the Greyhound Political Action Committee which gives to candidates of both parties, "based on their attitude on the free enterprise system." Jennrich, p. 53. Although he was not always happy with President Jimmy Carter, he planned to vote for his re-election. "He uses Greyhound buses in his campaigns," exulted Trautman, "so he can't be all bad." Jennrich, p. 53. According to informed sources, former President Richard Nixon wanted to join Trautman's old law firm of McCutcheon, Doyle, Brown, Trautman and Enerson, in San Francisco. Trautman allegedly became irate over Nixon's offer, threatening to withdraw his influence from the firm if the former chief executive was accepted.

[17]David Ogilvie, *Confessions of an Advertising Man*. New York: Atheneum, 1963, p. 45.

[18]In later years, this phrase earned the enmity of English purists and poets from all over the country. Its meter was all wrong, they said; it did not "scan." It should have been, "It's such a comfort to take the bus, and leave the driving *all up* to us." Two professors of English, from the Universities of Wisconsin and Indiana, wrote scathing letters demanding that the offending phrase be erased from the side of the buses, and from Greyhound literature.

[19]Ogilvie, p. 45.

[20]Some sources say that Walter Grosvenor was "relieved of duty" on the Greyhound account by a new president of Grey-North, and that Greyhound's fondness of Grosvenor helped to put them in mind to change agencies.

[21]*Wall Street Journal*, Oct. 11, 1977.

[22]By the time Kerrigan and others had bought Trailways, Stern and another GBJ staffer had formed the Stern-Monroe Advertising Agency. They won the Trailways account under the new management, headed by Kerrigan.

A few months after Grey-North lost the Greyhound account, Walter Grosvenor died of a heart attack. Another account executive, Abe Baum, stayed in Phoenix and ultimately became the assistant director of travel for the State of Arizona. Anthony

Wainright went to Dallas, via a short stint in New York, and then became Chairman of the Bloom Agency. Edward O'Connor opened a Central American Tour business in New Port Richey, Florida. Other Greyhound account personalities were scattered throughout the vast Grey empire.

Another matter of note is that shortly after the demise of the Greyhound account, Grey-North had some friendly dealings with its old antagonist, Amtrak. A group of Grey-North people made a presentation to Amtrak's marketing department, only to come in second. But in the fiercely competitive world of advertising, being second is just like being last—there are no "runner-up" prizes.

[23]See Rush Loving, Jr., "The Bus Lines are on the Road to Nowhere," *Fortune*, Dec. 1, 1978.

[24]See John Quirt, "How Greyhound Made a U-Turn," *Fortune*, March 24, 1980, pp. 139-40.

[25]Jennrich, *Nation's Business*, pp. 52-58.

[26]Ibid.

[27]Quirt, *Fortune, p. 139.*

[28]Ibid.

[29]Ibid.

[30]He was not the only person to do this. F.W. Ackerman was seventy when he was still Chairman of the Greyhound Corporation.

[31]For a time, however, Kerrigan retained control over Greyhound's Service Group, and bus manufacturing companies.

[32]Kerrigan Interview, Feb. 23, 1981. Also Dan McGowan, "Greyhound Lines Shake-Up Reveals Bitterness at the Top," *Arizona Republic*, Sept. 30, 1979, and Eric Pace, "Running Hard in Second Place," New York *Times* Dec. 14, 1980.

[33]*Arizona Republic*, Sept. 30, 1979. According to some reports, during the first month of Kerrigan's absence from Greyhound Lines, he vowed, "I shall return," and that this promise caused Trautman to deliver the quarter million "coup de grace" to get him completely out of the Corporation.

[34]Kerrigan Interview, Feb. 23, 1981.

[35]Ibid.

[36]*Arizona Republic*, Sept. 30, 1979. A week prior to the *Republic* interview, Kerrigan, like Trautman before him, talked to *Fortune*. Here, Kerrigan was quoted as saying, "I had no inherited right to run [Greyhound], but if Trautman wanted someone else, he could have let me know in a more open way." See "Back in the Driver's Seat: On a Different Bus," *Fortune*, Sept. 24, 1979, p. 15.

[37]Kerrigan Interview, Feb. 23, 1981. Apparently Trautman has once again decided to stay quiet on the Kerrigan matter. Repeated efforts by the author to interview him on the subject have not been successful. In a telephone conversation with Greyhound Vice-President for Public Affairs and Advertising, Dorothy Lorant, August 11, 1981, I was told that a conference of top Greyhound management had decided not to accommodate me on the Kerrigan-Trautman problems. She was "appreciative," however, that I did seek fairness and balance in reporting on the subject.

[38]Kerrigan Interview, Feb. 23, 1981.

[39]*Arizona Republic*, Sept. 30, 1979.

[40]Kerrigan Interview, Feb. 23, 1981.

[41]Dunikoski, like Chairman Trautman, isn't talking about it. In a less than cordial telephone call to the author's home on March 26, 1981, he informed me that he was "in the business of running a bus-line," not of giving interviews.

[42]Ironically, so it was reported, Lesko's son knew about his father's "change of status" at Greyhound before his father did. The son worked a summer-time job in the Corporation's mail room, and saw all the notices before they were to be announced.

[43]Kerrigan Interview, Feb. 23, 1981.

[44]*Fortune*, Sept. 24, 1979.

[45]Kerrigan Interview, Feb. 23, 1981.

[46]*Along the Greyhound Way*, May, 1979, p. 5.

[47]*Wall Street Journal*, May 9, 1979.

[48]Ibid.

[49]See Susan Carey, "Shake-Ups at Greyhound Leave Several Holes," *Arizona Republic*; October 31, 1980.

[50]See Dan McGowan, "Trautman Breaks His Silence on Greyhound Controversies," in *Phoenix Business Journal*, Dec. 1, 1980. Stanford and Harvard-educated Trautman was asked if the reports of his dictatorial manners were correct, and also if he had a "rubber-stamp" Board of Directors behind him. Trautman was quoted as saying, "I would be very happy to have you go down the hall [presumably of Greyhound Towers] and talk to anybody you want to about ... whether they really think I'm as mean as indicated." McGowan, p. 1. This silly suggestion was apparently not taken seriously by anyone. As for his Board of Directors, "I have good relations ... [and] I intend to keep them that way...." One way of doing just that is issuing gold Greyhound bus passes to all members of the Board.

It would appear from all the "re-organizations" that Trautman is not particularly a good judge of personnel. First, there was his "heir apparent" Kerrigan to go; then his "heir apparent" Swanson (who came to Greyhound, supported by consultants Booz, Allen & Hamilton, in a report that "read like a recommendation to canonize him." McGowan, p. 1. It should be recalled, too, that as legal counsel, Trautman gave the "crucial advice" that ultimately produced Greyhound's trauma in the Mt. Hood case, discussed at length in chapter eight. There were, apparently, in mid-1981, three leading contenders for Trautman's job as Chairman of the Greyhound Corporation. They were Ralph Batastini, Frank Nageotte, and John Teets, all of whom hold high positions within the organization. *The Arizona Republic*, August 21, 1981, ran a story in which it was revealed that Teets was named Chief Executive Officer of the Greyhound Corporation, a position that puts him in the number two spot, just below Trautman. Nageotte became Chief Operating Officer, making him the third man in the Corporation. Batastini became fourth in rank. One observer noted that "if all goes well," Teets is now in a good position to move into the chairmanship upon Trautman's planned retirement in August, 1982. The way Greyhound history has developed during the past few years, however, no one should regard this statement in any kind of absolute manner. See Susan Carey, "Greyhound Puts Its Vice Chairmen in Pecking Order," *The Arizona Republic*, August 21, 1981. Teets did, in fact, become chairman in 1982.

[51]New York *Times*, Nov. 2, 3, 1980.

[52]*Along the Greyhound Way*, Feb.1979, p. 1.

[53]Ibid. Trautman has subsequently said that he would like to see the ICC abolished. Jennrich, p. 53.

[54]*Fortune*, "Back in the Driver's Seat," p. 16.

[55]New York *Times*, Feb. 10, 1981.

[56]See Don Harris, "Skelly Quits Greyhound Over His O'Connor Views," *Arizona Quarterly*, July 17, 1981.

[57]See John Kolbe, "Rep. Jim Skelly: A Man Who Takes Issues, Ideas Seriously," *Phoenix Gazette*, July 23, 1981.

[58]*Arizona Republic*, July 17, 1981. In a telephone conversation with the author on August 11, 1981, Mrs. Lorant confirmed that she had been quoted correctly by the *Republic*.

[59]*Phoenix Gazette*, July 21, 1981.

[60]Ibid.

[61]Ibid.

[62]*Arizona Republic*, July 19, 1981.

[63]Ibid.

CHAPTER TEN

[1]Email, former Greyhounder, who would speak to me only on conditions of anonymity.

[2]Email, another Greyhounder, who would speak to me only on conditions of anonymity. This demand for anonymity was the same when I wrote the original Greyhound book. One might question the motives of anonymity; however, when several "anonymous" letters and emails tell me essentially the same thing, there must be kernels of truth somewhere.

[3]Radio TV Reports, Inc., Feb. 9, 1986.

[4]Ibid.

[5]Ibid.

[6]Ibid.

[7]Philip Beresfor, "Greyhound at Bay," *Sunday Times* (London), March 31, 1985.

[8]Ibid.

[9]Frederic D. Fravel, "The Greyhound Story, 1979-1990," Ecosometrics, Incorporated (Bethesda, Maryland, 1990), p. 18. This report was prepared for Greyhound Lines, Incorporated.

[10]David Freed, "Greyhound Bus Crushes Striking Driver," Los Angeles *Times*, March 4, 1990.

[11]Email, anonymous Greyhounder. In later years, Labor Secretary Robert Reich said, in considerable understatement, "The 1980s saw too much bitterness in labor-management relations." *In Transit,* July-Aug., 1993, p. 10.

[12]Craig Lentzsch Greyhound CEO, Interview (telephone), Jan. 12, 2001.

[13]Beresfor, "Greyhound ....," March 31, 1985.

[14]*In Transit*, April, 1990, p. 7.

[15]"Fred Currey Answers Questions About Greyhound," *Bus Ride*, May, 1990.

[16]Carlton Jackson, "Return to Tradition Could Win Passengers Back for New Owners of Greyhound Bus Line," *The Tennessean* (Nashville), May 5, 1987.

[17]Ibid.

[18]Beresfor, "Greyhound ....," March 31, 1985.

[19]Ibid.

[20]Ibid.

[21]Ed Stauss, "Greyhound Franchises," *Bus World*, Vol. 7, No. 4 (1985), p. 16.

[22]Ibid.

[23]Ibid.

[24]Ibid.

[25]Ibid, p. 18.

[26]Ibid.

[27]Ibid, p. 19.

[28]Ibid.

[29]Letter, Frederick Dunikoski to Domenic Sirignano, Feb. 13, 1986. Vincent Saalfield Collection.

[30]Ibid.

[31]Ibid.

[32]Ibid.

[33]Ibid.

[34]Lentzsch Interview.

[35]Jason Knott, "Greyhound Lines Ready to Take Off," *Metro Magazine*, Vol. 84, No. 4 (July/Aug., 1988), p. 42.

[36]Ibid.

[37]Jackson, "Return to Tradition ..."

[38]George Graveley, Interview with the author (telephone); Feb., 1987.

[39]Frederck G. Currey, Interview with the author (telephone), Feb., 1987.

[40]Domenic Sirignano, Interview with the author (telephone), Feb., 1987.

[41]"Fred Currey Answers Questions About Greyhound," *Bus Ride*, May, 1990, p. 76.

[42]Graveley Interview. Also Jackson, "Return to Tradition ...."

[43]Ibid.

[44]Knott, "Greyhound Lines ....," p. 42.

[45]Ibid.

[46]Ibid.

[47]Kristin Parsley, Email to the author, Feb. 13, 2001.

[48]Ibid.

[49]*Bus Ride*, Oct., 1989, p. 38.

[50]Ibid.

[51]Ibid., pp. 48, 49.

[52]Thomas C. Hayes, "Strike Hobbling Greyhound and Thousands of Its Riders," New York *Times*, March 3, 1990.

[53]"Emphasis on Customer Service, Larger Bus Fleet, New Facilities and Services All Add Up to Continued Growth for Greyhound Lines," *Bus Ride*, Oct., 1989, p. 38.

[54]Ibid.

[55]Ibid.

[56]Ibid., p. 39.

[57]"Currey Answers Questions ....," p. 76.

[58]Ibid.

[59]Ibid.

[60]Ibid.

[61]Ibid.

[62]Hayes, "Strike Hobbling ....," March 3, 1990.

[63]Ibid.

[64]Many ex-Greyhounders have confirmed this incident. They wish to remain anonymous.

[65]James La Sala, "They've Got It Backwards," In *Transit,* Vol. 98, No. 4 (May-June, 1990), p. 2.

[66]"U.S. Greyhound Locals Forced to Strike; Company Implements Proposal Rejected by 92%," *In Transit*, Vol. 98, No. 3 (April, 1990), p. 6.

[67]Ibid.

[68]Frederick G. Currey; Interview with the author (telephone), Jan. 17, 2001.

[69]Lentzsch Interview, Jan. 12, 2001.

[70]Hayes, "Strike Hobbling ....," March 3, 1990.

[71]Bob Baker, "Both Sides in Bus Strike Miles Apart: The Union and Company Are Pursuing Diverse Public Strategies. Greyhound Chairman Does Not Expect a Settlement Soon," Los Angeles *Times*, March 13, 1990.

[72]Ibid.

[73]"U.S. Greyhound Locals ....," *In Transit*, April, 1990, p. 21.

[74]Ibid. In 1991 Metzenbaum sponsored a bill in Congress to prohibit employers from permanently replacing workers on strike. It was defeated by a vote of 55-41. See 102 cong. 2 sess: June 11, 1992.

[75]"Currey Answers Questions ....," p. 78.

[76]Ibid.

[77]Bob Baker, "Finding a Dream Job in a Strike: Companies Facing Walkouts Increasingly Turn to Permanent Replacement Workers. They Find Plenty to Defy Labor Solidarity for More Pay," Los Angeles *Times*, Dec. 18, 1990.

[78]"Currey Answers Questions ...."

[79]David Freed, "Greyhound Bus Crushes Striking Driver," Los Angeles *Times*, March 4, 1990.

[80]Baker, "Both Sides ....," March 13, 1990.

[81]Ibid.

[82]Ibid.

[83]Ibid.

[84]Bill Vann, *The Case of Roger Cawthra: Anatomy of a Labor Frame-Up*, Southfield, Connecticut: Labor Publications, 1993, pp. 1-46. It must be kept in mind that Mr Vann presented just one side of the case.

[85]Ibid., p. 34. Numerous telephone calls to ATU president, James La Sala, to clarify this matter, have gone un-returned. ATU general counsel, Robert Molofsky, did call.

[86]Vann, p. 41.

[87]Ibid., p. 42.

[88]Dean Murphy, "Riding Out the Battle of the Buses ....," Los Angeles *Times*, April 8, 1990.

[89]Ibid.

[90]Ibid.

[91]Ibid.

[92]Ibid.

[93]Ibid.

[94]"Dignity: Greyhound Members Fight for Us All," *In Transit*, Vol. 98, No. 4 (May-June, 1990), p. 10.

[95]Ibid.

[96]Currey Interview, Jan. 12, 2001.

[97]Ibid.

[98]"Strikers at Greyhound Feel Forgotten," New York *Times*, March 3, 1991.

[99]Robert E. Oliver, "What a Difference a Year Makes," *Bus World*, Vol. 15(a), No. 3 (Winter, 1992), p. 33.

[100]"Greyhound Files for Chapter 11," *Times* (London), June 6, 1990.

[101]"U.S. Greyhound Locals ....," *In Transit*, April, 1990, p. 21.

[102]Kristin Parsley, Email to the author, Feb. 13, 2001.

[103]"Strikers at Greyhound Feel Forgotten," New York *Times*, March 3, 1991.

[104]*The Daily News* (Bowling Green, Kentucky), Jan. 21, 2001. The only place where unions are growing seems to be in the public sector, in governments, especially on the federal level.

[105]The *Atlantic Monthly*, Vol. 287, No. (Feb., 2001), p. 262.

[106]Ibid.

[107]Ibid.

[108]Ibid.

[109]Robert E. Oliver, "Greyhound Tries Green," *Bus World*, Vol. 15, No. 2 (Winter 1992), p. 7.

[110]Even though Russell's Guide was for a time without Greyhound schedules, it did not cease publication. It continued with the schedules of many other bus companies.

[111]Oliver, "What a Difference ..., p. 33.

[112]"Greyhound Lines, Inc. 85 Years of Changing for the Better," *Bus World*, Vol. 22, No. 12 (Dec., 1999), p. 6.

[113]Ibid.

[114]The back pay was challenged by a former Greyhound employee, Richard D. Jenkins, in a case that went into the courts. See *In Transit*, Vol. 104, No. 1 (Jan.-Feb., 1996), p. 7. The case was dismissed by the courts and

the money ultimately distributed. Robert Molofsky, General Counsel for ATU, Interview with the author (telephone), Jan. 25, 2001.

[115]"Greyhound Members Ratify Agreement, Final Details in Negotiation," *In Transit,* Vol. 101, No. 4 (July-Aug., 1993), pp. 8-9.

[116]Baker, "Finding a Dream ...." Los Angeles *Times*, Dec. 18, 1990.

[117]"Greyhound Members....," p. 10.

[118]Lentzsch Interview, Jan. 12, 2001.

[119]Frank Lorenzo was the famous, or infamous—whichever way one looked at him—"union buster" of a few years before at Eastern Airlines.

[120]"Greyhound Members ....," p. 3.

[121]Ibid.

[122]Warren S. George, "Re-Organizing Greyhound," *In Transit*, Vol. 102, No. 2 (March-April, 1994), p. 5.

[123]Robert E. Oliver, "Greyhound: Fighting for Its Life," *Bus World*, Fall, 1994, p. 25.

[124]Ibid.

[125]Ibid.

[126]Ibid.

[127]Robert E. Oliver, "Greyhound Looks to the Future," *Bus World*, Vol. 13, No. 3 (Spring, 1992), p. 9.

[128]"Motorcoach Deregulation at Crossroads," *Metro Magazine*, Vol. 89, No. 3 (March/June, 1993), p. 50.

[129]Oliver, "Greyhound: Fighting ....," p. 25.

[130]Lentzsch Interview, Jan. 12, 2001.

[131]Ibid.

[132]Oliver, "Greyhound Fighting ....," p. 27.

[133]Kristin Parsley, Email to the author, Feb. 13, 2001.

[134]Ibid.

[135]Lentzsch Interview, Jan. 12, 2001.

[136]Ibid.

[137]*Bus Ride*, Jan. 1996, p. 47.

[138]Ibid.

[139]Ibid.

[140]Greyhound Lines, Inc. 1998 Annual Report.

[141]Ibid.

[142]Ibid.

[143]Ibid.

[144]"Greyhound Members Ratify Contract—By Telephone," *In Transit*, Vol. 106., No. 6 (Nov.-Dec., 1998), p. 13.

[145]Robert Tomsho, "Greyhound Drives Down New Road in Quest for Success—CEO Lentzsch's Fence-Mending Helps Turn Around Bus Company's Fortune," *Wall Street Journal*, Feb. 25, 1998.

[146]Lentzsch Interview, Jan. 12, 2001.

[147]Ibid.

[148]"Tomsho, "Greyhound Drives Down New Road ...." Feb. 25, 1998.

[149]Ibid.

[150]Robert Molofsky (General Counsel, ATU), Interview with the author (telephone), Jan. 25, 2001.

[151]Tomsho, "Greyhound Drives Down New Road ....," Feb. 25, 1998.

[152]Ibid.

[153]Ibid.

[154]Ibid.

[155]Ibid.

[156]Ibid.

[157]http://www.greyhound.com/company/timeline.shtml

[158]Greyhound, 1998 Annual Report. Also Ralph Borland, Interview with the author (telephone), Jan., 2001.

[159]Borland Interview; also Lyn Brown, Interview with the author (telephone), Jan., 2001.

[160]Borland Interview.

[161]Fran Durbin, "Greyhound Lines Becomes 1st Bus Company to Join ARC," *Travel Weekly*, Vol. 58, No. 67 (Aug. 23, 1999), p. 4.

[162]Tim Teeboom, "Commemorating 85 Years of Trail Blazing," *Bus World*, Vol. 22, No. 11 (Nov., 1999), p. 11.

[163]"Memphis Children and Senior Citizens to Retrace Route of Underground Railroad; FedEx and Greyhound Lines Sponsor Educational Journey," *Greyhound PR Newswire*, June 5, 2000.

[164]See Margaret Allen, "Greyhound Hopes to Team with Package Delivery Company," *Dallas Morning Journal,* Jan. 14, 2000.

[165]"Greyhound Relocates Melbourne Terminal," *Greyhound PR Newswire*, June 15, 2000.

[166]*Greyhound PR Newswire*, June 27, 2000.

[167]Ibid., July 17, 2000.

[168]Ibid., Aug. 14, 2000.

[169]Ibid, June 27, 2000.

[170]"Safety Board Blasts Greyhound's Policies in Report on Accident," *Wall Street Journal*, Jan. 6, 2000.

[171]Kristin Parsley, Email to the author, Feb. 13, 2001.

[172]Ibid.

[173]Ibid.

[174]Christopher Reynolds, "Travel Insider; Airlines Buses, Hotels Address Accessibility; As More Complaints Come in, Travel-Related Businesses Are Being Forced to Improve Their Facilities for the Wheelchair-bound," Los Angeles *Times*, Jan. 23, 2000.

[175]Ibid.

[176]Dan Wallach, "Texas Transportation Department Gives Greyhound $282,150 to Improve Services," *The Beaumont Enterprise*, July 23, 2000.

[177]Oliver August, "Canadians Acquire Greyhound," London *Times,* Oct. 20, 1998.

[178]"Laidlaw's Quarterly Loss More Than Doubles to $542 Million," *Canadian Press*, July 12, 2000.

[179]Ibid.

[180]Frank Swoboda, "Greyhound Seeks Financing Sources; Firm Running Low on Operating Funds," *The Washington Post*, Aug. 16, 2000.

[181]Katherine Yung, "Troubled Laidlaw to Restructure, but Won't Sell Greyhound Bus Lines," *Dallas Morning News*, July 14, 2000.

[182]Katherine Yung, "Greyhound Sale Not in Laidlaw's Plans," *The Dallas Morning News*, July 13, 2000.

[183]Ibid.

[184]"Greyhound Seeks Financing," Greyhound PR Newswire, Aug. 16, 2000.

[185]Kristin Parsley, Email to the author, Feb. 13, 2001.

[186]Don Phillips, "Board Asks Greyhound to Explain Financial Problems," *The Washington Post*, Aug. 19, 2000.

[187]Ibid.

[188]Timothy Pritchard, "Relief for Laidlaw," New York *Times*, Sept. 21, 2000.

Bibliography

I. Original Sources

Dissertations, Theses, Letters and Speeches.

Ady, Robert M. "Changing Impacting Facility Location Decisions in the New Decade." Kansas City, MO, Oct. 21, 1980.

Allen, Steve. Letter to the author, Dec. 30, 1980.

Chandrawatna, Pradit. *The Greyhound Corporation.* Unpublished ms. Thesis, Univ. of Tenn., 1957.

Dunikoski, Frederick. Letter to Domenic Sirignano, Feb. 13, 1986. (Vincent Saalfield Collection).*

Ellis, Herman A. *Southwestern Greyhound Lines: A Historical Sketch.* Unpublished ms. College of Commerce, Univ. of Kentucky, 1952.

Schueneman, Laura. "George." Short story to author.

Van Sickle, C.L. (MacMurray Enterprises); letter to the author, June 5, 1981.

Interviews

Adkins, John. June 30, 1980.

Borland, Ralph. Jan. 2001 (telephone).*
Brown, Lynn. Jan. 2001 (telephone).*

Currey, Frederick G. Feb. 1987 (telephone),* Jan. 17, 2001 (telephone).*

Gravely, George. Feb. 1987 (telephone).*

Kelley, Verne. July 28, 1981.

Kerrigan, James. Feb. 23, 1980.

Lentzsch, Craig. Jan. 12, 2001 (telephone).*

Molofsky, Robert. Jan. 25, 2001.*

Simmons, E.W. June 30, 1980.

Sirignano, Domenic. Feb. 1987 (telephone*).

White, Kenneth. June 30, 1980.

*Indicates new listings.

MSS

American Heritage Center, University of Wyoming, Laramie, WY.

Broad, Khourie & Schulz, San Francisco.

Grey-North Archives, Chicago.

Motor Bus Society Archives, Trenton, NJ.

II. Secondary Sources

The Atlantic Monthly, Vol. 287 (Feb., 2001).*

Byrd, Russell A. *Russ's Bus*. Los Angeles: Wetzel Printing, 1945.

Campbell, Hannah. *Why Did They Name It——?* New York: Ace Books, 1971.

The Daily News. Bowling Green, KY, Jan. 21, 2001.*

D'Essen, Lorraine. *Kangaroo in the Kitchen*. New York: McKay & Co., 1959.

Fravel, Frederic D. *The Greyhound Story, 1979-1990*. Bethesda, MD: Ecosometrics, 1990.*

Kahn, Roger. *The Boys of Summer*. New York: New American Library, 1973.

McCullough, Edo. *World's Fair Midways*. New York: Exposition Press, 1966.

Meier, Albert, and John Hoschek. *Over the Road*. Trenton, NJ. Motor Bus Society, 1975.

Murphy, Dean. "Riding Out the Battle of the Buses..." Los Angeles *Times*, April 8, 1990.*

Olgivie, David. *Confessions of an Advertising Man*. New York: Atheneum, 1963.

Rae, John B. *The American Automobile: A Brief History*. Chicago: Univ. of Chicago, 1965.

Redden, R. Sr. *Greyhound 1926 to 1948: A Portfolio*. Lynn, MA: Private printing, 1980.

Vann, Bill. *The Case of Roger Cawthra: Anatomy of a Labor Frame-Up*. Southfield, CT, 1993.*

Magazines and Recent Newspapers

Allen, Margaret. "Greyhound Hopes to Team with Package Delivery Company, *Dallas Morning Journal*, Jan. 14, 2000.*

Along the Greyhound Way. Feb., 1979, May, 1979, March, 1980.

Asch, Nathan, "Cross Country Bus." *The New Republic*, Vol. 78 (April 25, 1934).

August, Oliver. "Canadians Acquire Greyhound." London *Times*, Oct. 20, 1998.*

"Back in the Driver's Seat: On a Different Bus." *Fortune*, Sept. 24, 1979.

Baker, Bob. "Both Sides in Bus Strike Miles Apart ...." Los Angeles *Times*, March 13, 1990.*

Baker, Bob. "Finding a Dream Job ..." Los Angeles *Times*, Dec. 18, 1990.*

Beresfor, Philip. "Greyhound at Bay." London *Sunday Times*, March 31, 1985.*

Burroughs, Robert A. Article in *Motor Coach Age*. April, 1973.

Bus Transportation, Vol. 1 (June, 1922).

"Coast to Coast." *Bus Age*, Vol. 7, No. 12 (Dec., 1925).

Durbin, Fran. "Greyhound Lines Becomes 1st Bus Company to Join ARC." *Travel Weekly*, Vol. 58, Issue 67 (Aug. 23, 1999).*

Drury, W.T. "Looking Backwards." *Backfire*, Oct., 1946.

"Fred Currey Answers Questions About Greyhound." *Bus Ride*. May, 1990,* Oct., 1989.*

Freed, David. "Greyhound Bus Crushes Striking Driver." Los Angeles *Times*, March 4, 1990.*

Freeman, Lewis R. "The Bus: A New Giant in Transportation." *American Magazine*, Sept., 1929.

George, Warren S. "Re-Organizing Greyhound." *In Transit*, Vol. 102, No. 2 (March-April, 1994).*

"Greyhound and Yelloway Unite." Greyhound Ltd., Vol. 1, No. 7 (March, 1929).

"Greyhound Bares Its Teeth at Amtrak." *Business Week*, June 9, 1973.

"Greyhound Lines, Inc. 85 Years of Changing for the Better." *Bus World*, Vol. 22, No. 12 (Dec., 1999).*

Greyhound 1998 Annual Report.*

"Greyhound Seeks Financing." Greyhound PR Newswire, Aug. 16, 2000.*

"Greyhound Still Growing." *Fortune*, Sept., 1944.

Gruber, William. "Greyhound Alive, Doing Well." *Chicago Today*, April 19, 1972.

Guzek, M.C. "Mike." "A Million Miler at the Wheel." *Popular Mechanics*, June, 1939.

Hayes, Thomas C. "Strike Hobbling Greyhound and Thousands of Its Riders." New York *Times*, March 3, 1990.*

"How Greyhound Grew Up from a Mere Pup." *Motorman, Conductor, and Motor Coach Operator*, March, 1954.

http://www.greyhound.com/company/timeline.shtml*

In Transit, "Greyhound Locals Forced to Strike," Vol. 98, No. 3 (April, 1990).*

In Transit, "Dignity: Greyhound Members Fight Us All," Vol. 98, No. 4 (May-June, 1990).* Vol. 104, No. 1 (Jan.-Feb., 1996).*

In Transit, "Greyhound Members Ratify Agreement...." Vol. 101, No. 4 (July-Aug., 1993).* Vol. 106, No. 6 (Nov.-Dec., 1998).*

Jackson, Carlton. "Return to Tradition Could Win Passengers Back for New Owners of Greyhound Bus Lines." Nashville *Tennessean,* May 5, 1987.*

Jenrich, John H. "The Lawyer Who Rides and Drives Greyhound." *Nation's Business*, Feb., 1980.

"Jitney Into Giant." *Fortune*, Vol. 10, No. 2 (Aug., 1934).

Knott, Jason, "Greyhound Lines Ready to Take Off." *Metro Magazine*, Vol. 84, No. 4 (July/Aug., 1988).*

"Laidlaw's Quarterly Losses More Than Double to $542 Million." *Canadian Press*, July 12, 2000.*

La Sala, James. "They've Got It Backwards." *In Transit*, Vol. 98, No. 4 (May-June, 1990).*

Loving, Rush, Jr. "The Bus Lines Are on the Road to No-Where." *Fortune*, Dec. 1, 1978.

McGowan, Dan. "Trautman Breaks His Silence on Greyhound Controversies." *Phoenix Business Journal,*" Dec. 1980.

"Memphis Children and Senior Citizens...Retrace Underground Railroad." Greyhound PR Newswire, June 5, 2000.*

Newsweek, Aug. 22, 1936.

Oliver, August. "Canadians Acquire Greyhound." London *Times*, Oct. 20, 1998.*

Oliver, Robert. "Greyhound Fighting for Its Life." *Bus World*, Fall, 1994.*

Oliver, Robert. "Greyhound Looks to the Future." *Bus World*, Vol. 89, N. 3 (May/June, 1993).

Oliver, Robert E. "Greyhound Tries Green." *Bus World*, Vol. 15, No. 2 (Winter, 1992).*

Oliver, Robert E. "What a Difference a Year Makes." *Bus World*, Vol. 15 (a), No. 3 (Winter, 1992).*

Phillips, Don, "Board Asks Greyhound to Explain Financial Problems." *Washington Post*, Aug. 19, 2000.*

Pritchard, Timothy. "Relief for Laidlaw." New York *Times*, Sept. 21, 2000.*

Quirt, John. "How Greyhound Makes a U-Turn." *Fortune*, March 24, 1980.

Radio TV Reports, Inc., Feb. 9, 1986.*

Reader's Digest, Aug., 1946.

Reynolds, Christopher. "Travel Insider...Airlines, Buses, Hotel...." Los Angeles *Times*, Jan. 23, 2000.*

The Sagebrush, Vol. XXIX, No. 16 (Feb. 6, 1952).

Selby, Earl, and Miriam. "Time to Get Amtrak on Track." *Reader's Digest*, April, 1977.

Stauss, Ed. "Greyhound Franchises." *Bus World*, Vol. 7, No. 4 (1985).*

"Strikers at Greyhound Feel Forgotten." New York *Times*, March 3, 1991.*

Swoboda. "Greyhound Seeks Financing Sources; Firm Running Low on Operating Funds." *The Washington Post*, Aug. 16, 2000.*

Teeboom. "Commemorating 85 Years of Trail Blazing." *Bus World*, Vol. 22, No. 11 (Nov., 1999).*

Tomsho, Robert. "Greyhound Drives Down New Road in Quest for Success ..." *Wall Street Journal*, Feb. 25, 1998.*

Tropical Breezes, Vol. 1, No. 16 (June, 1949).

Wall Street Journal. "Safety Board Blasts Greyhound's Policies in Report on Accident," Jan. 6, 2000.*

Wallach, Dan. "Texas Transportation Department Gives Greyhound $282,150 to Improve Services." *Beaumont Enterprise*, July 23, 2000.*

Yung, Katherine. "Greyhound Sale Not in Laidlaw's Plans." *Dallas Morning News*, July 13, 2000.*

Yung, Katherine. "Troubled Laidlaw to Restructure, but Won't Sell Greyhound Bus Line." *Dallas Morning News*, July 14, 2000.*

III. Government Documents

Greyhound Lines, Inc. v United States of America and Inter-State Commerce Commission, 308 F. Supp, 1033 (1970).

Interstate Commerce Commission; Mount Hood Stages, Inc.—Petition for Modification, No. MC-F-9136 (April 5, 1968).

Mt. Hood Stages v The Greyhound Corporation, 555 F. 2d 687 (1977).

102 Cong. 2 sess, June 11, 1992.*

A Survey of American Attitudes Toward Transportation. Washington: Dept. of Transportation, 1978.

United States and Interstate Commerce Commission v The Greyhound Corporation, 370; F. Supp. 881 (1974).

United States v Greyhound Corporation 363 F. Supp. 525 (1973).

IV. Newspapers

The Arizona Republic, 1979-1981.

Boston *Herald-American*, 1977.

Chicago *Daily Tribune*, 1950.

Chicago *Tribune*, 1980.

Duluth *Herald*, 1951.

Laramie *Boomerang*, 1970.

Los Angeles *Times*, 1978.

New York *Herald-Tribune*, 1946.

New York *Times*, 1933, 1935, 1937, 1940-1945, 1951-1957, 1958-1960, 1964-1965, 1967-1968, 1970, 1972, 1975, 1979, 1980-1981.

Park City Daily News (Bowling Green, KY), 1980.

Phoenix *Gazette*, 1981.

The Wall Street Journal, 1966, 1969, 1975, 1976-1977, 1979.

V. Miscellaneous

Various interviews and letters from bus drivers' conventions, trade journals, etc.

Index